EMPLOYER ENGAGEMENT

Making Active Labour Market Policies Work

Edited by
Jo Ingold and Patrick McGurk

First published in Great Britain in 2023 by

Bristol University Press
University of Bristol
1–9 Old Park Hill
Bristol
BS2 8BB
UK
t: +44 (0)117 374 6645
e: bup-info@bristol.ac.uk

Details of international sales and distribution partners are available at bristoluniversitypress.co.uk

© Bristol University Press 2023

British Library Cataloguing in Publication Data
A catalogue record for this book is available from the British Library

ISBN 978-1-5292-2299-9 hardcover
ISBN 978-1-5292-2302-6 ePdf
ISBN 978-1-5292-2301-9 ePub

The right of Jo Ingold and Patrick McGurk to be identified as editors of this work has been asserted
by them in accordance with the Copyright, Designs and Patents Act 1988.

Cover design: Andrew Corbett
Front cover image: 123rf/aleksandrs
Bristol University Press uses environmentally responsible print partners.
Printed and bound in Great Britain by CPI Group (UK) Ltd, Croydon,
CR0 4YY

Contents

List of Figures and Tables

Figures

Tables

List of Abbreviations

3f	Women Workers Union (Denmark)
ADE	Australian Disability Enterprises
ALMP	active labour market policy/programme
AMU	arbejdsmarkedsuddannelser (labour market training)
AOF	Workers Educational Association (Denmark)
ATA	Apprenticeship Training Agency (UK)
CAEHRS	Commercial Agreement for Employment and Health Related Services (UK)
CESI	Centre for Economic and Social Inclusion (UK)
CPA	contract package area
CSR	corporate social responsibility
DESE	Department for Employment, Skills and Education (Australia)
DWP	Department for Work and Pensions (UK)
EEO	Equalising Employment Opportunities (Australia)
ERA	Employment, Retention and Advancement (UK)
FE	further education
HE	higher education
HR	human resource
HRM	human resource management
IfA	Institute for Apprenticeships (UK)
JCP	Jobcentre Plus (UK)
JR	Jobrotation (Denmark)
JSA	Jobseekers' Allowance (UK)
LJP	Local Jobs Program (Australia)
NAS	National Apprenticeship Service (UK)
NDIS	National Disability Insurance Scheme (Australia)
NFP	not-for-profit (organization)
NPM	New Public Management
OECD	Organisation for Economic Co-operation and Development
PES	public employment service
PPN	Prime Providers Network (UK)

SBWA	sector-based work academy (UK)
SE	supported employment
SEO	Small Employer Offer (UK)
SHRM	strategic human resource management
SME	small- and medium-sized enterprise
TfL	Transport for London (UK)
TU	trade union
UC	Universal Credit (UK)
UI(F)	unemployment insurance (funds)
VET	vocational education and training
WE	Work Experience (UK)
WP	Work Programme (UK)

Notes on Contributors

Orla Baker has close to 15 years' experience in business development gathered across several industries including: employment services; science technology engineering and mathematics (STEM); international development; not for profit; education and social welfare. She has a passion for building relationships with teams, individuals and organizations to achieve exceptional results. Orla holds a double degree in Teaching and Arts from the University of Adelaide.

Irmgard Borghouts is Endowed Professor of HRM and Social Security at Tilburg University, the Netherlands. Her multidisciplinary expertise lies in the fields of employment security, labour market policy, social security and inclusive HRM. She is scientific lead of the Academic Collaborative Center Inclusive Labor Market and director of the People Management Centre.

Thomas Bredgaard is Professor at the Centre for Labour Market Research at Aalborg University (Denmark). His research interests include employer engagement in active labour market policies, disability and employment, flexicurity, evaluation and public management.

Tony Carr has worked in employment and skills for almost 20 years. He is a prevalent voice for improving employer services within employment and skills programmes. He has supported many employability organizations in employer engagement strategy design and training of employer engagement staff. He has advised commissioning agencies in the UK, Australia, France, Germany, The Netherlands and the United Arab Emirates on employer engagement practices.

Emma Crichton is Executive Director at Growth and Innovation at Asuria. Emma has over 30 years' experience in human services. As part of Asuria's global expansion, she has led a significant global business development strategy including in Sweden and the United Kingdom. Emma has a Bachelor of Arts with a double major in Sociology and Social Work from Deakin University, Melbourne.

Tanja Dall works in the Department of Sociology and Social Work, Aalborg University. Her research focuses on social work and professionalism in public employment services, with a particular interest in how professionals collaborate with clients, other professionals and employers in efforts to include disadvantaged unemployed in the labour market.

David Etherington is Professor of Local and Regional Economic Development at Staffordshire University. Prior to working in the university sector, David worked in local government on economic and social regeneration policy. His research interests include Marxist political economy, welfare, work, employment relations, labour and social movements.

Charissa Freese is Endowed Professor of HRM and Social Security at Tilburg University, The Netherlands. Her expertise is in the field of HRM policies for vulnerable workers. In addition, she is Vice-Dean at TIAS School for Business and Society and extra-ordinary professor at the School of Industrial Psychology and Human Resource Management and the WorkWell Research Unit of the Faculty of Economic and Management Sciences at the North-West University, South Africa.

Anne Green is Professor of Regional Economic Development at City-REDI (Regional Economic Development Institute) at the University of Birmingham. Her research interests span employment, non-employment, regional and local labour market issues, progression in work, skills strategies, progression in work, urban and rural development, migration and commuting, associated policy issues and evaluation.

Tom Gustafson is Vice-President of People and Culture for Bed Bath & Beyond's Supply Chain organization. His career has been in HR and supply chain at Coca-Cola, Best Buy, Gap and Bed Bath & Beyond at Sephora. Tom's most recent work of note is engineering and executing a strategy to employ a large number of individuals with disabilities in Sephora's US supply chain.

Andrew Hamilton worked as a corporate sales and marketing specialist before using these 'commercial' skills in the not-for-profit sector more than 20 years ago, commencing as a volunteer board member with Foresters Community Finance, before joining Social Ventures Australia. Executive roles then followed with Goodstart Early Learning and Open Minds before founding the specialist consulting firm Social Scaffolding in 2015. Andrew has a B.Comm and MBA from Griffith University.

William Hanson has over 14 years of leadership consulting experience in a wide range of settings including business, the military, medical, educational and agricultural. Published in a variety of journals, he conducts research in business and educational settings with a focus on leadership, professional and ethical development, and culture. Dr Hanson has over 25 years of military leadership experience and experience as board member and officer for four community organizations.

Jo Ingold is Associate Professor of Human Resource Management at Deakin Business School, Deakin University, Melbourne. She has a background in central government research and policy and in the non-profit sector. Her research focuses on employment programme design and delivery, employer engagement and workforce inclusion.

Martin Jones is Professor of Human Geography and Vice-Chancellor at Staffordshire University. Martin works on the interface between economic and political geography and research interests include state theory, process of state intervention and the devolved geographies of local and regional economic development.

Matthias Knuth is a retired sociologist who directed a research unit at the Institute for Work, Skills and Training (IAQ) in the University of Duisburg-Essen. He was in charge of several evaluation studies of German active labour market programmes. He also served as president of the German Association for Social Science Labour Market Research.

Flemming Larsen is Professor at Aalborg University. His research focuses on labour market and social policy, both from a political science and public administration perspective. At present he is co-leader of the research centre CUBB, which in cooperation with local welfare agencies tries to develop co-creation and user involvement in employment services through system innovation. Flemming has participated in several international research networks and projects and has published widely internationally.

Mikkel Bo Madsen works at the Department of Sociology and Social Work, Aalborg University. His research focuses on the intersection of social work and employment policies, in recent years with a particular focus on the professional involvement of employers and workplaces in policies for disadvantaged unemployed.

Patrick McGurk is Reader (Associate Professor) in Management Practice at Queen Mary University of London. His research concerns employment and skills, leadership development and diversity management. Additionally,

Patrick is Associate Dean for Education in the School of Business and Management.

Richard Meredith is Teaching Fellow at Queen Mary University London. His research interest is employer engagement with state employment and skills schemes, particularly in the case of the UK. He has 24 years' public sector experience (including the UK Public Employment Service) and 14 years' industry experience in employer intermediary services (including Business Link and Train to Gain).

Jeffrey Moore is Professor of Management at Anderson University (South Carolina). He was raised in France and received his PhD from the University of Nice Sophia – IAE. Leading the Anderson University research team, they work with Walgreens, Sephora, Bed Bath & Beyond and WinCo to study their disability employment practices and impact on team members and organizational culture.

Omolola Olaleye is Doctoral Researcher at Queen Mary University of London. Her research interests include the role of apprenticeships in broadening diversity in organizations and facilitating career advancement for young people of minority ethnic heritage. Other research interests include social mobility and youth labour market experiences.

Paul Sissons is Professor of Work and Employment at the University of Wolverhampton. His recent research has examined wage progression for low-paid workers; sub-national approaches to development and ideas around inclusive growth; the links between skills, business models and productivity; and the place-based impacts of creative freelancing.

Rik van Berkel is Associate Professor at the Utrecht School of Governance, The Netherlands. His research interests include activation and welfare-to-work policies, the frontline delivery of these policies, and the engagement of employers and the role of their HRM policies in promoting the labour-market inclusion of vulnerable labour-market groups.

Jay Wiggan is Senior Lecturer in Social Policy at the University of Edinburgh. His research interests include the politics of welfare reform and the governance of active labour market policy in the UK.

Acknowledgements

My interest in employer engagement first manifested at the end of my PhD, which compared policies to assist jobless partnered women into work in the UK, Denmark and Australia. I was left with the question, 'What about employers in all of this?' At the time, finishing my PhD in 2010 mid-global recession and as the first in my family to university, I felt green and that I didn't have a sensible research agenda. I was fortunate to be awarded a post-doc at Leeds University Business School and my obsession with employer engagement in active labour market policies and programmes flourished. I want to heartily thank everyone who supported my research while I was at Leeds, including the Economic and Social Research Council who funded my Future Leaders Grant. Along the way I have met fantastic people, in both the employability sector and in the academic world.

I long thought this book was needed but wasn't sure whether I was the person to take the lead, or what editing a book even involved, and am grateful to Mel Simms for the frank pep talks! I am so very grateful to Patrick McGurk for being willing to be on this journey with me. We came up with a wish list of fantastic potential contributors and, to our delight, they all said yes. I am grateful to all our wonderful co-authors who committed their time and energy to this book, especially during a time of global turmoil and my own family emigration to Australia. I want to sincerely thank Bristol University Press and our editor Paul Stevens and the team for supporting this project throughout. It has been a pleasure to work with you all.

I am forever grateful for the unfailing support of my adopted family, the Ingolds, particularly my mother- and father-in-law, my sister-in-law Suzey, my adopted aunts and late grandfather. I owe a particular debt to my husband, Chris, who has always been my rock, from when I changed course at Bristol from English to Social Policy, through the decision to undertake my PhD and beyond. I am so lucky to be supported by Chris and our son, Zack, who both put up with my quirks and obsessions (including boring them rigid about activation policies). Neither of my parents lived to see this book but I am grateful to you both for the path you set me on. My parents' relationship with work was as a necessity rather than a love; work that involved multiple jobs and didn't always pay the bills; tough manual labour that wrecked their bodies – this experience growing up no doubt led to my interest in employment and unemployment. I am lucky every single day to do what I do and to be surrounded by wonderful people, both professionally and personally.

Jo Ingold
Melbourne, June 2022

I spent the first half of my career in further education and from the start I was interested in engaging employers in the classroom, work experience and field visits. Spending most of my professional life in inner London, I became passionate about employers – and the state – doing the right thing and opening their doors to young people and other workers who wouldn't normally have access. As I progressed my academic career and moved into higher education, I found I was able to bring together my passion and interests by combining the study of human resource management, employment, training, skills and education.

For the inspiration to specialise in employer engagement research, I principally have to thank my erstwhile colleague Professor Ian Greer. Ian articulated for me this important gap in the employment relations literature and introduced me to Jo Ingold, with whom I went on to co-edit this collection. I also want to thank Jo especially for inviting me to collaborate, being the driving force of this book and introducing me to her extensive network of leading scholars in the field. It has been nothing but a pleasure to work with Jo and our co-contributors. Working with Paul Stevens and the team at Bristol University Press has been similarly pleasurable and effortless.

On a personal note, I wish to thank my wife Valerie and our daughters Leah, Hannah and Gabi for bearing with me during the years of my obsessive pursuit of my academic work, and for the interest they have shown in what even I can see is a somewhat obscure area. I also have to thank my father, John McGurk, who, through his dedication, intellectual curiosity and good humour, continues to be my main inspiration.

Patrick McGurk
London, June 2022

Introduction: Why Is Employer Engagement Important?

Jo Ingold and Patrick McGurk

For centuries governments have been exercised by the challenge of how to deal with individuals in the population who are not in paid labour. It is a highly politicized issue, cutting across a range of policy domains including macro-economics, labour markets, social security, education and health. In the early part of the 20th century countries in the Global North introduced some form of public employment service provision, or 'labour exchange' (Price, 1998). Active labour market policies (ALMPs)[1] as we now know them first emerged in the 1950s in Sweden under what is known as the 'Rehn-Meidner model' after the two economists who conceived them (Bonoli, 2010). Their aims were equality of wage distribution, sustainable full employment, modernization of Swedish industry and addressing the recurrent problem of labour shortage. The idea of ALMPs subsequently spread to France, Italy, Germany and elsewhere. Following the 1970s oil shocks and economic depression, there was a shift away from 'activation' aiming to provide occupations and activities for jobless individuals and to address mass unemployment, as well as temporary jobs and training programmes in the public sector, amounting to job creation.

These early indicators of the importance of the demand side of labour markets (employers) were largely left behind in the 1990s when a 'new wave' of 'active labour market policies and programmes' emerged. The diffusion of ALMPs across countries was aided by supra-national institutions such as the European Commission and the OECD[2] promoting ALMPs as key policy solutions (Ingold and Monaghan, 2016), leading to some considerable convergence in the direction and focus of them. However, there was also a 'reorientation' of ALMPs away from the goal of job creation and towards incentivizing work over 'welfare' and providing employment assistance to address what was perceived as the key policy problem: the mismatch of workers with jobs. This inevitably led to a shift away from 'passive' public spending on cash transfers through social security benefits towards supply-side measures oriented around increasing the 'employability' of individuals by 'activating' them for work.

ALMPs have historically been provided by the public employment services (PES), but the contracting-out of services to for-profit and non-profit organizations is now a feature across a variety of countries. ALMPs involve a spectrum of mechanisms, ranging from assistance with coaching and job search, employability skills training (CVs, interview skills), paid, subsidized or unpaid work placements/work trials, 'social activation' for non-employment-related obstacles to employment (for example housing, alcohol/drug use) through to workfare/work for your benefit[3] and sanctions for non-compliance. ALMP approaches have been categorized as 'human capital' (involving a focus on education, training or work experience) and 'work-first' (quickest way into work) (Lødemel and Trickey, 2000). Work-first has also been termed enablement or 'workfare' (Dingeldey, 2007), although in practice interventions are typically combined.

To date, the defining feature of ALMPs since the 1990s has been a focus on the supply side of the labour market, that is, jobseekers. This has been thrown into sharp relief by mechanisms in the related policy domain of social security that have focused on the tightening of eligibility and conditionality for benefits to reduce in-flows and 'welfare dependency' (WelCond Project, 2018), and the extension of ALMPs beyond unemployed groups to other 'economically inactive' cohorts, key examples being lone parents (see Wiggan and Knuth; Green and Sissons in this volume) and disabled people (Hanson and Moore; Moore, Hanson and Gustafson; Hamilton in this volume). Consideration of the demand side (employers) has largely been absent from policies. This is despite the axiom that employers are critical to such programmes' success, whether that be measured by job outcomes, or 'sustainability' of jobs beyond job placement (often measured at the six-month point). This is not to say that there are no examples of 'demand-side' interventions. For example, wage subsidies can be categorized as operating both on the demand and supply sides, given that by definition they reduce costs to employers (Robertshaw, forthcoming). Other ways of engaging employers have included partnering with them to design training and work placements and work trials (McQuaid and Lindsay, 2005; Salognon, 2007; Lindsay et al, 2018). Martin (2014) has argued that ALMPs should not be merely 'fair-weather' instruments but suggests that effective activation strategies can help to make labour markets more resilient to adverse demand shocks, and that a mix of ALMP strategies needs to be adjusted according to labour demand, placing employers at the forefront. Swank and Martin

(2001, 2004, 2012) were among the first to argue that a key determinant of employer involvement in social policies was the role of employers via employers' representative organizations (national and peak). However, critiques of the shortcomings of ALMPs have drawn attention to the lack of attention to the demand side within policymaking and programme design and delivery (for example van Berkel et al, 2017 and Bredgaard, Ingold and van Berkel, this volume). Peck and Theodore (2000) have argued that ALMPs merely re-shuffle the 'jobs queue' at the lower end of the labour market, exacerbating the 'low-pay, no-pay cycle' (Shildrick et al, 2010).

Academic scholarship has been similarly slow to address the topic of 'employer engagement' in ALMPs, largely because of persistent hard boundaries between academic disciplines. It is worth providing a note on the definition of 'employer engagement', a term that has been used somewhat interchangeably with the terms 'employer participation' and 'employer involvement' in relation to employment and skills policy by policymakers, evaluators and researchers (van Berkel et al, 2017: p 505; see also Ingold and Valizade, 2015). Scholars have attempted to define employer engagement both theoretically and empirically. Ingold and Stuart (2015) have argued that there are 'two faces' to employer engagement in ALMPs: 'employer involvement with programmes and the engagement between providers and employers' (p 443). Bredgaard (2017) has distinguished between employers' attitudes towards engagement and their actual behaviour. Van Berkel et al (2017) put forward a broader definition of employer engagement as 'the active involvement of employers in addressing the societal challenge of promoting the labour market participation of vulnerable groups' (p 503). Van Berkel et al (2017) have also argued that human resource management (HRM) can bring novel insights to the study of ALMPs by focusing on the 'public dimension' of HRM, including how it can inform inclusive recruitment practices to promote the employment and retention of disadvantaged individuals.

The majority of studies of ALMPs to date have been within the social and public policy spheres, so have tended to focus predominantly on either institutional or governance issues. Where they have focused on agency, this has been on 'downstream' actors (Wright, 2012) affected by policies or programmes, or on frontline actors involved in implementation such as street-level bureaucrats and street-level organizations. The latter is a welcome development that has paved the way for examination of the role of employer-facing staff involved in delivering ALMPs (Ingold, 2018). However, there still remains a lack of scholarship focused on what Wright (2012) calls 'upstream' policy actors (employers) who are critical to the success of policies. In recent years, there have been attempts to correct this omission (see for example Lambert and Henly, 2013; McGurk, 2014; Ingold and Stuart, 2015; Bredgaard and Halkjær, 2016; Orton et al, 2019), including through the fusion of HRM approaches with social and public policy literature (for example McGurk, 2014; Simms, 2017).[4]

Building on this emerging new direction, this book is the first on the topic of employer engagement in ALMPs (although Mann et al (2014) provide comprehensive coverage of employer engagement in schools) and it uniquely brings together for the first time in one volume leading authors from across the disciplines of social and public policy, economics and business and management/HRM to critically examine employer engagement in ALMPs across a range of country contexts. The book adopts a thematic approach that spans the three levels macro, meso and micro, from the national level of policy, through the middle level of policy mediation and implementation to the everyday level of workplaces and employer practice. The text sets out a conceptual framework for analysing employer engagement, provides empirical contributions to inform both HRM and public policy scholarship and promotes collaborations between the disciplines. It also presents case studies from practitioners, in order to strengthen understanding of employer engagement practice. The chapters in the volume also cover a range of jobseeker groups, who have been subject to various policy interventions, including: disabled people/people with disabilities (Hanson and Moore; Moore, Hanson and Gustafson; Hamilton); lone parents, refugees and older workers (especially Wiggan and Knuth); and ethnic minorities (McGurk and Olaleye). The book seeks to observe national differences and explore key themes pertinent to employer engagement within one volume while moving towards a more integrative conceptualization.

The country selections themselves are distributed between what could be referred to as varying welfare regimes, or different types of market economy, which could be divided several ways. The book chapters examine the UK,[5] the USA, Australia and a northern European cluster of Denmark, Germany and The Netherlands. Australia features as a stand-alone case study at micro level (Hamilton) and in comparison with the UK. The UK is considered at national (macro) level (McGurk and Olaleye), sub-national (meso) level (Green and Sissons) and the level of the workplace (micro) (McGurk and Meredith). There are specific case studies of Denmark, one focusing on the political-economic (macro) level and the other examining the sub-national (meso) level of municipalities (Dall, Larsen and Bo Madsen); and of The Netherlands that focuses on the workplace (micro) level (Borghouts and Freese). The USA is represented in two chapters, an empirical chapter on Sephora (Hanson and Moore) and a case study of the same company, this time co-authored with Sephora's Vice-President (Hanson, Moore and Gustafson). Our international comparative perspective is far from exhaustive and was informed by two elements: firstly, the country expertise of our contributors, who themselves were selected on the basis of their expertise on this still relatively novel topic; secondly, an attempt to cover the countries at the vanguard of active labour market policies and programmes, particularly Denmark, the UK and Australia. Three of the chapters in the collection are devoted to international comparison, specifically between the UK, Denmark and The Netherlands (Bredgaard, Ingold and van Berkel), between the UK and Australia (Baker, Ingold, Crichton and Carr) and between the UK and Germany (Wiggan and Knuth). Given the dominance of employer engagement scholars in northern Europe and North America, the book is limited to the Global North although we recognize this as a key limitation. It is hoped that the book will stimulate scholarship in both Global North and Global South and across the fields of social and public policy, the sociology of work and human resource management.

Outline of the book

Part I of the book focuses on the macro level (national policy and institutions). In Chapter 2, Thomas Bredgaard, Jo Ingold and Rik van Berkel introduce a 'varieties of employer engagement' framework for analysis of ALMPs, since each country context has fundamentally different problem definitions, target groups, governance modes and policy instruments and, by implication, different consequences for the relationship between employers, employment services and jobseekers. The chapter provides a comprehensive review of scholarship on employer engagement and argues for the centrality of organizations' HRM policies and practices as gatekeepers to labour market entry, integration, retention and progression, although these have been largely absent from activation scholarship. The chapter draws on the exemplars Denmark, the UK and The Netherlands to illustrate the three main varieties of employer engagement in activation policies: regulating, facilitating and negotiating demand.

In Chapter 3, David Etherington and Martin Jones situate employer engagement and the labour market within a political economy approach, examining the connections between the state, state intervention and the politics of representation in contemporary capitalism. Focusing on the example of Jobrotation in Denmark, Etherington and Jones illustrate how such a model integrates both supply-side and demand-side dimensions of ALMPs and point to key lessons for other countries. They emphasize the importance of four elements of the Danish system that are key to shaping successful employment and skills policy: high union densities and membership; active trade union involvement in social dialogue; a developed system of collective agreements; and devolved authorities in labour-market policymaking.

In Chapter 4, Patrick McGurk and Omolola Olaleye provide a critical discussion of the principal ways in which employers in England have engaged with Further and Higher Education since the early 2000s to improve workforce skills. The chapter develops an under-explored perspective on the apprenticeship debate, namely integral attempts to increase workforce diversity through apprenticeships, so far with limited success, thereby demonstrating the piecemeal and fragmented nature of related diversity initiatives. McGurk and Olaleye demonstrate how, despite continual efforts to put employers in the 'driving seat' of skills reform, the voluntaristic institutional framework in England has persistently produced weak employer engagement, in which employers tend to act as purchasers and volunteers, rather than commissioners or co-producers.

Finally for Part I, in their practitioner case study (Chapter 5), Orla Baker, Jo Ingold, Emma Crichton and Tony Carr reflect on the historical challenges posed by the omission of employers as stakeholders from the development of programme commissioning frameworks. Examining developments in the UK and Australia, Baker, Ingold, Crichton and Carr examine both commissioner- and provider-led initiatives to facilitate collaboration amongst providers, in order to more effectively engage employers and better service employers and jobseekers. The case study suggests that the UK has travelled further than Australia along what is a very protracted and unstable path towards collaboration. Persistent issues in both countries include how to better foster collaboration and the need for commissioners of services to work across departmental silos, and to consider collaboration at the stage of policy and programme design, rather than expect providers to 'retrofit' their delivery within highly competitive commissioning models.

In Part II we turn to the meso level of organizations and actors involved in delivery of ALMPs. In Chapter 6, Anne Green and Paul Sissons explore ALMP approaches and practices in the UK alongside a wider national discourse about increasing good work. The chapter evaluates the extent to which ALMPs are a 'weak link' in seeking progress towards good work: firstly, as a result of the historically embedded nature of the employer engagement function within particular types of networks of employers; and secondly how this has been supported by a work-first system. Green and Sissons argue that within this there is only limited scope for the PES to engage with a good work agenda; however, labour and skills shortages offer ALMPs an opportunity to capitalize on some upward pressures on job quality to move from work-first to career-first approaches.

In Chapter 7, Tanja Dall, Flemming Larsen and Mikkel Bo Madsen investigate the 'black box' of employer engagement by examining the day-to-day work of the staff in PES who are involved with employer engagement. Based on a five-year study of municipalities in Denmark, Dall, Larsen and Bo Madsen propose a framework to understand this black box – how and why employer engagement may facilitate successful outcomes for vulnerable unemployed people – and analyse how the PES can involve employers in the endeavour of recruiting unemployed individuals with social, mental and physical disabilities. Based on examination of these micro-processes, Dall, Larsen and Bo Madsen conclude that employer engagement does not merely entail employers being socially responsible on paper; it also involves the employing organizations as a whole, including managers on all levels, supervisors, human resource (HR) staff, union representatives and existing employees (topics addressed in Part III).

Chapter 8 sees Jay Wiggan and Matthias Knuth examine changing patterns of employment participation during the last 40 years and, within this context, employers' views of benefit claimants and the PES. Drawing on a number of examples of demand-led ALMPs in the UK and Germany intended to integrate a variety of claimant groups (long-term and short-term unemployed; lone parents; sick and disabled people; older jobseekers; newly arrived refugees) into the labour market, Wiggan and Knuth explore the integrative capacity of employers in terms of the extent to which they are willing and/or able to recruit benefit claimants and/or participate in the services offered by the PES to facilitate this. Wiggan and Knuth conclude that this comparison demonstrates a contradiction between political imperatives and economic business.

In the practice case study for Part II (Chapter 9), Andrew Hamilton examines the Australian government's attempts to assist more people with disabilities to enter the mainstream workforce, drawing on a case study involving the co-design and implementation of a supported employment-service delivery model designed to empower people with disabilities to achieve their career ambitions. The chapter identifies specific recommendations to increase the employment of people with disabilities, including employer education and awareness; the re-contextualization of employment around a skills match between an individual and the employer, rather than just filling diversity quotas; reviewing of recruitment and progression processes within organizations; and the importance of solution-focused 'co-design' between participants, employers and government agencies.

In Part III we examine the micro (workplace) level of employer engagement. In Chapter 10, Patrick McGurk and Richard Meredith examine employers' recruitment of staff via ALMPs through the lens of corporate HR strategy. They demonstrate how employer engagement in the UK is focused in the typically low-waged sectors of retail, hospitality, social care and cleaning. Using Lepak and Snell's (1999) model of HR architecture, the chapter presents a case study of a supermarket retailer to demonstrate how engagement is driven by strategic imperatives while also sustained or constrained by local management. On one hand, McGurk and Meredith demonstrate the strong influence of internal strategic and operational factors in both enabling and constraining engagement; on the other, they show how internal factors interact with external factors through relationship with the local intermediary and local managers' navigation of the changing welfare benefits system.

In Chapter 11, Irmgard Borghouts and Charissa Freese demonstrate how bringing together the two scientific domains of HRM and social security is critical to gaining insight into how HRM policy can be optimally aligned with work and social security policy, and how this policy can in turn facilitate HRM policy aimed at sustaining employment. Taking strategic HRM as a starting point, the chapter focuses on 'inclusive HRM' activities that facilitate labour market transitions. Borghouts and Freese put forward a conceptual model of 'inclusive HRM policy', including four labour market transitions for vulnerable (potential) workers that focus on job-to-job transitions and the intersection of HRM and social policies. They suggest how these transitions relate to the internal, external and 'outside' labour market and how inclusive HRM can be aligned with the public system of social security.

In Chapter 12, William Hanson and Jeffrey Moore examine the environmental conditions, pressures and processes that promote an inclusive, adaptive organization necessary for recruiting and retaining large numbers of disabled people into the workforce. Hanson and Moore argue that shrewd business leaders look to recruit from among the disabled population to gain significant competitive advantages but, while both internal and external pressures can create the need for organizations to adapt to new conditions, it is leadership that shapes the pressures and conditions for building a successful, inclusive organization. Drawing on elements of complexity leadership theory and integrating empirical data from cases of large corporations across the retail, pharmaceuticals, manufacturing and luxury brands sectors, they set out key strategies for fostering the necessary conditions and pressures that can lead to productive, lasting change and robust, inclusive organizations.

Finally for Part III, in the practice case study (Chapter 13), Jeffrey Moore, William Hanson and Tom Gustafson trace the journey by which the US subsidiary of luxury brand LVMH (Sephora) created inclusive workplaces. The case demonstrates the advantages of hiring disabled employees (who outperform their non-disabled counterparts) and sets out key recommendations to other organizations wanting to gain a competitive advantage through an inclusive culture.

The book ends with a conclusion (Chapter 14) that reflects on the themes identified in the three Parts and integrates evidence from the different countries and areas of policy examined, in order to present a theoretical extension to existing scholarship. It also sets out an agenda for embedding demand-side approaches in future scholarship, policymaking and practice.

Notes

[1] Policies and programmes are also referred to interchangeably as 'activation' (particularly in northern Europe) and welfare to work (commonly used in the USA, UK and Australia. Policies refers to the overarching direction and programmes to the specific activities (for example the New Deal programmes introduced by the Labour government in the UK in 1998).

[2] The 1994 OECD Jobs Study and Restated 2006 Strategy, and the European Commission European Employment Strategy (1997) were critical.

[3] For example 'Work for the Dole' in Australia or *nyttejobs* in Denmark.

[4] See *Human Resource Management Journal Special Issue: Employer engagement*, 27(4).

[5] The term 'UK' (United Kingdom) refers to the political entity that governs the whole of Great Britain (England, Wales and Scotland) as well as Northern Ireland. However, in relation to employment and skills, owing to the nature of their devolution settlements, particularly Scotland and Northern Ireland, and to a lesser extent Wales, operate different regulations. The chapters in this book therefore use the term UK when generalizing internationally and making international statistical comparisons; however, when dealing with specific regulations relating to employment and skills, they refer specifically to England, Scotland, Wales or Northern Ireland, to 'England and Wales' or to 'Great Britain', depending on the regulatory regimes in question.

References

Bonoli, G. (2010). 'The political economy of active labour-market policy', *Politics & Society* 38(4): 435–57.

Bredgaard, T. (2017). 'Employers and active labour market policies: typologies and evidence', *Social Policy and Society* 17(3): 365–77.

Bredgaard, T. and Halkjær, J. (2016). 'Employers and the implementation of active labour market policies', *Nordic Journal of Working Life Studies* 6(1): 47–59.

Dingeldey, I. (2007). 'Between workfare and enablement – The different paths to transformation of the welfare state: A comparative analysis of activating labour market policies', *European Journal of Political Research* 46, 823–51.

Ingold, J. (2018). 'Employer engagement in active labour market programmes: The role of boundary spanners', *Public Administration*, DOI: 10.1111/padm.12545.

Ingold, J. and Monaghan, M. (2016). 'Evidence translation: an exploration of policymakers' use of evidence', *Policy and Politics* 44(2): 171–90.

Ingold, J. and Stuart, M. (2015). 'The demand-side of active labour market policies: A regional study of employer engagement in the work programme', *Journal of Social Policy* 44(3): 443–62.

Lambert, S. and Henly, J. (2013). 'Double jeopardy: The misfit between welfare-to-work requirements and job realities.' In E. Brodkin and G. Marston (eds) *Work and the welfare state: Street-level organizations and workfare politics*, Washington, DC: Georgetown University Press, pp 69–84.

Lepak, D.P. and Snell, S.A. (1999). 'The human resource architecture: toward a theory of human capital allocation and development', *Academy of Management Review* 24(1): 31–48.

Lindsay, C., Pearson, S., Batty, E., Cullen, A.M., Eadson, W. (2018). 'Co-production and social innovation in street-level employability services: Lessons from services with parents in Scotland', *International Social Security Review* 71(4): 33–50.

Martin, C. (2004). 'Corporatism from the firm perspective: employers and social policy in Denmark and Britain', *British Journal of Political Science* 25(1): 127–48.

Martin, C.J. and Swank, D. (2004). 'Does the organization of capital matter? Employers and active labor market policy at the national and firm levels', *The American Political Science Review* 98(4): 593–611.

Martin, C.J. and Swank, D. (2012). *The political construction of business interests: Coordination, growth, and equality*, Cambridge: Cambridge University Press.

Martin, J. (2014). Activation and active labour market policies in OECD countries: stylized facts and evidence on their effectiveness, IZA Policy Paper no. 84.

McGurk, P. (2014). *Employer engagement: A human resource management perspective*, University of Greenwich Business School Working Paper WERU7, London: University of Greenwich.

McQuaid, R.W. and Lindsay, C. (2005). 'The concept of employability', *Urban Studies* 42(2): 197–219.

Orton, M., Green, A., Atfield, G. and Barnes, S.A. (2019). 'Employer participation in active labour policy: From reactive gatekeepers to proactive strategic partners, *Journal of Social Policy* 48(3): 511–28.

Peck, J. and Theodore, N. (2000). '"Work first": workfare and the regulation of contingent labour markets', *Cambridge Journal of Economics* 24: 119–38.

Price, D (1998) *Office of hope: A history of the employment service*, London: Policy Studies Institute.

Robertshaw, D. (forthcoming). 'Lost in categorisation? Employment subsidies – bringing the beneficiaries back in', *Journal of Social Policy*. https://doi.org/10.1017/S0047279422000216

Salognon, M. (2007). 'Reorienting companies' hiring behaviour: An innovative "back-to-work" method in France', *Work, Employment & Society* 21(4): 713–30.

Shildrick, T., MacDonald, R., Webster, C. and Garthwaite, K. (2010). *The low-pay, no-pay cycle: Understanding recurrent poverty*, Report for Joseph Rowntree Foundation, York: JRF.

Simms, M. (2017). 'Understanding employer engagement in youth labour market policy in the UK', *Human Resource Management Journal* 27(4): 548–64.

van Berkel, R., Ingold, J., McGurk, P., Bredgaard, T. and Boselie, P. (2017). 'An introduction to employer engagement in the field of HRM: blending social policy and HRM research in promoting vulnerable groups' labour market participation', *Human Resource Management Journal Special Issue: Employer Engagement* 27(4): 503–13.

WelCond Project (2018). *Final findings report: Welfare conditionality project 2013–2018*, York: Welfare Conditionality Project: www.welfareconditionality.ac.uk

PART I

The Macro Level: Political Economy and Policies

2

Varieties of Policy Approaches to Employer Engagement in Activation Policies

Thomas Bredgaard, Jo Ingold and Rik van Berkel

Introduction

There is a growing interest in the role of employers in the delivery and success of activation policies. In this chapter, we put forward a typology of policy approaches to employer engagement in activation policies. We identify three main policy approaches: regulation, facilitation and negotiation. The policy approaches rely on different assumed problems and different target groups of unemployed and apply different types of governance and policy instruments. The typology that we put forward can be used to classify national policy approaches in the emerging field of employer engagement in activation policies.

The chapter begins with a discussion of the growing attention for employer engagement in activation policies and research. In the second section, we describe the typology of policy approaches to employer engagement. The third section illustrates the typology by analysing and comparing recent developments in activation policies aimed at strengthening the role of employers in the UK, Denmark and The Netherlands. We conclude with a discussion of our contribution to debates about the role of employers in activation policies.

Activation policies and employer engagement

In more than three decades of active welfare state and labour market reforms, and a vast associated scholarly literature, the role of employers has received surprisingly little attention in policies, debates and research. Since the early

1990s, when the diffusion of active labour market policies accelerated across a range of countries, activation policies have mainly focused on the supply side of the labour market. Their objectives have been to motivate unemployed people through supportive and disciplinary measures to actively look for jobs, develop their skills and competences and be more flexible with respect to the kinds of jobs they are willing to accept (Dingeldey, 2007; Bonoli, 2013; Ingold and Stuart, 2015; Bredgaard, 2018).

Similarly, activation researchers have mainly focused on the supply side. Scholars have been preoccupied with classifying and categorizing different types of (supply-side) activation policies, such as workfare versus enabling regimes (Dingeldey, 2007); labour market attachment versus human capital approaches (Lødemel and Trickey, 2000); and liberal versus universal types (Barbier and Ludwig-Mayerhofer, 2004). In these classifications, the role of employers has been secondary and different policy approaches to employer engagement have largely been neglected.

The supply-side orientation in activation policies individualizes the problem of unemployment (Cole, 2008). By targeting the behaviour, skills, attitudes and motivation of jobseekers while ignoring the role of employers and their organizations in promoting labour market participation, activation policies have failed to address the demand side of the labour market. Consequently, the personnel (human resource management – HRM) policies and practices of organizations in acting as gatekeepers to labour market entry, integration, retention and progression have been largely absent from activation scholarship. Focusing activation policies on the supply side and increasing pressures on jobseekers to accept any available job may even have allowed employers to worsen conditions of employment rather than invest in them to make jobs more accessible and attractive for jobseekers (Peck and Theodore, 2000; Standing, 2011).

Demand-side policies aimed at promoting labour market participation have never been fully absent, though; some of them even precede the activation era. Examples include anti-discrimination legislation, aimed at combating discrimination practices in the recruitment and selection processes of employers (Frøyland et al, 2019). The Rehn–Meidner model that effectively introduced activation policies during the 1950s in Sweden also centred on demand-side drivers (Erixon, 2010). A demand-side approach that has probably intervened most deeply in organizational and HRM practices but received little attention in mainstream activation policies and debates, concerns programmes aimed at disabled people, such as 'supported employment' where participants are placed in ordinary jobs and then trained and supported by counsellors and job specialists (Bond et al, 2008; Beyer et al, 2010). However, the wave of activation reforms and policies in the 1990s largely abandoned programmes of this kind in favour of supply-side approaches.

During the 2000s, approaches in activation policies oriented to the demand side gradually started to re-emerge. Immervoll and Scarpetta (2012), for example, suggest that across the Organisation for Economic Co-operation and Development (OECD), demand-side incentives increased while direct job creation (for example through public jobs) decreased. Two types of factor contributed to this reorientation of activation policies towards the demand side.

First, activation policies produced modest effects, especially for disadvantaged jobseekers (Kluve, 2010; Martin, 2014; Bredgaard, 2015). This issue gained relevance with the broadening of the target groups of activation policies towards groups that are more difficult to employ, including people with disabilities and health issues, long-term unemployed people with complex personal and social problems, lone parents, refugees and others. In combination with a stronger policy focus on (quick) labour market integration, this broadening of target groups created significant challenges in many countries regarding the development of programmes and interventions that could support disadvantaged jobseekers in labour market integration and engage employers in activation policies. At the same time, studies suggested that employer engagement in activation policies contributes positively to the outcomes and cost-effectiveness of activation policies (Hasluck and Green, 2007; Johansson, 2008; Rosholm and Svarer, 2011; van Gestel et al, 2018).

Second, debates emerged about new forms of governance and the decreasing capacities of governments to successfully address social issues, especially those considered 'wicked problems' (Head and Alford, 2015). This debate emphasized the importance of the involvement of core stakeholders in developing and implementing policies and interventions aimed at solving social problems successfully (Emerson et al, 2011). Evidently, employers are core stakeholders in promoting the labour market participation of marginalized jobseekers (for example, older workers, disabled jobseekers or ethnic minorities). At the same time, new governance models and instruments were introduced into public administration and shifted the focus from new public management towards co-creation and new public governance (Lascoumes and Le Galès, 2007; Martínez Lucio and Stuart, 2011; van Berkel and Leisink, 2013).

In combination, the modest effects of supply-side activation policies and the realization that employers are core stakeholders in the labour market inclusion of marginalized groups of jobseekers created a growing interest in exploring employer engagement in activation policies. In this chapter, we use the concept 'activation policies' as a common denominator for active labour market policies, welfare-to-work policies and employment policies that aim at moving unemployed individuals from outside to inside the labour market. Similarly, the concept 'employer engagement' is used as a common denominator for the public and scholarly interest in employers' 'involvement', 'participation' and 'inclusion' in activation policies. The concept of employer engagement closely relates to the notions of 'demand-side' (Ingold and Stuart, 2015; Bredgaard, 2018; Dinan, 2018), 'demand-led' (Fletcher, 2004; Gore, 2005) or 'demanding' (Frøyland et al, 2019) approaches in activation policies. Other authors use concepts such as 'employer participation' (Orton et al, 2019), 'employer orientation' (Sowa et al, 2015) or 'employer-oriented' labour market policies (Castillo, 2019). Each of these concepts addresses the growing attention in activation policies to the role of employers in realizing policy objectives. Although employers may have other reasons to engage in policies and programmes than to realize policy objectives or solve wicked problems, in this chapter we adopt a policy and design focus and examine how activation policies address the role of employers in promoting labour market participation.

Varieties of policy approaches to employer engagement

As mentioned, there is a growing body of research on employer engagement in activation policies. There are a number of studies in specific countries leading to first steps in conceptualizing the demand-side-oriented approach in activation, as well as in analysing diversity in these approaches (for example, Sheehan and Tomlinson, 1998; Fletcher, 2004; Gore, 2005; Farnsworth, 2006; Salognon, 2007; van Kooy et al, 2014; Mandal and Osborg Ose, 2015; Sowa et al, 2015; Bredgaard and Halkjær, 2016; Taylor et al, 2016; van Gestel et al, 2018; Aksnes, 2019; Castillo, 2019; Frøyland et al, 2019).

There are also some typologies of different types of programme and approaches to employer engagement. For instance, Ingold and Valizade (2015) distinguish between typologies that focus on categorizing (1) the type of employer participation or (2) the motives for employer participation in activation policies. In the first group, Martin (2004a, 2004b) uses a scale with different degrees of participation and combines it with the ideological position of the employers. Similarly, Nelson (2013) uses a five-point scale to compare employer participation in activation policies in Denmark and Germany. Ingold and Valizade (2015) compare degrees of employer engagement in the UK and Denmark by distinguishing between employers that are 'instrumentally engaged' and 'relationally engaged'. In the second group of typologies that categorize motives for participation in activation policies, there is recognition of other types of motivation than short-term economic self-interest. For example, Aa and van Berkel (2014) conceptualize employers as either clients or co-producers and identify three types of employer motivation in The Netherlands: (1) employers recruiting new workers through a public recruitment channel, (2) employers that are motivated to reduce their wage costs and (3) employers motivated by corporate social responsibility (CSR). Coleman et al (2014) identify four types of motivation for recruiting unemployed young people: (1) altruistic motive, (2) opportunistic motive, (3) responsive motive and (4) strategic motive. Similarly, Orton et al (2019) suggest that employers can be 'reactive gatekeepers' or 'proactive strategic partners'. Bredgaard (2018) distinguishes between attitudes and behaviour of employers and conceptualizes four different types of employer response to active labour market policies (committed employers, dismissive employers, sceptical employers and passive employers).

However, a shortcoming of these attempts to categorize and conceptualize employer engagement to date is that they focus on the micro level: individual employers. We extend this literature by focusing on variations in policy approaches to employer engagement, that is, the type of governance, policy design and instrument selection that occurs prior to employer engagement in activation. We intend to link policy design and instruments at the macro level with the meso and micro levels of organizational practice and delivery. The typology is inspired by the literature on modes of governance and policy instruments (Schneider and Ingram, 1990; Bemelmans-Videc et al, 1998; Osborne, 2001; Jordan et al, 2005).

The three policy approaches to employer engagement are regulation, facilitation and negotiation. They are set out in Table 2.1, in which these policy approaches to employer engagement are compared along various dimensions. Evidently, they are ideal types and theoretical constructs, and concrete activation policies are very likely to reveal mixes of them. Nevertheless, we believe that these ideal types are fruitful because they help to identify various policy logics underlying the engagement of employers in promoting the labour market participation of marginalized groups (see Table 2.1).

The first dimension, definition of the problem, refers to what each of the policy approaches considers to be the core problem in promoting the labour market participation of unemployed jobseekers. The second dimension, target groups, refers to the specific group of jobseekers that is expected to benefit from each type of employer engagement and indicates that the approaches are not mutually exclusive, but can be combined to address different target groups. The third dimension, governance modes, specifies the underlying assumptions about governance and implies the change in governance modes towards new public management and new public governance that has created a growing interest in employer engagement. The fourth dimension refers to the underlying policy assumption about the role of employers in activation policies. The final dimension, main policy instruments, provides examples of the main types of instruments deployed in each of the policy approaches.

The regulation approach: The rationale for regulation is to prevent discrimination in the recruitment practices of employers. The best-known

Table 2.1: Varieties of policy approaches to employer engagement in activation

	Regulation approach	Facilitation approach	Negotiation approach
Problem definition	Avoid discrimination by changing the recruitment and selection practices of employers	Provide adequate and qualified labour and serve the recruitment needs of employers	Collaborate with employers on job matches, job design and job retention
Target groups	Disadvantaged jobseekers further away from the ordinary labour market	Jobseekers close to the regular labour market that are 'fit' and 'ready' to work	Disadvantaged jobseekers further away from the ordinary labour market
Governance mode	Old public administration	New Public Management	New Public Governance
Policy assumption about employer's role	Employers as passive subjects and utility maximizers	Employers as customers	Employers as co-producers
Main policy instruments	'Sticks' (regulation)	'Carrots' (subsidies)	'Sermons' (information)

example of this approach, anti-discrimination legislation, aims at preventing discrimination in hiring practices and existed prior to activation. However, it focuses on employees and jobseekers in general rather than the groups targeted for activation specifically. At the same time, many of the groups whose protected characteristics (gender, ethnicity, disability) were addressed through anti-discrimination legislation are over-represented among the groups targeted for activation, for example disabled people, ethnic groups and older workers. Anti-discrimination legislation can be combined with quota regulations to promote the labour market participation of disabled people (Borghouts-van de Pas and Freese, 2017). Quota regulations existed before the introduction of activation policies but in some countries have been introduced as part of them (Sargeant et al, 2018). Regulation is a typical example of 'old public administration' and regards employers as passive subjects of government control and sanctions. The dominant policy instrument is 'the stick', that is, laws either prohibiting particular actions or mandating certain actions from employers. To make enforcement effective, 'the stick' may be accompanied by negative incentives that punish undesired actions (taxes and fines) or by positive incentives that stimulate desired actions (subsidies). The approach addresses employers and their organizations as legal subjects expected to comply with legal regulations and as utility maximizers that are responsive to punishment or reward. Despite the rise of new modes of governance and new (softer) policy instruments, regulation still constitutes a vital part of the 'package' that countries develop in their activation policies. This underlines what Jordan et al (2005) called the 'resilience of regulation' in the context of new governance and new policy instruments.

The facilitation approach: The rationale for the facilitation approach is not to change but to facilitate the recruitment practices of employers by providing an adequate and qualified supply of labour. Compared to the regulation approach, this policy approach relies more strongly on the roles of labour market intermediaries, that is, the public, private or community-sector agencies responsible for implementing activation policies. It has a strong service orientation and emphasizes interactions between these employment agencies and employers, and services provided by these agencies to employers. Compared to the 'policies against the market' of the regulation approach, this is 'policies with the market' (Esping-Andersen, 1985). The underlying governance mode is New Public Management (NPM), which pervaded public administration and public employment service from the 1990s (Hood, 1991). NPM was a critique of the inefficiencies of regulation and a promotion of market mechanisms in public governance (Osborne, 2001). The core characteristic of this approach is in line with what the literature denotes as 'demand-led' policies (Gore, 2005). The approach operates on the basis that labour market interventions such as training should focus on the employees that employers need, thus matching local jobseekers to existing vacancies (McCollum, 2012). It follows from this, that the primary target group are jobseekers that are close to the regular labour market and considered 'fit' and 'ready' to work (Ingold, 2018). Employers are addressed as clients, and their specific recruitment needs are met by proposing suitable candidates for available vacancies and by providing candidates who have the training or education considered necessary to make matches successful, thus giving measures oriented to the supply side a clear demand-led dimension. In this policy approach, employers' recruitment needs are considered fixed and non-transformable in the matching process (Gore, 2005; Frøyland et al, 2019). This is one of the reasons why this approach has been criticized for de facto principally benefiting jobseekers close to the labour market (Fletcher, 2004). Focusing exclusively on the recruitment process rather than organizational HRM practices in a broader sense (Devins and Hogarth, 2005; McCollum, 2012) results in facilitating demand rather than necessarily stimulating it or negotiating roles for jobseekers further from the labour market. The policy instruments the facilitating demand approach involves are 'carrots' (including subsidies). This can take the form of free recruitment and selection services, and training and education for jobseekers, to stimulate employer engagement in hiring jobseekers. Rather than obliging them to act, these measures aim to induce employers to act voluntarily by appealing to their needs and wants, often their immediate labour needs. Wage subsidies for a 'trial period' of job training are often used to engage employers in this type of activation approach.

The negotiation approach: The negotiation approach also has a strong focus on services provided by labour market intermediaries but addresses some of the weaknesses of the facilitation approach and targets disadvantaged jobseekers, who are more difficult to 'sell' to employers. The negotiation approach deals with a broader range of HRM issues than recruitment and selection in addressing the inclusiveness of organizations. It considers employer preferences and practices as alterable rather than fixed (Salognon, 2007; Frøyland et al, 2019). Organizational and HRM characteristics that are relevant to matching processes are thus considered subjects for negotiation. The origins of this approach are found in 'Supported Employment' and related programmes (Griffin et al, 2008). Supported Employment programmes focus specifically on people with disabilities and may therefore provide valuable insights into the conditions supporting the labour market inclusion of individuals furthest from that market.[1] This approach also broadens the role of labour market intermediaries, who are crucial actors in the negotiating process and in providing organizations with the support that they need to become more inclusive. The policy approach is rooted in the ideas of partnership, collaboration and co-creation, which are characteristic of New Public Governance (Osborne, 2006; Torfing et al, 2014). The main policy instrument in the negotiation approach is 'sermons', that is, information and persuasion. We see a combination of policy tools in use. One type are capacity tools (providing information and resources). The negotiation process aims at creating shared values, beliefs and learning, for example concerning the societal value of and business case for hiring and placing jobseekers (Simms, 2017). Given the focus on negotiation, employers are addressed as co-producers or partners in activation programmes.

To illustrate how these three policy approaches to engaging employers in activation are combined in practice, the next section compares examples of employer engagement in the UK, Denmark and The Netherlands. Our selection of cases from these countries is not meant to be representative of activation policies in these countries; rather, they were selected as helpful in illustrating how the different policy approaches are implemented and combined in different national and institutional contexts.

Policy approaches to employer engagement in the UK, Denmark and The Netherlands

Although the welfare regimes of the UK, Denmark and The Netherlands vary considerably (Esping Andersen, 1990), and likewise their varieties of capitalism (Hall and Soskice, 2001), all three countries have witnessed attempts to promote employer engagement in activation policies. Nevertheless, the differences between the countries do resonate in the ways in which employer engagement developed, as we will see when we use our typology of policy approaches to employer engagement to analyse these developments.

The regulation approach

A striking similarity between the three countries is that enforcing employer engagement in activation policies through 'hard' regulation is practically absent, apart from anti-discrimination legislation. In terms of the policy instruments distinguished by Schneider and Ingram (1990), hard regulation includes authority tools and negative incentives such as sanctions and charges. Anti-discrimination legislation focuses on protected characteristics (such as gender, race, age, disability) and this intends to have an impact on employers' recruitment and selection practices, as well as other dimensions of the HR cycle, such as onboarding, reward, recognition and progression. However, as a main activation challenge in changing the recruitment and selection practices of employers, regulation is arguably limited aside from its core assumption that employers are law-abiding subjects. In some cases the characteristics protected by legislation map onto specific target groups of jobseekers (although not necessarily). The reluctance to employ hard regulation in the context of activation policies has different backgrounds.

In the UK, successive governments have demonstrated limited commitment to changing employers' recruitment practices within a range of policymaking domains reflective of the UK's position as the most liberal labour market regulatory regime in Europe. In the UK, reluctance to adopt hard regulation is embedded in a broader context of lack of institutionalized forms of employer engagement in labour market issues. In Denmark and The Netherlands, there is a strong tradition of including the 'social partners' (government, trade unions, employer representatives) in policymaking (Becker, 2001; Schreuder, 2001; Bredgaard and Madsen, 2018). This means that policymakers can rely on social partners' capacities for self-regulation and voluntary engagement rather than hard regulation. In Denmark, regulation of employers' personnel practices, for example through employment quotas, is generally considered a violation of the voluntarist 'Danish model' of labour regulation and in conflict with the much praised 'flexicurity' in which there are limited restrictions on companies' recruitment and dismissal practices. In The Netherlands, the well-known 'Polder model' that institutionalizes the engagement of both employers and trade unions in labour market issues through decentralized responsibility and consensual decision making can be considered a source of reluctance to introduce hard regulation.

Interestingly, in both The Netherlands and Denmark policymakers threatened to introduce quotas if employers did not voluntarily engage in recruiting 'disadvantaged' jobseekers. In the Danish case, as part of reforming the disability pension system the social-democratic government of the late 1990s created a new category of 'flexible jobs' for persons with permanently reduced working ability (for example, jobseekers with disabilities). It threatened employers that, if they did not create a specific number of flexible jobs within five years, the government would have to introduce quotas instead. The threat was never actioned as flexible jobs quickly became popular among eligible participants, employers and jobcentres (Gupta and Larsen, 2008). Currently about 100,000 individuals in Denmark work in these flexible jobs, which is equivalent to 2.5 per cent of the adult population. One third of all workplaces in Denmark employ at least one person in a flexible job (Bredgaard and Halkjær, 2016). In the Dutch case, each year specific targets are set for the number of jobs that should be created by public and private employers; a quota regulation will be enacted if organizations fail to achieve these yearly targets. In the UK, businesses are not threatened with sanctions if they fail to engage with programmes.

The 'carrots' (subsidies) offered by the three countries differ more notably. In the UK few positive financial incentives exist to encourage employers to engage in activation programmes. However, quasi-wage incentives that are not strictly wage subsidies in the true sense have been used as 'sweeteners' for employers alongside activation programmes for specific groups, for example the Youth Contract Wage Incentive for long-term unemployed young people.

In The Netherlands and Denmark, by contrast, there are numerous examples of economic subsidies and other types of positive incentive for employers, which seek to stimulate their engagement in activation policies and the recruitment of unemployed jobseekers, some of which we will return to later in the chapter. Economic incentives are based on the notion that employers are utility maximizers and such incentives can work to offset the risks to employers of employing individuals with employability-related or other barriers to work.

The facilitation approach

Providing qualified and motivated labour to fill vacancies has always been a *leitmotif* for the public employment service and became even more prominent with the active labour market reforms in the 1990s. The objective of activation policies was to train, motivate and assist the unemployed in active job search and thereby reduce structural unemployment (Barbier and Ludwig-Mayerhofer, 2004; Dingeldey, 2007; Bonoli, 2013). The United Kingdom, Denmark and The Netherlands were pioneers in introducing activation policies.

In Denmark and The Netherlands, municipalities play a core role in delivering activation policies and facilitating local labour supply. Dutch municipalities were made increasingly responsible for the funding of social assistance benefits, which provided a strong incentive to reduce the number of social assistance recipients by making activation more effective. In Denmark, financial incentives for local jobcentres to prioritize an activation strategy with local employers instead of municipal activation projects were enhanced. In both countries, promoting an employer orientation in activation policies was a core strategy in making municipal activation more effective. The Dutch Council of Work and Income expressed this view quite clearly in a report in 2009 (RWI, 2009, p 28): 'Demand-oriented reintegration projects are an essential lubricant for the functioning of the labour market: it combines effective reintegration with solving personnel shortages'. In Denmark, several impact evaluations have suggested that activation programmes delivered by (private) employers perform better, measured by participants' subsequent employment rates and income, than activation programmes carried out by the local jobcentres or other public institutions (Rosholm and Svarer, 2011).

In the UK, the trajectory has been towards centralization of employment services. The Work Programme (WP) that ran from 2011 to 2017 constituted the largest single activation programme and represented a centralizing of activation policy and an expansion of contracting out through the Department for Work and Pensions as purchased. This gave a greater role to a larger range of labour market intermediaries, with 39 'Prime' providers across the UK, predominantly from the private sector but also from the voluntary and social enterprise sectors. However, since the WP ended in 2017, the Work and Health programme is the main, centralized activation programme; it is targeted at jobseekers who have been unemployed for two years or more and who have a health condition or disability. Since the 'new wave' of the 1990s, UK activation has been dominated by cheaper, 'work-first' programmes predominantly targeted at the longer-term unemployed, based on evidence that those unemployed for six months or less are able to 'self-service' and return to employment quickly. Consequently, additional programmes, such as the WP, have targeted individuals further away from the labour market. This suggests that the dominant approach taken by the UK to employer engagement was to facilitate demand with pockets of good practice focused on negotiating demand (see next section).

The instruments and tools that labour market intermediaries in the three countries could use to facilitate demand reveal differences and similarities. Dutch and Danish labour market intermediaries utilize a larger set of policy instruments in engaging employers and in facilitating their recruitment needs. For example, intermediaries in these countries can inform employers about financial incentives such as subsidies or work experience programmes that are more numerous than the UK offers. Intermediaries in all countries also use services like job fairs and 'meet and greet' events at which employers can meet unemployed clients, vacancy databases and assistance in job brokering.

As mentioned, employers are treated as clients whose current recruitment needs are the starting point of the services the intermediaries provide. However, as examples within this policy approach demonstrate, activities focus on serving the immediate recruitment needs of employers. This allowed a programme such as the WP to operate at scale by channelling large numbers of unemployed individuals towards vacancies posted by employers (particularly large employers), with the probability that some would become employed (Ingold, 2018). Such interventions may serve to successfully fill employers' immediate vacancies, at least in the short term, but might not result in sustainable matches in the longer term, or overcome organizations' HRM practices that exclude groups or individuals from work.

The negotiating approach

This type of employer engagement is the most recent development in all three countries. While the facilitation approach can be characterized as a 'bottom-up' approach mainly developed by labour market intermediaries under pressure of performance targets and the need to improve the effectiveness and outcomes of activation policies, the rise of the negotiating approach in the three countries surveyed reveals a more diverse pattern.

The main activation challenge in the Danish Flexible Jobs scheme and the Dutch Job Agreement was to match jobseekers with employers by changing employers' recruitment practices. The target group for the Flexible Jobs scheme was persons with permanently reduced working ability who would not be able to work in ordinary employment, while the Job Agreement focused on promoting the participation in the regular labour market of people unable to earn statutory minimum wage independently because of reduced work capacity attributable to physical, mental or psychological disabilities. The Dutch and Danish policies reveal a mix of policy instruments: regulation (the quota threat), incentives (among others, wage subsidies) and capacity tools (services provided by intermediaries), and information.

In the UK, the WP was introduced during the 2008/9 Global Financial Crisis amidst rising unemployment, including youth unemployment, and specifically targeted at individuals who were long-term unemployed, at risk of long-term unemployment (particularly young people), or disabled or with a long-term limiting health condition and assessed as 'fit for work'. The programme was built on the classic instruments of New Public Management: a 'payment by results' incentive framework for providers delivering the programme and a 'black box' delivery model without prescription from central government. The WP was a supply-sided programme focused on moving 'harder to help' individuals into employment; however, as labour market intermediaries, WP providers recognized that, to place individuals in lasting employment, investment in employer engagement or 'business development' teams were critical to programme outcomes, giving rise to a range of demand-side activities within programme delivery. In aggregate, the WP performed poorly for individuals furthest from the labour market but relatively successfully for those closer to the regular market (House of Commons, 2013). In the UK, there were numerous examples of provision of information and resources about programmes for employers and individuals on caseloads, and information and resources were provided to unemployed clients about job vacancies. A core driver for these initiatives and for building more intensive relationships with employers was the WP's focus on 'hard to employ' groups of jobseekers. The processes of negotiating demand involved managing expectations: those of jobseekers about available jobs in the labour market, and those of employers about the available candidate pool. They also involved leveraging employers' HR and CSR 'logics' (Simms, 2017) to create shared values and beliefs that might facilitate successful placements of individuals and build ongoing and trusted relationships with employers that could form the basis for repeated engagement and placements.

Conclusions

There is a growing awareness and literature on the role of employers in activation policies. The turn towards the demand side of the labour market is related to dissatisfaction with inadequate results of supply-side policies and expansion of activation policies to target new groups with problems besides unemployment. We contribute to this debate by identifying three different policy approaches to employer engagement and by illustrating their implementation in three countries pioneering activation (UK, Denmark and The Netherlands). We label the three policy approaches to employer engagement in activation policies the regulation approach, the facilitation approach and the negotiation approach.

The regulation approach is the traditional way of addressing employers in labour market policy, by prohibiting discriminatory practices or prescribing particular practices for recruiting marginalized groups of jobseekers (for example, older workers, disabled jobseekers or ethnic minorities). In this approach, employers are considered passive subjects of law and regulation. In our three case countries, anti-discrimination legislation has been employed, but there is a general reluctance to use hard regulation, although Danish and Dutch policymakers have threatened to use quotas and sanctions if employers did not voluntarily participate in activation programmes.

The facilitation approach considers employers as customers for the services of labour market intermediaries. The objective of this type of activation policy is to provide employers with qualified and motivated labour to fill vacancies and reduce structural unemployment. The target groups are those unemployed who are closest to the regular labour market. Facilitation of an adequate labour supply has always been a core objective of public employment services and became more prominent with the emergence of activation policies from the early 1990s. The UK, The Netherlands and Denmark were among the countries pioneering the transformation from passive to active labour market policies, and therefore, also among the first to apply the facilitation approach. This approach, however, is not particularly successful in helping the most disadvantaged unemployed, those with multiple and complex barriers to labour market integration.

The negotiation approach considers the preferences of employers as alterable and intervenes on the demand side of the labour market. Job specialists and other intermediaries strive to negotiate between jobseekers with complex problems beyond unemployment and the recruitment and personnel practices of employers, and match the former with the latter. This involves a mutual process of co-production and adaptation. In the UK, no activation policy exists that provides an institutionalized basis for this type of negotiation, but initiatives have emerged in a 'bottom-up' fashion that are less systematic and more piecemeal than the Danish and Dutch cases. In Denmark and The Netherlands, national programmes and frameworks seek to negotiate a balance between the disadvantaged unemployed and employers, such as the Flexible Jobs schemes and the Job Agreement.

Current literature has not paid sufficient attention to these variations in policy approaches to employer engagement. Previous conceptualizations of employer engagement tend to focus on country case studies and the micro level, individual employers. We have tried to contribute to this literature by identifying variations in policy approaches and linking the policy design and instruments at the macro level with the meso and micro levels of organizational practice and delivery. As the cases from the United Kingdom, Denmark and The Netherlands show, the engagement of employers in activation policy is predominantly promoted in a voluntary rather than obligatory way. The cases also show that specific policy programmes often combine elements of the three policy approaches to employer engagement.

In future research, this typology can be used to compare activation approaches in different countries, including the different levels of governance and service delivery. A research agenda for future studies should include, on one hand, an examination of the development of policy approaches to employer engagement that uses a comparative perspective and explores institutional and contextual characteristics that help to explain specific employer engagement configurations; and on the other, and perhaps most importantly, studies should examine the impact of varieties of employer engagement and the extent to which they contribute to a more inclusive labour market.

Note

[1] Frøyland et al (2019) argue that these programmes combine supply-oriented and demand-oriented approaches (denoting this approach as a 'combined approach') in the sense that they focus on the match between supply and demand, and on providing support (through professional 'employment specialists' or 'job coaches') to jobseekers, employees and employers.

References

Aa, P. and van Berkel, R. (2014). 'Innovating job activation by involving employers', *International Social Security Review* 67(2): 11–27.

Aksnes, S.Y. (2019). 'Engaging employers in vocational rehabilitation: Understanding the new significance of knowledge brokers', *Journal of Vocational Rehabilitation* 50(1): 73–84.

Barbier, J.-C. and Ludwig-Mayerhofer, W. (2004). 'Introduction', *European Societies* 6(4): 423–36.

Becker, U. (2001). '"Miracle" by consensus? Consensualism and dominance in Dutch employment development', *Economic and Industrial Democracy* 22(4): 453–83.

Bemelmans-Videc, M., Rist, R. and Vedung, E. (1998). *Carrots, sticks and sermons: Policy instruments and their evaluation*, London: Transaction Publishers.

Berkel, R. and Leisink, P. (2013). 'Both sides now: Theoretical perspectives on the link between social and HR policies in promoting labour market participation.' In P. Leisink, P. Boselie, M. van Bottenburg and D. Hosking (eds) *Managing social issues: A public value perspective*, Cheltenham: Edward Elgar, pp 143–62.

Berkel, R., Ingold, J., McGurk, P., Boselie, P. and Bredgaard, T. (2017). 'An introduction to employer engagement in the field of HRM: Blending social policy and HRM research in promoting vulnerable groups' labour market participation', *Human Resource Management Journal* 27(4): 503–14.

Beyer, S., Urries, F. and Verdugo, M. (2010). 'A comparative study of the situation of supported employment in Europe', *Journal of Policy and Practice in Intellectual Disabilities* 7(2): 130–36.

Bond, G., Drake, R. and Becker, D. (2008). 'An update on randomized controlled trials of evidence-based supported employment', *Psychiatric Rehabilitation Journal* 31(4): 280–90.

Bonoli, G. (2013). *The origins of active social policy. Labour market and childcare policies in a comparative perspective*, Oxford: Oxford University Press.

Borghouts-van de Pas, I. and Freese, C. (2017). 'Inclusive HRM and employment security for disabled people: An interdisciplinary approach', *E-Journal of International and Comparative Labour Studies* 6(1): 9–33.

Bredgaard, T. (2015). 'Evaluating what works for whom in active labour market policies', *European Journal of Social Security*, 17(4): 436–453.

Bredgaard, T. (2018). 'Employers and active labour market policies: Typologies and evidence', *Social Policy & Society* 17(3): 365–77.

Bredgaard, T. and Halkjær, J. (2016). 'Employers and the implementation of active labour market policies', *Nordic Journal of Working Life Studies* 6(1): 47–59.

Bredgaard, T. and Madsen, P.K. (2018). 'Farewell flexicurity? Danish flexicurity and the crisis', *Transfer: European Review of Labour and Research* 24(4): 375–86.

Castillo, D. (2019). 'Employer-oriented labour market policies in Sweden: Creating jobs and the division of labour in the public sector', *International Social Security Review* 72(2): 75–95.

Cole, M. (2008). 'Sociology *contra* government? The contest for the meaning of unemployment in UK policy debates', *Work, Employment & Society* 22: 27–43.

Coleman, N., McGinigal, S., Thomas, A., Fu, E. and Hingley, S. (2014). *Evaluation of the youth contract wage incentive: Wave two research*, DWP Research Report no. 864, London: Department of Work and Pensions.

Devins, D. and Hogarth, T. (2005). 'Employing the unemployed: Some case study evidence on the role and practice of employers', *Urban Studies* 42(2): 245–56.

Dinan, S. (2018). 'A typology of activation incentives', *Social Policy & Administration* 53(1): 1–15.

Dingeldey, I. (2007). 'Between workfare and enablement – The different paths to transformation of the welfare state: A comparative analysis of activating labour market policies', *European Journal of Political Research* 46: 823–51.

Emerson, K., Nabatchi, T. and Balogh, S. (2011). 'An integrative framework for collaborative governance', *Journal of Public Administration Research and Theory* 22(1): 1–29.

Erixon, L. (2010). 'The Rehn–Meidner model in Sweden: Its rise, challenges and survival', *Journal of Economic Issues* 44(3): 677–715, DOI: 10.2753/JEI0021-3624440306.

Esping-Andersen, G. (1985). *Politics against markets: The social-democratic road to power*, Princeton, NJ: Princeton University Press.

Esping-Andersen, G. (1990). *The three worlds of welfare capitalism*, Princeton, NJ: Princeton University Press.

Farnsworth, K. (2006). 'Capital to the rescue? New Labour's business solutions to old welfare problems', *Critical Social Policy* 26(4): 817–42.

Fletcher, D. (2004). 'Demand-led programmes: Challenging labour market inequalities or reinforcing them?' *Environment and Planning C: Government and Policy* 22: 115–28.

Frøyland, K., Andreassen, T. and Innvaer, S. (2019). 'Contrasting supply-side, demand-side and combined approaches to labour market integration', *Journal of Social Policy*, doi:10.1017/S0047279418000491.

Gore, T. (2005). 'Extending employability or solving employers' recruitment problems? Demand-led approaches as an instrument of labour market policy', *Urban Studies* 42(2): 341–53.

Griffin, C., Hammis, D., Geary, T. and Sullivan, M. (2008). 'Customized employment: Where we are; where we're headed', *Journal of Vocational Rehabilitation* 28: 135–39.

Gupta N.D. and Larsen, M. (2008). *Evaluating labour market effects of wage subsidies for the disabled – the Danish Flexjobs scheme*, Working Paper 07:2010, Copenhagen: SFI.

Hall, P.A. and Soskice, D. (2001). *Varieties of capitalism – the institutional foundations of comparative advantage*, Oxford: Oxford University Press.

Hasluck, C. and Green, A. (2007). *What works for whom? A review of evidence and meta-analysis for the Department of Work and Pensions*, Research Report No 407. London: DWP.

Head, B. and Alford, J. (2015). 'Wicked problems: Implications for public policy and management', *Administration & Society* 47(6): 711–39.

Heins, E. and de la Porte, C. (2015). 'The sovereign debt crisis, the EU and welfare state reform', *Comparative European Politics* 13(1): 1–7.

Hood, C. (1991). 'A public management for all seasons?' *Public Administration* 69: 13–19.

House of Commons Work and Pensions Committee (2013). *First report of Session 2013–2013 HC162 Can the Work Programme work for all user groups?*, London: The Stationery Office.

Immervoll, H. and Scarpetta, S. (2012). 'Activation and employment support policies in OECD countries. An overview of current approaches', *IZA Journal of Labor Policy* 1: 9.

Ingold, J. (2018). 'Employer engagement in active labour market programmes: The role of boundary spanners', *Public Administration*, DOI: 10.1111/padm.12545.

Ingold, J. (2021). 'Employers' perspectives on benefit conditionality in the UK and Denmark', *Social Policy & Administration* 54(2): 236–49.

Ingold, J. and Stuart, M. (2014). *Employer engagement in the Work Programme*, CERIC Policy Report No. 5: Centre for Employment Relations, Innovation and Change (CERIC), Leeds: Leeds University Business School.

Ingold, J. and Stuart, M. (2015). 'The demand-side of active labour market policies: a regional study of employer engagement in the work programme', *Journal of Social Policy* 44(3): 443–62.

Ingold, J. and Valizade, D. (2015). *Employer engagement in active labour market policies in the UK and Denmark: A survey of employers*, Policy Report no. 6, Centre for Employment Relations, Innovation and Change (CERIC), Leeds: Leeds University Business School.

Johansson, P. (2008). 'The importance of employer contacts: Evidence based on selection on observables and internal replication', *Labour Economics* 15: 350–69.

Jordan, A., Wurzel, R. and Zito, A. (2005). 'The rise of "new" policy instruments in comparative perspective: Has governance eclipsed government?' *Political Studies* 53: 477–96.

Kluve, J. (2010). *Active labor market policies in Europe: Performance and perspectives*, Essen: Springer.

Lascoumes, P. and Le Galès, P. (2007). 'Introduction: Understanding public policy through its instruments – from the nature of instruments to the sociology of public policy instrumentation', *Governance* 20(1): 1–21.

Lødemel, I. and Trickey, H. (eds) (2000). *'An offer you can't refuse': Workfare in international perspective*, Bristol: Policy Press.

Mandal, R. and Osborg Ose, S. (2015). 'Social responsibility at company level and inclusion of disabled persons: The case of Norway', *Scandinavian Journal of Disability Research* 17(2): 167–87.

Martin, C. (2004a). 'Reinventing welfare regimes: Employers and the implementation of active social policy', *World Politics* 57(1): 39–69.

Martin, C. (2004b). 'Corporatism from the firm perspective: Employers and social policy in Denmark and Britain', *British Journal of Political Science* 25(1): 127–48.

Martin, J. (2014). *Activation and active labour market policies in OECD countries: Stylized facts and evidence on their effectiveness*, IZA Policy Paper no. 84.

Martínez Lucio, M. and Stuart, M. (2011). 'The state, public policy and the renewal of HRM', *The International Journal of Human Resource Management* 22(18): 3661–71.

McCollum, D. (2012). 'The sustainable employment policy agenda: What role for employers?' *Local Economy* 27(5–6): 529–40.

Nelson, M. (2013). 'Revisiting the role of business in welfare state politics: Neocorporatist versus firm-level organisation and their divergent influence on employer support for social policies', *Comparative European Politics* 11(1): 22–48.

Orton, M., Green, A., Atfield, G. and Barnes, S.-A. (2019). 'Employer participation in active labour market policy: From reactive gatekeepers to proactive strategic partners', *Journal of Social Policy*: https://doi.org/10.1017/S0047279418000600.

Osborne, S.P. (ed) (2001). *The new public governance: Emerging perspectives on the theory and practice of public governance*, Abingdon: Routledge.

Osborne, S.P. (2006). 'The new public governance?' *Public Management Review* 8(3): 377–87.

Peck, J. and Theodore, N. (2000). '"Work first": Workfare and the regulation of contingent labour markets', *Cambridge Journal of Economics* 24: 119–38.

Rosholm, M. and Svarer, M. (2011). 'Effekter af virksomhedsrettet aktivering i den aktive arbejdsmarkedspolitik [Effects of company-based activation programmes in ALMP]': https://star.dk/media/1332/effekter-af-virkso mhedsrettet-aktivering.pdf

RWI (2009). *Match! Publiek-private en regionale samenwerking bij vacature-vervulling [Match! Public-private and regional collaboration in filling vacancies]*, The Hague: RWI.

Salognon, M. (2007). 'Reorienting companies' hiring behaviour: An innovative "back-to-work" method in France', *Work, Employment & Society* 21(4): 713–30.

Sargeant, M., Radevich-Katsaroumpa, E. and Innesti, A. (2018). 'Disability quotas: Past or future policy?' *Economic and Industrial Democracy* 39(3): 404–21.

Schneider, A. and Ingram, H. (1990). 'Behavioural assumptions of policy tools', *The Journal of Politics* 52(2): 510–29.

Schreuder, Y. (2001). 'The Polder model in Dutch economic and environmental planning', *Bulletin of Science, Technology & Society* 21(4): 237–45.

Sheehan, M. and Tomlinson, M. (1998). 'Government policies and employers' attitudes towards long-term unemployed people in Northern Ireland', *Journal of Social Policy* 27(4): 447–70.

Simms, M. (2017). 'Understanding employer engagement in youth labour market policy in the UK', *Human Resource Management Journal* 27(4): 548–64.

Sowa, F., Reims, N. and Theuer, S. (2015). 'Employer orientation in the German public employment service', *Critical Social Policy* 35(4): 492–511.

Standing, G. (2011). *The precariat: The new dangerous class*, London: Bloomsbury Academic.

Taylor, S., Carnochan, S., Pascual, G. and Austin, M. (2016). 'Engaging employers as partners in subsidized employment programs', *Journal of Sociology and Social Welfare* 43(1): 149–70.

Torfing, J. and Triantafillou, P. (2014). 'What's in a name? Grasping new public governance as a political-administrative system', *International Review of Public Administration* 18(2): 9–25.

Van Gestel, N., Oomens, S. and Buwalda, E. (2018). 'From quasi-markets to public–private networks: Employers' engagement in public employment services', *Social Policy & Administration,* DOI: 10.1111/spol.12469.

Van Kooy, J., Bowman, D. and Bodsworth, D. (2014). *Understanding employer engagement programs for disadvantaged jobseekers*, Victoria: Brotherhood of St Laurence.

3

Political Economy of the Inclusive Labour Market Revisited: Welfare through Work in Denmark

David Etherington and Martin Jones

Introduction

This chapter draws attention to the wider political economy of the labour market, and in particular provides a framework for a deeper, nuanced understanding of social processes and institutional relations in and through which employer engagement is framed. Our perspective takes on board an analytical framework that views a welfare regime as embodying historically formed class (struggle) relations, in which policies are contingent upon the balance of social forces and specific forms of political struggle. Struggles tend to be centred around both the redistribution of income and access to power resources and representation structures. In relation to representation we refer to both elected local and national government, and systems of political exchange such as social dialogue and corporatist networks (Jessop, 2016).

Esping-Andersen's (1990) concept of welfare regimes as systems of power and negotiation between key interests and actors helps us understand the social and political dynamics of labour regulation. He argued that the redistributive and potentially inclusive dimension of a welfare regime is contingent on labour movement power and influence. The historic development of industrial capitalism in the Scandinavian countries, including Denmark, involved the formation of a highly developed trade union movement and systems of collective bargaining. In earlier work (Etherington and Jones, 2004a) we argued that 'welfare through work' in Denmark is shaped largely by the industrial relations framework and the key role that trade unions (TUs), labour movement organizations and the public sector play in labour market policy.

This chapter suggests that four key elements of the Danish system are crucial in shaping employment and skills. The first is that high union density and membership make TUs important actors. In Denmark, the TUs manage unemployment insurance (UI) benefits (the Ghent system), which are important in connecting trade unions to unemployment policies. All these elements combined are crucial to employer engagement in labour market policy. Second, and linked to this, is the TUs' active involvement in social dialogue and bargaining around employment policy and relatedly, third, a developed system of collective agreements where unions negotiate changes and improvements to welfare and skills policies (Valizade et al, 2022). The fourth and final element is the central role and importance of local government (and the local welfare state) and devolved authorities in labour market policy. The geographies of labour market development within a highly devolved system mean that institutions and actors operate within the same geographical boundaries, making coordination and collaboration more straightforward.

In the early 1990s the Danish trade unions put forward the idea of 'Jobrotation' as a way of sharing work and addressing the high rates of structural unemployment. Jobrotation (JR) involves unemployed people being given direct job training, and unskilled employees being released to update their training and education. The unemployed 'substitutes' receive work experience at TU-negotiated rates, as well as vocational training. The employed obtain additional vocational training and the firm (or public sector organization) benefits through an 'upskilled' workforce, without losses in employment/production (Etherington, 1997, 1998). JR has been supported and coordinated by the Danish Workers Educational Association along with the TUs, with cooperation from the management of the firm or public sector organization and labour market authorities. It is important to emphasize here that as an innovation JR was, and remains, possible because of the way that social dialogue is embedded into policy and delivery. This approach to labour market policy was hailed by the EU as a 'win–win' and a vehicle for inclusion (Eurofound, 2018).

Drawing on JR as a case study, this chapter considers how the Danish 'model' offers lessons for addressing the pressing issues of developing an 'inclusive labour market'. The chapter demonstrates that employers are only one player in the institutional arrangements required for a genuinely inclusive labour market. The next section outlines the Danish welfare and labour-market model. This focuses on a more detailed account of the nature of governance, social dialogue and TU involvement in labour market policy and how this has shaped the JR model. A key research question is how, following the challenges posed by the 2008 economic crisis, Denmark's response to the COVID pandemic has influenced labour market inclusion. Here we highlight the continued interest by both national government and the trade union movement in JR.

Denmark as a redistributive model?
Collective bargaining and social dialogue

Danish social democracy and the Nordic model were born of mass struggle at the end of the 19th century, which established the TU movement's rights to association, representation in policy decision making through the creation of tripartite bodies (TUs; employers; local government) and a series of welfare reforms embracing social insurance, health and universal benefits (Etherington and Jones, 2004a).

Several institutional factors have contributed to maintain relatively high levels of union membership and density (70–80 per cent) in the Nordic countries, even after the culmination of post-Second World War unionization in Europe in the 1970s. Firstly, the presence and wide-ranging functions of unions in the workplace have facilitated acceptance and support of unions as a 'matter of fact' in Nordic working lives (Lind and Knudsen, 2018). Collective agreements cover wages and all issues around working conditions, with a co-determination system and co-determination committees at the occupational and local levels. 'Social partners' establish general wage scales and terms and conditions at the overall level (state, region or municipality), which are then integrated into individual agreements for different occupations. Additionally, the key role of social partner bodies in labour market and welfare policies has been an important historical feature of welfare state-building in Denmark through a highly decentralized local government system with responsibilities for a wide range of welfare, social and health services, as well as managing social assistance for people who are unemployed (and not covered by insurance). An important part of the collective agreement system is the role of employer associations which, compared with the UK, are highly organized. The main employer association – the Danish Employers Association (Dansk Arbejdsgiver) – has to approve the agreements negotiated (Lind and Knudsen, 2018).

Unemployment Insurance Funds

All the Nordic countries except Norway have unemployment benefit systems administered by the trade unions (the Ghent system, so named as it originated and still operates in Belgium). In Denmark the Ghent system has a long history, with the TUs managing UI benefits since the 1930s. These benefits are based on individual contributions during employment and, in the event of unemployment, claimants receive their benefit from the UI office, which tends to be run by the relevant sector trade union (Høgedahl and Kongshøj, 2017).

Most wage earners in the Nordic Ghent countries are therefore simultaneously members of both a trade union and a union-controlled

Unemployment Insurance Fund (UIF, or *A-kasse*). However, workers often associate trade union and UIF membership and thus conflate them; becoming a member of a UIF is an important reason for joining their present trade union (Lind and Knudsen, 2018). In 2002 the centre-right government introduced a series of reforms to UI benefits covering benefit rate, duration, eligibility and the level of state financing; as well as the relationship between UI benefits and alternative social assistance. In theory, such changes have made UIFs less attractive and consequently eroded their role as a recruiting mechanism for the associated trade unions (Kjellberg and Lyhne Ibsen, 2016).

Whilst there have been a number of changes in the UI system, which can be seen to weaken the foothold of the trade unions in the labour market, nevertheless the system is the envy of many countries. TUs provide an important link between the unemployed and the activation system, form a vehicle for providing services for the unemployed and provide signposting to various activation schemes and job offers. In this way they play a crucial role for involvement with Jobrotation schemes. In some instances, they have proved so effective that there have been joint initiatives between the jobcentres and UIF in promoting activation for the long-term unemployed (Etherington, 2008).[1] Additionally, the municipalities often promote their collaboration with TUs in the services that trade unions offer for their members – for example the Copenhagen municipality.[2]

Preserving the social safety net

One of the key features of successful engagement by workers with the labour market is access to an adequate social safety net. Table 3.1 shows some basic indications of welfare and social support in Denmark compared with countries with similar economies. The table shows the large extent to which the social safety net in Denmark has been maintained. For example, Denmark's investment in childcare is one of the highest in the EU and still maintained after the economic crisis broke out. Moreover, the proportion of households having great/moderate difficulties in affording childcare is also significantly lower in Denmark than in the UK. The corollary to this is that the proportion of households in Denmark who gave financial reasons as a factor in not using childcare for children below school age was just 0.7 per cent compared with 25.9 per cent in the UK (EC, 2018, p 18).

Factors that determine individual in-work poverty include the increasing numbers of women entering the labour force, a high proportion of whom take part-time/low-paid employment. As the table shows, this is significantly higher in the UK than in Denmark (Filandri and Struffolino, 2018). The replacement rate of benefits (that is, benefit levels as a percentage of average wages) is significantly higher in Denmark, with 2.5 per cent of GDP spent

Table 3.1: Social expenditure indicators – childcare, in-work poverty and benefit replacement rates

	Percentage of children aged 0–5 in formal childcare	Percentage having great/ moderate difficulty in affording childcare	Percentage of individuals defined as 'working poor'	Replacement rates of benefits (%), average for single person, couple (one earner, two children)
UK	28	16.7	23.0	32
Denmark	70	3.8	8.3	47
Sweden	51	6.2	16.7	45
Finland	32	4.3	14.9	n/a
Germany	32	3.9	24.9	42
Netherlands	52	10.9	18.7	29
Belgium	43	14.3	12.8	64
France	48	12.9	15.9	45

Source: For childcare, EC (2018), adapted from table 4, p 18; for working poor, Filandri and Struffolino (2018) adapted from table 2, pp 144–5; and for benefit replacement rates, Spicker (2017), adapted from table 4.1, p 62

on unemployment benefits in Denmark, compared with 0.2 per cent in the UK (Esser et al, 2013).

Given the context – the dominant Danish dual earner model – women who stay at home are few. The Nordic countries are the only states to provide a 'work-welfare' choice for women, making female work as an end in itself relatively desirable, as family benefits are high and are always paid to the mother. The universal breadwinner model aims to achieve gender equity by promoting female employment and in this model both men and women are viewed as breadwinners (Ingold and Etherington, 2013; Rostgaard, 2014).

Labour market governance, social partners and Jobrotation

Jobrotation and the business model

Job rotation (JR) is essentially a labour market tool that aims to increase the skills base of businesses, particularly small- and medium-sized enterprises (SMEs), whilst maintaining levels of production. The idea sprang from a period of high unemployment, but at the same time firms were experiencing severe skills shortages. The JR model was established originally over a trial period from 1994 to 2003, and a legal enabling instrument was established in 2003 by the state. As highlighted in the previous section of this chapter, the unemployed act as substitutes (or backfill) for employees who can be released to undertake vocational or other forms of training. Unemployed substitutes would be paid the rate for the job at the relevant collective agreement rate. This approach was welcomed by the social partners because it enabled employers to release unskilled workers in order to upgrade their skills and solve recruitment and skill shortages. The trade unions, who were well positioned within the policy arena, gained considerable control and influence in representing unemployed interests in gaining work-based training, as well as shaping the vocational training programmes that were delivered to existing employees (Etherington, 2008). At the same time employers viewed JR as a means by which workers could be trained via a planned and coordinated training strategy involving the key social partners.

JR was piloted in 1994 in Fibertex, a medium-sized textile factory in Aalborg (North Jutland) operating in an area of high structural unemployment. The company was struggling with a workforce that required retraining to adapt to changing technologies and work organization. The trade union discourse focused on the need to distribute work and most of the ideas around JR were initially around sharing work: the unemployed would be offered employment and training opportunities within a supervised and mentored work and training programme, enabling the company to release workers for training without losing production capacity (Etherington and Jones, 2004a, 2004b).

The dynamic for expanding the use of JR in Denmark was the introduction of various leave schemes under reforms in 1994, including education leave. Participation in the schemes was funded by the state via educational budgets and unemployment benefits as well as the European Commission European Social Fund. The leave schemes were intended to raise the qualification profile of low-skilled, unemployed and employed people. However, it is important to emphasize that the JR model is underpinned by the inclusion of education and training as part of activation programmes – something which has arisen from pressures from the social partners and the TUs representing unskilled workers (Madsen, 2015). An integral feature of the JR model is that the unemployed receive pre-employment counselling and training as well as in-work mentoring and support throughout the programme. Much of this has been provided by the Workers Educational Association (AOF). The model allows organizations to retain staffing levels whilst upskilling their workforce, and at the same time provide high-quality employment and training for unemployed people. Significantly, JR has linked welfare-to-work and lifelong learning policies, invoking the need for organizations to provide the necessary adjustments through HR and organizational policies to integrate newcomers to the workplace. The other key feature of the Danish reforms and the introduction of JR is the strengthening of the skills system, regional labour market institutions and corporatist modes of governance with equal representation for the TUs, local government and employers on the Regional Labour Market Councils.

At national level, the National Advisory Council for Initial Vocational Education and Training monitors developments in society and the labour market and highlights trends influencing vocational education and training (VET). The Council then makes recommendations to the Ministry of Education regarding the VET programmes and their labour market relevance. At a regional and local level, VET colleges and social partners work together to enhance VET programmes to meet the needs of the local business environment. This is supported by local training committees (*lokale uddannelsesudvalg*), which ensure close contact between VET colleges and the local business environment. Labour market training (*arbejdsmarkedsuddannelser* – AMU) is designed according to short-term labour market forecasts focused on specific occupations. One assessment of the Danish skills system underlines the importance of the role of the social partners in developing skills:

> Denmark has established a sophisticated CVET system that offers employers and employees a wide variety of training offers to choose from. Danish social partners play a prominent role in setting up the system of formal employee training and assuring that the content is up to date and the quality is maintained at a high level. Bipartite committees at the sectoral and local level as well as tripartite committees at the national level ensure that there is a constant exchange of views as to how the system should evolve and where skills needs exist. (Zibrowius, 2017, p 15)

Already we can see a multiplicity of actors and institutions engaged with the employment and skills system. The various training committees involve equal representation of the social partners including trade unions and representatives of the employers via business associations linked to various economic sectors. It is important to emphasize here that the Danish employers are relatively organized: their national organization (Danskarbejdsgiver – Danish Employers Association) ensures that employer representatives are involved with decision making on skills policy (Emmenegger and Seitzl, 2020). Particularly important to note is the role the TUs play in shaping the skills agenda.

Three key, interrelated elements enable integration of policy and its relative effectiveness. One element is the influence of collective agreements on training. Financing measures are regulated by national laws determining allowances (which may support training leave); the remaining features of training leave, such as eligibility or duration, are decided by the social partners through collective agreements at sectoral or company level or through individual agreements between employers and employees.

Second, the geography of labour market policy ensures that institutions and actors operate within the same geographical boundaries. Most aspects of labour market and welfare policies are devolved to the municipalities, which develop employment and welfare policies while also managing activation programmes. Local authorities play a major role in activating marginalized groups in the labour market and call on their social and health services to support their activation programmes. The local authorities are also represented on the regional councils, which enables them to articulate and promote their interests in economic and social policy.

Third, other labour market institutions such as the AMU organizations, which operate at a regional level, are relatively autonomous and have the scope to develop and implement their own training initiatives. This enables them to respond to changing conditions in the labour market without involving complex negotiations with central government to obtain permissions and approvals for schemes.

It is through this type of integrated approach that JR has been coined a 'welfare-through-work' model, in that activation programmes are linked to workplace strategies around recruitment and vocational education and training. The essence of JR is that it raises important issues around how people can be retained in employment and appropriate strategies that are required to achieve this (see Figure 3.1).

For funding JR takes advantage of existing labour market funding including budgets for:

- a wage subsidy (benefit topped up to the collective agreed wage rate/wage for unemployed substitutes), which can involve some matching payment by employers;
- pre-employment mentoring and training, accessing existing programmes run by the regional vocational training centres (that is, AMU funding to providers such as the AOF);
- in-work training for unemployed substitutes – generally provided by the employment services/municipalities; and
- vocational training for existing employees – this is provided through the regional labour market institutions with the AMU playing a crucial role.

Jobrotation and 'social clauses'

In 1995, a transnational network was established by the AOF and funded under the European Social Fund Adapt Programme to coordinate 35 projects in 15 countries. The idea and concept of JR has subsequently gained considerable ground within European policy circles, reflected by EU support

Figure 3.1: The Jobrotation model

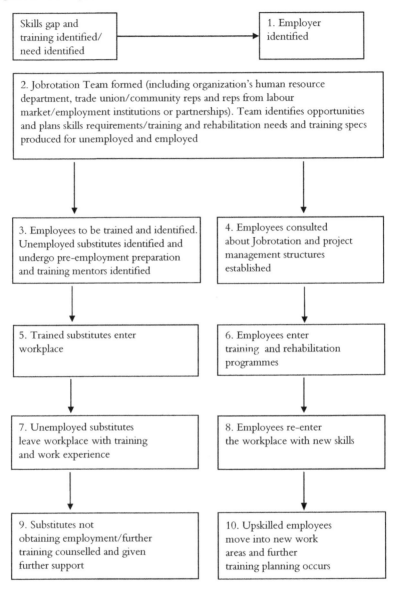

for a JR Network ('EU Jobrotation'). Between 1996 and 1999, 1,802 Danish organizations used JR involving 80,287 employees and 16,957 substitutes. JR has been put forward as a tool for promoting equal opportunities and labour market inclusion (Kruhøffer, 2007). At an EU Conference organized in 2000 in Italy it was reported that:

[w]ithin the framework of the innovative initiatives for the enhancement of human resources, particularly as far as the fight against unemployment and the total increment of the 'Italy System' quality are concerned, the method of Job Rotation has proved to be particularly fitting to the new legislation in Italy, in order to develop an Equal Opportunity policy for (and between) both male/female workers, and male/female unemployed. (EU Jobrotation, 2000, p 3)

One of the attributes of Jobrotation, therefore, has been its scope to build in a gender and equality perspective to encourage positive action in relation to employment and training opportunities. These are important principles and criteria to adopt in assessing the effectiveness of activation programmes and employer engagement. The construction of notions of gender equality in Denmark grew out of 'combined effects of a strong feminist mobilization and favourable political opportunity structures [which] enabled female policymakers to use the state as an arena for political activism for advancing gender equality and for adopting women-friendly policies' (Borchorst and Siim, 2007, p 221; Etherington, 2008).

Social and population changes in relation to increasing immigration and the rise in non-standard employment have created challenges for women's access to labour market policies. A survey carried out by Etherington (2008) found that JR was used in a variety of organizational and workplace contexts. One of the issues identified in terms of the potential for JR was to promote gender equality but, despite the advanced nature of social support and childcare provision, this did not necessarily lead to gender equality in the labour market. It was with this in mind that the (former) Women Workers Union (KAD; now the 3f union), which represented 100,000 women workers in many unskilled jobs in the manufacturing and service sectors, internally organized its involvement with JR by establishing a national and regional secretariat geared to advise and support local shop stewards in the development of JR. KAD established a 'national model' to be used in a variety of workplaces to enable JR to upgrade the skills of women workers. JR has rapidly become regarded as a tool to promote equality of opportunities in the workplace and to combat occupational segregation of the labour market. In this respect, JR has offered considerable opportunities for women to gain access to further vocational and professional qualifications.

More recently a survey carried out by the Centre for Policy on Ageing (2016) highlighted the continuing interest in JR in Denmark and as an instrument for promoting learning for older workers. JR in effect brings together the different elements of the employment and skills system so that policy makers can focus on targeting particular groups. As the Centre put it:

[w]hile it may be difficult to disentangle the effects of individual elements within the Danish adult education system on overall wage levels and labour force participation rates for older workers, it is clear that the emphasis on lifelong learning, education and training at all ages, has a positive effect on labour force participation rates in older age. (Centre for Policy on Ageing, 2016, p 5)

The public sector has also used JR as a vehicle for implementing organizational training strategies and combining the upgrading of qualifications – particularly for women workers – and improving service delivery. For example, in one local authority JR has been used in the social and health sector involving 'teams' of unskilled workers, with home care assistants, assistant nurses, cleaning and kitchen staff and unskilled workers in the parks department, enabling the unemployed to obtain basic gardening skills and those workers to undertake some basic education such as maths, English, Danish, communications and psychology. Drawing up this type of educational portfolio is typical of JR schemes, in that courses undertaken do not necessarily involve purely work-related training, but seek to foster, as part of an employability model, broader and transferable education and skills. Similarly, evaluative research undertaken by the (former) North Jutland Labour Market Council has revealed that the key motivation for Aalborg City Council's involvement in JR, in relation to childcare nursery provision, is to update professional qualifications by releasing workers to undertake further education and training. As part of the JR model, replacements from the unemployment register receive job-related and basic vocational training and, by doing this, the Council addresses labour shortages in the sector (Etherington and Jones, 2004b).

The JR experience in Denmark has been varied. In the private sector, for instance, an electronic company producing loudspeakers with over 500 employees has implemented JR through a union management training committee. This has involved identifying training needs, producing a training plan for the company and assessing the financial implications involving the labour market authorities and the firm (Etherington, 2008). In many ways training strategies in that company tend to be focused around breaking down demarcations and enabling labour to become more flexible and multiskilled at the same time. Elsewhere the extent of union involvement is also interesting, as it extends *beyond* the immediate workplace.

Economic and COVID crisis, challenges and opportunities

During the 2000s there was a decline in the use of JR for a number of reasons: lower rates of long-term unemployment; a shift towards 'work-first' active labour market policies; and resource limitations given that setting up programmes demanded substantial initial funding to support training and in-work subsidies (Etherington, 2008). The other challenge relates to the shift to a more work-first regime and may be key to developing JR. Denmark has installed a complex system of work-related conditions for accessing social assistance and UI so that increasingly more people are under pressure to take up job offers. This raises a number of issues around how disadvantaged groups will move away from the cycle of work and welfare (Ingold, 2020).

Within the sphere of ALMP, there is active engagement by just a few employers, in the main those incentivized by the wage subsidy schemes. There is evidence that these encourage the recruitment of unemployed people, but among certain types of employers who employ predominantly unskilled workers. Wage subsidies can also tend to act as a means of 'parking' the unemployed, as Bredgaard and Halkjaer (2016) report:

> firms where the economic situation had worsened within the last years were more likely to participate in the wage subsidy scheme. The empirical evidence thus indicates that firms may use subsidized labor as a means of coping with economic hardship leading to distortion of competition and crowding out. (Bredgaard and Halkjaer, 2016, p 57)

The pressure to move people into employment quickly (through targets and managing limited budgets) (Andersen et al, 2017) has been accompanied by even more stringent conditions and increased use of sanctions on claimants (Ingold, 2020; Larsen and Caswell, 2020).

The development of JR and an inclusive labour market faces a challenge in relation to the rise in precarious and atypical employment, which predominates in certain sectors of the economy such as services, hotels and catering. Trade unions face difficulties in recruiting and unionizing workers, particularly from Black and Minority Ethnic and refugee communities. Special measures for immigrants (lower-level benefits) have implications for gender equality too as policies tend to reinforce social and gender divisions between Danish-born women and female migrants in the labour market. Accordingly, new forms of inequality among women are an obstacle to achieving gender equality from the perspective of ethnic and religious minorities. This issue is underlined in Lotte Hansen's study of the unionization of cleaners in Copenhagen, in which precarious work is being negotiated through forging new forms of solidarity among the workforce through network building by TU officials and activists (Hansen, 2019).

Overall, the Nordic countries (including Denmark) have coped relatively well in response to the economic and COVID crises (Alsos and Dølvik, 2021). Following the pandemic Denmark, in contrast to other countries such as the UK, retained a strong public sector (Mailand and Thor Larsen, 2017; Etherington, 2020). As Greve et al (2020) have observed:

Denmark and Norway had lower rates of lower public sector debt, and only Finland had a public sector deficit in 2019. Thus, compared with most other countries, the social democratic welfare states were in a favourable macro-economic position to cope with the pandemic. This solid fiscal assessment is also shared by prominent international bond rating agencies. (Greve et al, 2020, p 297)

A second feature is that Denmark has retained its social protection system, in particular compensation for those made unemployed or furloughed. The unemployment benefit replacement rate (as of 2019) is 90 per cent up to a maximum monthly rate of €2,527 compared with around 17 per cent (around €500) in the UK (TUC, 2020a, p 8). The third feature is the role of the social partners. Social dialogue provides opportunity structures and space for the TUs to promote their agendas. Not surprisingly the unions are vocal in favour of social and employment protection, as well as the extension of skills and training for employment and the unemployed (Eurofound, 2020b).

This said, in the face of the 2008 economic crisis and the COVID pandemic there have been calls from various bodies, including the trade unions and Danish Local Government Association, to develop JR more widely and try to overcome the limitations of primarily work-first approaches (Eurofound, 2018). An example of this is the promotion of JR within the public sector (municipalities) by the Local Government Association, along with a number of TUs, as a way of increasing in-work vocational training and progression (Kommunernes Landsforegningen/Danish Local Government Association, 2016).

A tripartite agreement between the government and the social partners (trade unions and employer associations) introduced a new, temporary, short-time work scheme (August 2020, to cover COVID lockdown), promoted as a work-sharing scheme (*arbejdsfordelingsordning*), as a way of preventing redundancies (Eurofound, 2020a). The scheme paid out supplementary UI benefits (at a level 20 per cent higher than normal) to workers who were sent home for some of their normal working time and the work sharing agreement implies that employees in the companies that chose to make use of the measure would work between 50 per cent and 80 per cent of the time. The rest of the working time, they were furloughed. They received full pay when at work and unemployment benefit for the time at home. The normal unemployment benefit rate was increased by 20 per cent, that is, to a maximum of DKK23,000 (€3,087). In addition, non-insured people (that is, employees not members of an unemployment benefit fund) received the same benefit rate. An employers' contribution primarily financed the increased unemployment benefit rate. The original work-sharing scheme deducted time not at work from the number of unemployment hours allowed while still receiving a benefit rate; the temporary work-sharing agreement set this mechanism on hold, so that time not at work did not count as unemployment time (see Kvist, 2021).

The focus on work sharing and the distribution of work has led one of the largest trade unions, Forbundet for Offentlig Ansatte (FOA, 2021), to call for developing JR. This renewed interest relates to an increase in the use of JR between 2010 and 2014.[3] Again, the trade unions and the social partners are taking the lead to ensure that employers address the training needs of workers who are vulnerable to unemployment. This focus on skills and training follows an existing agreement signed in 2020 between the social partners to support the salary costs of apprenticeships via an Employer Reimbursement Fund.[4]

Conclusions

A survey of European labour market policies in the face of and after the 2008 crisis pointed to the increasing policy focus on austerity cuts and greater orientation to work-first policies (Hastings and Heyes, 2016). The COVID crisis has raised the debate even further about a number of issues such as the impact of austerity on labour markets, the role of social dialogue, conditionality and job retention in the labour market (Etherington, 2020). The overall trend towards the rise in atypical employment, precarious work and the platform economy has been a feature of the Danish labour market, as in other countries, and this will have implications for the way TUs and labour market authorities respond. Based on recent evidence there is no doubt that unionization and collective agreements will present opportunities for marginalized, low-paid workers to acquire skills (Ilsøe et al, 2020).

The significance of JR, and the future roles it may play, relate to the way it is situated within these ongoing political struggles around the maintenance of trade union influence on social dialogue and different areas of employment and social policy in Denmark. Even in the context of the COVID crisis, austerity and work–first politics, other discourses are still evident, centring on the links between JR and issues of social solidarity. For example: building connections between the employed and unemployed as a vehicle for shaping a relevant and comprehensive adult vocational education system; the possibilities for influencing the politics of social inclusion and gender/ethnic equality within labour-market policy; and a mechanism for improving the delivery of public services by increasing the education and skills of low-skilled workers. In this way JR encapsulates many progressive aspects of the Danish welfare model and it remains an important instrument of struggle. For shifting the agendas within the workplace and enhancing union representation in relation to training, it is seen as an important feature of local government initiatives in relation to addressing the needs of marginalized groups in the labour market (Etherington and Jones,

2004a; Eurofound, 2018). Moreover, this chapter has demonstrated that employers are only one player in the institutional arrangements required for a genuinely inclusive labour market, and that employers' engagement is effective when situated within a social dialogue that collectivizes a 'logic of collective action', as Offe (1985) would put it, which would not occur with employer-led training fostered just around employers and subject to serial market and policy failures.

In addition to this, an important question for future critical policy and political analysis is whether initiatives such as JR will evolve as an adaptation of workfare, and a continuation of the 'new paternalism' found in North America, or whether they will be deployed as pilots for more inclusive and radical labour market instruments, perhaps indicative of social solidarity, that could provide a space within which to challenge contemporary neoliberal orthodoxy. As highlighted in the previous section, the JR idea has been adopted in a number of EU countries and conferences have revealed that there were strong social as well as economic factors for doing this (EU Jobrotation, 2000). The UK Trades Union Congress (TUC) has called for a job retention scheme that would operate on principles similar to JR with an emphasis on training and employment rights linked to subsidized employment (TUC, 2020b). In the UK, the existing infrastructure and funding regimes can bring about similar initiatives. For example, the devolved authorities have given priority to inclusive growth, policy integration and the deployment and alignment of apprenticeship with other funding programmes (Etherington and Jones, 2016; Etherington et al, 2020).

Watching this political space will prove to be crucial for observing welfare regimes as evolving systems of power and negotiation between key interests and actors (after Esping-Andersen, 1990) and for getting deeper insights into the social and political dynamics of labour regulation in Denmark and beyond.

Notes
[1] This information was provided in an interview with a senior officer of the 3f trade union in Copenhagen in June 2016.
[2] https://international.kk.dk/artikel/how-can-my-trade-union-help-me-when-i-am-une mployed
[3] www.eurofound.europa.eu/observatories/emcc/erm/support-instrument/job-rotation
[4] www.cedefop.europa.eu/en/news/denmark-political-agreement-secures-apprenticesh ips-during-and-after-covid-19-crisis

References
Alsos, C. and Dølvik, J.E. (eds) (2021). *The future of work in the Nordic countries: Opportunities and challenges for the Nordic working life models*, Copenhagen, Nordic Council of Ministers.

Andersen, N.A., Caswell, D. and Larsen, F. (2017). 'A new approach to helping the hard-to-place unemployed: The promise of developing new knowledge in an interactive and collaborative process', *European Journal of Social Security* 19(4): 335–52.

Borchorst, A. and Siim, B. (2007). 'Gender equality: Woman-friendly policies and state feminism – theorizing Scandinavian gender equality', *Feminist Review* 9(2): 207–24.

Bredgaard, T. and Halkjaer, T. (2016). 'Employers and the implementation of active labour market policies', *Nordic Journal of Working Life Studies* 6(1): 47–59.

Bredgaard, T. and Madsen, P.K. (2018). 'Farewell flexicurity? Danish flexicurity and the crisis', *Transfer.* 1–12, DOI: 10.1177/1024258918768613.

Centre for Policy on Ageing (2016). 'Foresight Future of an Ageing Population – International Case Studies Case Study 2: Training older workers in Denmark': www.cpa.org.uk/information/reviews/CPA-Intern ational-Case-Study-2-Training-older-workers-in-Denmark.pdf

Emmenegger, P. and Seitzl, L. (2020). 'Social partner involvement in collective skill formation governance: A comparison of Austria, Denmark, Germany, The Netherlands and Switzerland', *Transfer* 26(1): 27–42.

Esping-Andersen, G. (1990). *Three worlds of welfare capitalism*, Oxford: Polity.

Esser, I., Ferrarini, T., Nelson, K., Palme, J. and Sjoberg, O. (2013). *Unemployment benefits in EU Member States*, Brussels: Employment Social Affairs and Inclusion.

Etherington, D. (1997). 'Trade unions and local economic development – Lessons from Denmark', *Local Economy* 12: 267–74.

Etherington, D. (1998). 'From welfare to work in Denmark: An alternative to free market policies?' *Policy and Politics* 26(2): 147–61.

Etherington, D. (2008). *New welfare spaces: labour market policies in the UK and Denmark,* Saarbrücken: VDM Dr Mueller.

Etherington, D. (2020). *Austerity, welfare and work: Exploring politics, geographies and inequalities*, Bristol: Policy Press.

Etherington, D. and Ingold, J. (2012). 'Welfare to work and the inclusive labour market: A comparative study of activation policies for disability and long-term sickness benefit claimants in the UK and Denmark', *Journal of European Social Policy* 30(1): 22–44.

Etherington, D. and Jones, M. (2004a). 'Beyond contradictions of the workfare state? Denmark, welfare-*through*-work, and the promises of job-rotation', *Environment and Planning C: Government and Policy* 22: 129–48.

Etherington, D. and Jones, M. (2004b). 'Whatever happened to local government? Labour market policy in the UK and Denmark', *Policy and Politics* 32(2): 137–50.

Etherington, D. and Jones, M. (2016). 'Inclusive labour market instrument: Jobrotation': https://ersa.org.uk/blog/job-rotation-idea-whose-time-has-come

Etherington, D., Jones, M. and Ingold, J. (2020). 'Jobrotation: An idea whose time has come?' Blog presented to seminar organized by the Employment Related Services Association, July: https://ersa.org.uk/blog/job-rotat ion-idea-whose-time-has-come

EU Jobrotation (2000). 'European Conference Mainstreaming Jobrotation', 12 May, Rome: www.arcidonna.it/mainstreaming/pdf/jobattiinglese.pdf

Eurofound (2018). 'Job rotation': www.eurofound.europa.eu/observator ies/emcc/erm/support-instrument/job-rotation

Eurofound (2020a). *New temporary tripartite agreement on work sharing, case DK-2020-36/1251 (measures in Denmark)*, COVID-19 EU PolicyWatch, Dublin: http://eurofound.link/covid19eupolicywatch

Eurofound (2020b). *COVID-19: Policy responses across Europe*, Luxembourg: Publications Office of the European Union.

European Commission (2018). *Barcelona objectives on the development of childcare facilities for young people*, Brussels: European Commission.

Filandri, M. and Struffolino, E. (2019). 'Individual and household inwork poverty in Europe: Understanding the role of labor market characteristics', *European Societies* 21(1): 130–57.

Forbundet for Offentlig Ansatte (2020). *En Indsats Mange Resultater Jobrotation*, Copenhagen: FOA.

Greve, B., Blomquist, P., Hvinden, B. and van Gerven, M. (2020). 'Nordic welfare states – still standing or changed by the COVID-19 crisis?' *Social Policy Administration* 55: 295–311.

Hansen, L.L. (2019). *Perspectives of worker solidarity in changing times*, Frederiksberg: Frydenlund Academic.

Hastings, T. and Heyes, J. (2016). 'Farewell to flexicurity? Austerity and labour policies in the European Union', *Economic and Industrial Democracy*: 1–23, DOI: 10.1177/0143831X16633756.

Høgedahl, L.K. and Kongshøj, K. (2017). 'New trajectories of unionization in the Nordic Ghent countries: Changing labour market and welfare institutions', *European Journal of Industrial Relations* 23(4): 365–80.

Ilsøe, A., Jesnes, K. and Hotvedt, M. (2020). 'Social partner responses in the Nordic platform economy.' In K. Jesnes and S. Oppegaard (eds) *Platform work in the Nordic models*, Oslo: Fafo, pp 68–78

Ingold, J. (2020). 'Employer perspectives on benefit conditionality in the UK and Denmark', *Social Policy and Administration* 54: 236–49.

Ingold, J. and Etherington, D. (2013). 'Work, welfare and gender inequalities: An analysis of activation strategies for partnered women in the UK, Australia and Denmark', *Work Employment and Society* 27(4): 621–38.

Jessop, B. (2016). *The state: Past, present, future*, Cambridge: Polity Press.

Kjellberg, A. and Lyhne Ibsen, C. (2016). 'Attacks on union organizing: Reversible and irreversible changes to the Ghent-systems in Sweden and Denmark.' In T.P. Larsen and A. Ilsøe (eds) *Den Danske Model set udefra komparative perspektiver på dansk arbejdsmarkedsregulering: Et festskrif t til professor emeritus Jesper Due og og professor emeritus Jørgen Steen Madsen*, Copenhagen: Jurist- og Økonomforbundets Forlag, pp 279–302.

Kommunernes Landsforegningen (KL – Danish Local Government Association) (2016). *Tredobbelt Gevinst – Erfaringer med jobrotation paa kommunale Arbejdsplads*, Copenhagen: KL.

Kruhøffer, J. (2007). *Job rotation in Europe as the feasibility environment for the Jobrotation e-Service,* Berlin: AOF.

Kvist, J. (2021). *Social Protection and inclusion policy responses to the COVID-19 crisis*, Denmark: European Union European Social Policy Network (ESPN).

Larsen, F. and Caswell, D. (2020). 'Co-creation in an era of welfare conditionality', *Journal of Social Policy*, doi:10.1017/S0047279420000665.

Lind, J. and Knudsen, H. (2018). 'Denmark the long-lasting class compromise', *Employee Relations* 40(4): 580–99.

Madsen, P.K. (2015). *Upskilling unemployed adults. The organisation, profiling and targeting of training provision: Denmark*, Luxembourg: European Employment Policy Observatory.

Mailand, M. and Thor Larsen, P. (2017). *Bargaining and social dialogue in the public sector* (BARSOP), Copenhagen: University of Copenhagen FAOS.

Nordic Council of Ministers (2020). *TemaNord* 513.

Offe, C (1985). *Disorganized capitalism: Contemporary transformations of work and politics*, Cambridge: Polity.

Rostgaard, T. (2014). *Family policies in Scandinavia*, Stockholm: Frederich Ebert Stiftung.

Spicker, P. (2017). *What's wrong with social security benefits?* Bristol: Policy Press.

Trade Union Congress (2020a). *Fixing the safety net: Next steps in the response to the Corona virus*, London: TUC.

Trade Union Congress (2020b). *Why the UK needs a permanent short time work scheme*, London: TUC.

Valizade, D., Ingold, J. and Stuart, M. (2022). Employer participation in active labour market policies in the United Kingdom and Denmark: The effect of employer associations as social networks and the mediating role of collective voice. *Work, Employment and Society.* https://doi.org/10.1177/09500170211063094

Warming, K. (2019). *Discrimination against parents: Experiences of discrimination in connection with pregnancy and parental leave*, Copenhagen: Danish Institute of Human Rights.

Zibrowius, M. (2017). *Promoting social partnership in employee training: Denmark country report*, Cologne: German Economic Institute.

4

Skills, Apprenticeships and Diversity: Employer Engagement with Further and Higher Education

Patrick McGurk and Omolola Olaleye

This chapter provides a critical discussion of the principal ways in which employers in England have engaged with further and higher education in recent years to improve workforce skills. There is a specific focus on recent apprenticeship reforms as illustrative of the strongest form of employer engagement, involving employers as co-producers alongside colleges and universities. The final section of the chapter examines the broader role of employers in engaging with apprenticeships as a means to improve workforce diversity, thereby contributing towards the government's social mobility goals.

Employer roles in further and higher education in England

Employer engagement in England provides a critical case of how employers behave as stakeholders in a liberalized workforce development system. In other words, the English context illustrates what happens when next to no demands are made on employers to develop workforce skills, leaving them free to engage with education providers as they wish, while taking advantage of changing government incentives. By contrast, other advanced industrial democracies – and even the devolved administrations of Scotland, Wales and Northern Ireland – place clearer obligations on employers through more formalized institutional arrangements (see Bredgaard, Ingold and van Berkel, in this volume).

Further education (FE) in England encompasses the compulsory elements of education up until the age of 19 as well as post-compulsory education and training below the level of university degrees. Full-time FE provision is primarily provided by school sixth forms and sixth form colleges, which concentrate on university entrance qualifications, as well as FE colleges, which also provide the majority of part-time training for young people and adults. Alongside FE colleges are a growing number of private and non-profit training providers, commissioned by the state to provide both full- and part-time training courses. This institutional landscape – of FE colleges, alternative accredited training providers and, to a lesser extent, sixth form colleges and school sixth forms – is the primary site of workforce skills development in England. Employers play various roles, most notably in the provision of work experience placements and work-related experiences as part of training courses.

Higher education (HE) in England encompasses the provision of degree and degree-equivalent qualifications. Universities are the principal licensors of such qualifications, which are studied on both a full- and part-time basis. However, as in the FE sector, a growing number of private and non-profit providers, as well as some FE colleges themselves, are licensed to offer higher-level qualifications. These alternative providers tend to specialize in vocational and professional qualifications, particularly in business, law and information technology (Hunt and Boliver, 2019) and it is in this area that employer engagement is most prevalent. Nonetheless, there is a long-standing convention of employer involvement on the traditional, academic side of the sector, particularly in technical and engineering subjects, as well as a range of advisory board memberships and corporate sponsorships (such as of student scholarships and prizes, specific programmes of study, physical spaces and specific academic appointments). In more recent years, employer involvement in universities has taken on a new dimension through the introduction in 2017 of degree apprenticeships, which require detailed employer engagement with the curriculum design.

The past forty years or so have seen waves of unsuccessful government reforms to try to involve employers more centrally in the education and training system (Keep, 2020). Invariably, the driving argument behind such reforms has been that employers, as the actors closest to the specific and changing needs of local labour markets, are best placed to design and administer sufficiently flexible and responsive skills development (Grugulis, 2007). However, as studies by Payne (2008), Keep (2012) and Huddleston and Laczik (2012, 2018) have consistently demonstrated, the expectations placed on employers by policymakers have been both unclear and unrealistically wide-ranging. At the strategic level, employer engagement has often amounted to little more than a 'steadfast minority' of large, household-name employers acting in an advisory role (Payne, 2008), expressing the voices of increasingly internationalized corporations rather than locally rooted businesses or small and medium-sized enterprises (SMEs) (Keep, 2012).

At the more practical level, the expectations to co-design new vocational qualifications and provide workplace-based opportunities for learners have repeatedly stretched the limits of employers' technical knowledge and expertise, as well as their capacity to meet demand for industry visits, projects, internships, mentorships and the like (Huddleston and Laczik, 2012, 2018). Consequently, the default in UK employment and skills policy has been to resort to subsidized, central-government-driven initiatives (Grugulis, 2007; Keep, 2012). This has resulted in an institutional and cultural legacy of a very confused set of employer roles and responsibilities (Keep, 2020).

In its weakest form, employer engagement with further and higher education tends to constitute representation through advisory roles within networks and on boards in colleges and universities at various levels, as well as the more direct hosting of students on short-term, government-funded work placements. In its strongest form, employers are integrated into partnerships with colleges and universities at all levels, including collective representation through employer organizations and the co-production and funding of programmes of education and training.

To understand more clearly the various employer roles in further and higher education, similarly to previous conceptualizations in relation to government active labour market initiatives (Snape, 1998; van der Aa and van Berkel, 2014; Bredgaard, 2018; Orton et al, 2019), it helps to distinguish between the employer as 'client', and the employer as 'partner'. Additionally, across the client–partner spectrum, it is also helpful to distinguish between 'weak' and 'strong' employer engagement. The two interrelated distinctions produce a two-by-two matrix, which we offer as a clarifying conceptualization of employer roles in further and higher education.

As illustrated in Figure 4.1, the weak employer-client may be characterized as a 'purchaser' of educational or skills-development services provided by

Figure 4.1: Employer roles in further and higher education

	Employer as client	**Employer as partner**
Weak	Purchaser *e.g. buyer of skills development courses and short qualifications*	Volunteer *e.g. advisory board member, provider of work experience and internships*
Strong	Commissioner *e.g. board member of regional enterprise and development institution*	Co-producer *e.g. deliverer of apprenticeships*

colleges and universities. The strong employer-client on the other hand is a 'commissioner' of programmes of study, typically funded by the government. In parallel, the weak employer-partner may be characterized as a 'volunteer' who plays a supporting or advisory role in designing and providing learning and skills-development activities, but is not directly involved in programme management or assessment. The strong employer-partner may however be termed a 'co-producer' of educational programmes together with colleges and universities, including the sharing of responsibility for their design, funding, delivery, assessment and ongoing programme management.

In elaborating each of the four conceptualized roles in turn, we seek to illustrate that employer engagement with FE and HE in England is predominantly weak. The institutional arrangements and lack of incentives or obligations in such a market-liberalized environment serve to ensure that employers tend to act as purchasers or volunteers, rather than commissioners or co-producers. In effect, such an environment ensures that employers are only concerned in a limited way with the supply of skills, rather than with a significant contribution to longer-term and wider-ranging workforce development.

Employer as purchaser. In the purchaser role, the individual employer pays local colleges and to a lesser extent universities to design, deliver, assess and manage short courses towards the achievement of pre-defined learning outcomes and qualifications. Typically, such provision in colleges is known as 'bespoke training' or 'business development', and in universities as 'executive education'. Employers purchase such services with the aim of developing existing members of their staff. Employers may sponsor individual employees, as members of larger, mixed classes, or whole cohorts that are dedicated to a particular employer as part of a wider workforce development strategy. Such arrangements may be sporadic or long-standing, year after year, and colleges and universities will often deploy staff to manage ongoing relationships with employer-clients (see for example James Relly and Laczik, 2022). These relationships, especially long-standing ones, may therefore often feel like partnerships; but given the essentially transactional nature of the exchange, in which the employers do not influence the content or outcomes of the education and training provided, and may easily exit without consequences, the employer's role is effectively limited to that of purchaser.

Employer as volunteer. In the volunteer role, the employer – sometimes as part of an employer consortium or association – develops a partnership with a local college, university or associated education–business partnership network. Such partnerships may develop at both strategic and operational levels in a mutually reinforcing way. At operational level, the employer tends to facilitate the provision, for example, of guest speakers, conveners of workshops and careers/employability events at the college or university, and/or host fieldwork visits by its students. A slightly deeper level of operational engagement would involve the provision of mentorships for individual students and project teams, work experience placements and/ or fully paid internships. At the strategic level, usually in tandem with the range of operational engagements just described, representatives of individual employers or of groups of employers may serve on departmental or institution-level advisory boards, thereby contributing to a more systematic and planned approach to programmes of visits, work experience and the like, and even sponsoring full programmes of study (see Garner, 2015). Such sponsorship may go as far as compact agreements, in which employers commit to guarantee interviews or job offers to graduates of particular programmes of study. However, in England at least, where regional labour markets are very liberalized and uncoordinated, even the longest-standing, most formal partnerships between FE/HE and local employers are predicated on essentially informal and voluntary arrangements. At operational level, employer engagement may wax and wane, often with changes in key personnel. At strategic level, the consistency and robustness of engagement may also vary considerably, and even the most institutionalized examples of these arrangements, such as the Employment and Skills Boards of the early 2000s, were accused of being little more than 'talking shops' (Croden and Simmonds, 2008).

Employer as commissioner. In the commissioner role, key local employers are appointed as representatives of regional institutions in charge of workforce development budgets to oversee the provision of programmes of skills development and qualifications, usually by FE colleges or approved/registered training providers, to meet local labour market needs. There is a long history in England of government attempts to put employers in the driving seat by having private sector chairs of strategic planning boards and directly funding them to oversee workforce development (see the Technology and Enterprise Councils of the 1990s, the Regional Development Agencies of the 2000s and the Local Enterprise Partnerships of the 2010s) (and see Warner and Gladding, 2019). In this type of arrangement, colleges are commissioned to deliver 'off-the-shelf' and/or bespoke qualifications to specific numbers of school-leaver or adult learners, and are also held accountable for the management of programmes and their outcomes in terms of progression into employment, typically measured by the number of pre-employment placements, job-starts and employees retained up to six months. Employer-commissioners in this sense are therefore more strongly engaged than the employer-purchaser, as they have wider-ranging responsibilities and deeper involvement in the educational provision itself, if not sourcing training and development directly for their own employees, but for other employers in the region. Quite how the local employers are recruited and appointed to the regional institutions, however, has been the subject of concern about how representative of the local economy and society they are. Rather than be closely reflective of the local economy and society, such employers often represent the 'great and the good', typically large and influential employers with experience of public contracting, often from the sectors of finance, technology, construction and transport; there may also be a number of smaller but well-connected entrepreneurs (Jones, 1997; Payne, 2008; Etherington and Jones, 2016; McGurk and Meredith, 2018).

Employer as co-producer. In the co-producer role, the employer is directly involved at all stages of design, delivery, management and assessment of educational qualifications. While some employers have long been heavily involved as partners in the provision of specialist educational programmes in colleges and universities, the most salient contemporary example of such deep employer involvement is in the new English apprenticeship system. In 2012 the government invited sector-based employer groups known as 'Trailblazers' to develop their own apprentice standards, working on the advice of education professionals and requiring the approval of a new national regulatory body, the Institute for Apprenticeships (IfA). With time, new apprenticeship standards spanned traditional sectors such as construction and hairdressing as well as newer sectors such as technology, finance and media, and ranged from school- and college-level to advanced and university-level. The theoretical parts of the standards have to be delivered by a college, university or approved training provider during no less than 20 per cent of the working week, while the practical learning is delivered by the apprentice's employer. Theoretical and practical instruction are integrated and continuously assessed, including a third-party, 'end-point' assessor at the end of the typically three- or four-year apprenticeship. This represents a co-production model in that the employer is a senior partner in its relationship with further and higher education and is required to commit to strong, ongoing engagement (Keep, 2020). In practice, as always, the realities of the employer–education co-production model are complex and contradictory, as explored in the next section.

This opening section has sought to clarify the often-confusing roles that employers have to navigate in their engagement with FE and HE in England. While there are no neat measures of the proportions assumed by each of the four main employer roles, the experience of the past forty or so years clearly shows that the English liberalized, uncoordinated system produces far more purchasers and volunteers than it does commissioners or co-producers. In so far as employers are directly involved with education, it is mainly to support soft interventions concerned with developing students' and learners' skills rather than the systematic development of vocational and technical knowledge. The exception to this is the contemporary apprenticeship, which, in theory at least, adopts a co-production model. Given that apprenticeships appear to provide the strongest form of employer partnership with education in England, against the backdrop of an otherwise uncoordinated system of stakeholder relations, it is instructive to explore the actual potential and limits of this institutional arrangement.

Apprenticeships: employers as co-producers

Apprenticeships are not a new phenomenon in England and have existed since the 16th century, concentrated in the skilled artisan trades (Fuller and Unwin, 2007; Mirza-Davies, 2015). The forms and mechanisms through which apprenticeships are delivered have evolved, but the fundamental feature – on-the-job learning – is still a key component of contemporary apprenticeships. To understand the role of employers within contemporary English apprenticeships, it is helpful to note three recent developments:

1. the creation of 'Modern Apprenticeships' in the mid-1990s;
2. the establishment of the National Apprenticeship Service (NAS) in 2009; and
3. the introduction of Trailblazer apprenticeships in 2012, accompanied by a compulsory employer levy in 2017.

Modern Apprenticeships represented an attempt to emulate other European systems of vocational training and lay the ground for contemporary apprenticeships in England. The reforms by the Conservative government of the day introduced a range of new apprenticeships outside the traditional sectors of construction (dominated by men) and hairdressing (dominated by women) to broaden sectoral coverage, including the service sectors of retail, hospitality and business. With regard to employer involvement, in an ideological reaction against the tripartite model (Gospel, 1998), the responsibility for coordinating apprenticeships shifted away from state-trade union–employer decision-making bodies towards, at sector level, new, employer-led 'Industry Training Organizations' (later to become 'National Training Organizations', then 'Sector Skills Councils') and, at local level, to 'Training and Enterprise Councils' (later to morph into 'Learning and Skills Councils'). However, in reality, active engagement by employers in the design, delivery and assessment of the new qualifications proved minimal, effectively resulting in a state-driven system of apprenticeship training, increasingly delivered by private training contractors (Gospel, 1998; Ryan and Unwin, 2001; Grugulis, 2007).

The creation of the NAS under the Labour government of the 2000s and the surrounding reforms succeeded to some extent in consolidating what had become a very fragmented apprenticeship system. However, a myriad of new private training providers, known as Apprenticeship Training Agencies (ATAs), continued to play an increasingly significant role in delivering *both* the theoretical *and* the practical, instructional content of apprenticeships.

The dominant role played by ATAs, combined with the essentially state-driven management of apprenticeship places, served to distance employers further in practical terms. In addition, generally low expectations around apprenticeship quality and quality control, especially in relation to the school-leaver, 'apprenticeship-lite' qualifications ('Level 2' qualifications), and particularly in the service sectors of retail, business and social care, allowed widespread abuses of the funding system by training providers in collusion with some employers. The most prevalent abuse took the form of claiming funding for new apprenticeships that were in fact short-term, in-house training courses for existing employees. In short, the institutional framework that developed around apprenticeships incentivized the provision by training organizations – both ATAs and FE colleges – of quick, easy-to-deliver packages that might have qualified for apprenticeship funding, but resulted in poor quality and low returns for employers, apprentices and the government (Wolf, 2015).

Increasing employer dissatisfaction with the quality of apprenticeship training was an important driver behind the introduction of Trailblazer apprenticeships in 2012. The newly elected Conservative-led coalition government commissioned a root-and-branch review by high-profile entrepreneur Doug Richard (DBIS, 2012). The Richard Review, though very supportive of the apprenticeship brand, recommended radical reform in order to meet employers' needs. Richard argued that employers, as the 'real consumers' of apprenticeships, should be directly involved in the design of new Trailblazer apprenticeships (DBIS, 2012, p 13). Trailblazers were therefore developed from 2013 onwards by voluntary 'employer networks' in sectors as diverse as digital media, accountancy, advanced manufacturing and social care. The central principle – 'employer ownership' – marked a significant departure from the state-driven reforms characteristic of the English system since the introduction of Modern Apprenticeships.

Trailblazer apprenticeships had four key aims reflecting this principle:

> *Put employers in the driving seat*: Apprenticeships will be based on standards designed by employers, making them more relevant and therefore more attractive to existing and new employers.
>
> *Increase the quality of apprenticeships*: An apprentice will need to demonstrate their competence through rigorous and holistic assessment. This will focus on the end of the apprenticeship to ensure that the apprentice is ready to progress.
>
> *Simplify the system*: The new employer-designed standards will be short and easy to understand. They will describe the skills, knowledge and behaviour that an individual needs to be fully competent in an occupation.

Give employers purchasing power: Putting control of government funding for the external training of apprentices in the hands of employers, to empower businesses to act as customers, driving up the quality and relevance of such training. (DBIS, 2014; emphasis added)

The government proceeded to directly subsidize employers that recruited apprentices to Trailblazer frameworks (SFA, 2015). It also accepted Richard's other recommendations that sought to repair the damage inflicted on the credibility of many apprenticeships in previous years. He had recommended that the definition of an apprenticeship should be restricted to a 'new job or role' requiring substantive training, and that the training of existing workers should be delivered separately.

The newly elected Conservative majority government of 2015 saw, however, that it would take more than employer enthusiasm for the new standards and a direct subsidy mechanism to meet its ambitious recruitment targets of 3 million new apprenticeships by 2020 (Mirza-Davies, 2015). It was told by independent inspectors that many SMEs in particular 'did not want additional responsibilities for the organisation and bureaucracy of an apprenticeship' (Ofsted, 2015, p 29). Similarly, a government-commissioned survey of over 4,000 employers (Colahan and Johnson, 2014) reported that 26 per cent did not want any more influence over apprenticeship training, and that only 56 per cent felt empowered to change their training provider or the type of apprenticeship training provided. The government responded to such concerns by introducing a 'digital voucher' to ease employer choice and administration of apprenticeship provision, as well as announcing a compulsory levy on large employers (DBIS, 2015a).

The national employer levy was a radical and surprising step, especially for a neoliberal Conservative government. Following the advice of Professor Alison Wolf (2015), the levy was set at 0.5 per cent of the employer's pay bill in businesses where that bill is over £3 million. It was to be collected at source from payroll, offset against a £15,000 allowance and administered by a 'Digital Apprenticeship Service' (HM Revenue and Customs, 2016). The government estimated that the levy would raise nearly £3 billion, potentially doubling apprenticeship funding by 2019/20. The announcement of the levy received mixed support from employer groups. The UK body for large employers, the Confederation of British Industry, predictably called for the levy to be voluntary rather than prescriptive (Warrell and Gordon, 2015). The human resource managers' body, the Chartered Institute of Personnel and Development, surveyed businesses to find that only 39 per cent of large employers were committed in principle, with 31 per cent replying that a levy would mean reducing investment in other areas of training (Kirton, 2015). However, in the government's own consultation, the levy received a generally positive response, with half of respondents agreeing that a proportion of the apprenticeship funding raised from larger companies should be used to support apprenticeships (DBIS, 2015a).

The government pressed ahead and implemented the levy from April 2017. It was expected that less than 2 per cent of employers would pay the levy, although between them these large employers accounted for over half the country's workforce. Also, a commitment was made that levy contributors would be able to receive more back in training subsidies than they paid in, so long as this entitlement was used within two years, after which it would expire (Delebarre, 2015; HM Treasury and the Rt Hon. George Osborne MP, 2015; HM Revenue and Customs, 2016). In time, it was arranged that levy-paying employers would receive a 10 per cent top-up from the government on payments to training providers to fund their apprenticeship training, while employers not paying the levy would have to contribute only 10 per cent towards theirs (Powell, 2020). Additionally, various quality safeguards were introduced, including the requirement for at least 20 per cent of an apprentice's working time to be devoted to off-the-job learning, which could only be provided by a new list of approved training providers. Such providers included FE colleges, universities (mainly but not exclusively for the higher- and degree-level apprenticeships), some private providers and levy-paying employers with their own registered training licences. Similarly, only approved organizations were permitted to perform the final, qualifying, 'end-point assessments', in a shift away from in-house, continuous assessment.

So did the Trailblazer reforms succeed in engaging employers and placing them in the driving seat of technical and vocational education? As modelled, the percentage of levy-paying employers was small at only 1.3 per cent of employers (around 19,000 organizations), but accounted for approximately 60 per cent of the workforce; each paid on average around £140,000 in levy contributions, amounting to approximately £2.7 billion for the Treasury in the fiscal year 2017/18 (Powell, 2020). One stark indicator, however, of low employer engagement with the new apprenticeships was that only £370 million of the £2.7 billion that year was actually paid back out to apprenticeship training providers on the levy-paying employers' behalf (Powell, 2020). This means that many large employers simply paid the levy without making use of it to invest in apprenticeship training, in effect treating it as an additional tax, unrelated to their own workforce development. Moreover, the actual number of new apprentices recruited by employers dropped significantly in the two years after the levy was introduced. While 2016/17 had seen 495,000 apprenticeship starts, this dropped to 376,000 in 2017/18 and 393,000 in 2018/19, with the most significant drop among 16–19-year-olds (Powell, 2020).

Some of the drop in apprenticeship recruitment in the two years after the introduction of the levy may doubtless be attributed to teething problems with the new system. Also, given the disruption to employment caused by the coronavirus pandemic from 2020 (see next section), it may be too early to judge whether the levy will come to be viewed as a successful workforce development investment strategy, rather than an unproductive tax on large employers. However, Powell's (2020) policy review for the House of Commons Library offers a wider range of reasons for the drop in apprenticeship recruitment. Powell (2020) indeed cites problems with the new levy administration and the deterrent nature of the 10 per cent payment for SMEs; however, he also cites employers' reluctance to release apprentices for 20 per cent of their working time for off-the-job learning, as well as employer complaints about a general lack of suitable apprentice applicants and training providers.

Despite being (back) in the driving seat, therefore, the familiar complaints by employers about the supply side of the training system – notably the lack of work-ready skills in young people and the inappropriateness or poor quality of state-provided training – do not appear to have subsided with the introduction of the new apprenticeships. On the other hand, there are indications that part of the reduction in apprenticeship recruitment is linked to an employer-driven concern that, in the pursuit of numbers, too much quality was being traded off (Mason, 2020; Powell, 2020). In addition, there was a significant uptake in the new and more demanding higher-level and degree apprenticeships as a proportion of total apprenticeship starts, from 7 per cent in 2016/17 to 26 per cent in 2019/20 (Powell, 2020; Foley, 2021a). As Mason (2020) argues, in terms of employer engagement, '[t]he growth in Higher apprenticeships is potentially positive to the extent that it reflects employer willingness to commit new resources to employment-based training of graduate- and technician-level employees, rather than expect them to have acquired employability skills through full-time classroom-based education' (p 476). There are, however, serious concerns at government level that, rather than investing in new, advanced-level workforce development, some employers in collusion with universities have been simply 'rebadging' their sponsorship of existing management development programmes (including MBAs) as higher-level apprenticeships in order to access the state-provided training subsidy.

Not for the first time, therefore, employers' professed desire to collectively take charge of workforce development as their own best experts, or at least take responsibility as senior partners in a co-production arrangement with the colleges and universities (and even trade unions), must be called into question by their willingness to fall back on state-designed, -funded and -provided qualifications. For sure, not all employers are the same, and there are several examples of new, high-quality apprenticeships developed by employers in accordance with a co-production model. Mason (2020, p 476), for example, points to new apprenticeship standards for mechatronics technicians and IT infrastructure technicians, jointly designed by employers from a wide range of industries, and leading to transferable, recognized, higher qualifications for learners. But overall it is highly concerning that the latest bold and promising apprenticeship reforms do not yet show signs of significantly changing employer behaviour with regard to engaging with workforce development. It has to be wondered whether England's essentially liberal and voluntarist system will ever produce more than what Gospel (1998, p 450) described as 'high-skilled islands within a low-skilled sea'.

The failure in England to engage employers with FE and HE on the scale required for transformation towards widespread and deep partnerships is rooted in several structural factors, which have long been summarized and highlighted by commentators such as Keep (2012, 2014) and Keep and James (2011). In addition to confused roles and incentives for employers, even as co-producers, Keep (2020) cites: '"low road" competitive and product market strategies; poor employee relations, work organization and job design; and a failure to invest in the other components of a high-performance economy' (p 503). Yet Keep (2020) also highlights another crucial factor: the lack of collective and individual employer capacity in England, and how this factor is brought into sharp focus through comparative research on employer organizations as key actors in education and training systems (such as by Martin, 2005; Martin and Swank, 2012; Ingold and Stuart, 2015). As Keep (2020) argues, '[w]ithout [such employer organizations], government is left trying to deal with individual organisations, which imposes massive transaction costs and renders collective action extremely hard to contrive and sustain', thereby having to treat 'individual firms as atomised, individual customers in an [education and training] marketplace' (p 504). In addition, at individual employer level, Keep (2020) points to evidence that English firms lack up-to-date expertise in in-house training and approaches to work organization and job design that foster rich, informal, continuous learning.

In summary, the English model and experience of a marketized and voluntaristic education and training system, combined with a lack of collective and individual employer capacity, illustrate why employer engagement with further and higher education tends to be weak. It also helps explain how employers under such conditions tend to assume the roles of purchaser and volunteer, rather than commissioner or co-producer. In the next section, we explore this issue from a different angle.

Apprenticeship employers as promoters of workforce diversity

This final section of this chapter explores the perspective of diversity and inclusion in relation to apprenticeships, firstly by tracing the rhetoric of apprenticeship reform then by establishing and identifying the degree to which diversity and inclusion are incorporated in the agenda for apprenticeship reform to address skills shortages in England and Wales. We begin with an overview of the reforms, primarily from 2000, teasing out the degree to which diversity has been a key part of policy and plans for apprenticeships. Finally, we assess the progress made regarding the use of apprenticeships as a medium for workforce diversity by examining relevant data and evidence of success.

The principal aims of Modern Apprenticeships in 1994, introduced by the Conservative government of that time, were to improve the 'skills base' of the nation; to re-engage low-qualified young people 'back into training' (Ryan and Lőrinc, 2018, p 764); extend the apprenticeship programme to sectors without a history of apprenticeships, mainly services; and, notably, to offer training and employment opportunities to female and minority ethnic individuals,[1] who previously had not been offered equal access to apprenticeships and training, reflecting inequality in education, society and the labour market at large (Gospel, 1998). Figure 4.2 illustrates the evolution of policy interest and outcomes with respect to concerns about diversity.

By 1998, it became clear that the equal opportunity targets had not been met as only 3 per cent of apprentices then came from minority ethnic backgrounds; and furthermore only 40 per cent were female, and they were concentrated in traditionally female jobs, typically with lower wages owing to occupational segregation by gender in the labour market as a whole (Gospel, 1998). Minority ethnic students were more likely to have been taken on as apprentices in areas with a history of poor achievement, with only 48 per cent of them securing jobs upon completion compared to 72 per cent of white apprentices (Newton and Williams, 2013).

Between 2000 and 2010 policy reforms continued to take place, ranging from the Increased Flexibility programme to the Leitch Review of Skills in 2006 and the government's Skills for Growth agenda in 2009. The reforms at this time made no commitment to improving diversity and inclusion in apprenticeships. Instead, the focus appears to have been on improving the provision of apprenticeships and curriculum changes. Furthermore, there were limited strategies or policies designed to tackle gender imbalance and ethnic inequality in apprenticeships (Newton and Williams, 2013).

In 2013, following the 2012 Richard Review, apprenticeships were to become employer-orientated, although this had effectively been the case since the decline of union power in the early- to mid-1990s. This recommendation reaffirmed the government's desire to place control of apprenticeships firmly in the hands of employers, in line with its ideology of minimal state intervention. Employers were to be involved in the creation of recognized, industry-wide standards (developed by Trailblazer groups) that suited their industry's needs and provided the skills required, while the government pledged to set only 'a small number of criteria' (DBIS, 2013), which apprenticeship standards created by employers needed to meet to

Figure 4.2: Timeline of apprenticeship reforms and policies in England affecting diversity

Commitment to diversity, no target	No explicit diversity target		Diversity target		Unmet diversity target, continued disparities
1994	2006	2010	2015	2018	2021–present
Modern apprenticeship introduced	Leitch Review of Skills	Train to Gain ends	English apprenticeships: 2020 Vision	5 Cities Project launched	Coronavirus
	Train to Gain launched		Increase minority ethnic apprentices by 20% by 2020	Improve apprenticeship diversity in 5 major English cities	Apprenticeships start to decline
					Kickstart Scheme
1998	2009	2012	2017	2020	
Poor outcomes for ethnic and gender diversity	Skills for Growth	Richard Review of Apprenticeships	Apprenticeship levy introduced	Apprenticeship diversity target increase unmet	

ensure they were rigorous. Nevertheless, there was an accompanying commitment by the government to collect data to evaluate the impact of its proposed reforms on participation by gender, age, ethnicity, disability, apprenticeship level and sector (DBIS, 2013), and on accommodations made in terms of achievement at GCSE level,[2] particularly for those with disabilities. This would seem to indicate a re-emergent concern to promote wider access to apprenticeships and greater inclusivity.

The most explicit concern with equality and diversity came with the Conservative government of 2015, which stated its equality and diversity agenda through the publication of plans for apprenticeships in England. In a detailed report by the Department of Business, Innovation and Skills, *English Apprenticeships: Our 2020 Vision* (DBIS, 2015b), alongside a focus on economic recovery, productive capacity and improving the image of apprenticeships as a viable pathway into a career, the government set out an inclusion agenda by committing to increase the proportion of ethnic minority apprentices by 20 per cent by 2020. The strategy was to engage with minority ethnic youth to understand barriers restricting them from taking on apprenticeships as well as providing information and support targeted at this group. The document spells out the activities to be undertaken to achieve this, namely the establishment of a network of apprentice diversity 'champions' from employers and training providers committed to achieving greater diversity in apprenticeships; delivering campaigns on youth employment targeted at minority ethnic audiences; and working with the Local Enterprise Partnerships to increase understanding of employers' specific recruitment needs and to encourage and support employers to diversify their workforce by recruiting minority ethnic apprentices (DBIS, 2015b). In the same document emerged a commitment to using apprenticeships as a tool for enhancing social mobility 'to support young people to get the best start in life, through the opportunity that high quality education and training provides' (DBIS, 2015b). This was a 'game-changer' in that the government explicitly made a diversity commitment (while reiterating the role of employers) in apprenticeships.

Between 2010 and 2015, however, apprenticeship starts for young people aged below 25 grew sluggishly, increasing by only 4 per cent, compared to 17 per cent for over-25s (Social Mobility and Child Poverty Commission, 2016). As of 2020, data on apprenticeships showed that 84.9 per cent were white and 13.1 per cent were from minority ethnic backgrounds. Although this represents the highest degree of ethnic diversity since 2002 and an increase from 12.3 per cent in 2019 (Foley, 2021), the proportion of apprentices aged over 25 has remained higher than those between age 16 and 24 (Foley, 2020, 2021). The implication of this is that young people inadvertently lose out on opportunities to develop skills and build a career as opportunities are being given to apprentices of a much higher age. This is of concern; young people are missing out on opportunities for social mobility.

The government in 2015 had committed to improving apprenticeships and young people having a chance to climb the social mobility ladder. But they would not be able to do this if employers offer apprenticeships to older people or, in many cases, existing employees. The apprenticeship levy, which many employers viewed (and some continue to view) simply as a tax, encouraged employers to use the funds for training that they would have had to pay for anyway (Keep, 2020), leading to existing employees being placed on apprenticeship programmes instead of conventional training and development programmes. More recent research (Olaleye, unpublished) demonstrates how organizations sometimes use apprenticeships in place of professional qualifications, even for graduate recruits. This supports Keep's (2020) comment: 'the levy is often being gamed' (p 501). Olaleye's (unpublished) indicative findings reveal that some employers find it too cumbersome to navigate the required pastoral support for young people, particularly those who are new entrants into the world of work and/or recent school leavers. In other words, employers tend to find it easier, or have a preference, to work with older apprentices (that is, those over 16 years) who have some previous work experience or a Level 3 (college-level) qualification, particularly for the higher level apprenticeships.

Unsurprisingly, apprenticeships were affected by the economic consequences of the coronavirus pandemic on businesses and young people in particular – including those on apprenticeships. In April to September 2020, 82,400 fewer apprenticeships started than for the same period in 2019, which represented a 41 per cent fall (Powell, 2021, p 9). Prior to the pandemic, the proportion of young people not in employment, education or training had been on the decline since the 2008 financial crisis. Research by Tiley, Morris and Yusuf (2021) for the YMCA revealed that,[3] in May 2020, it became apparent that nearly 35 per cent of young people between 18 and 24 had lost their jobs, been placed on reduced hours or on furlough, as compared with 15 per cent of 35–44-year-olds (Tiley et al, 2021). Between March and July 2020 alone, 1,033 people were made redundant from apprenticeships and there was a drop from 84 per cent sustained employment upon completion of an apprenticeship to 55 per cent over the course of the pandemic (Tiley et al, 2021). During the crisis, the focus has clearly changed towards trying to keep young people in employment and training; so far no explicit target on diversity has been drawn up so, once more, the opportunity to use apprenticeships to improve equality, diversity and inclusion has taken a back seat. In the summer of 2021, as part of the Chancellor's Plan for Jobs and Kickstart Scheme launch, new funding was made available for apprenticeships – up to £3,000 for each new apprentice – to encourage employers to recruit and offer training and career opportunities to young people (Frazer, 2021; HM Treasury and the Rt Hon. Rishi Sunak, MP, 2021). However, given the failure of previous incentive schemes to increase the number of people under 25 being trained through apprenticeships, it would be premature to assume success for this plan, and it would be wise to exercise some healthy scepticism.

Apprenticeships in England are strongly characterized by the employer-led approach, perhaps a lasting consequence of policies from the Conservative governments of the 1980s and 1990s. The employer-led nature of apprenticeships means that employers have a significant role to play in the outcomes for apprentices. While the government has initiated action to support and encourage apprenticeship uptake, most recently in the form of the levy, there is still a high degree of employer power in decisions relating to apprenticeships – the simple decisions who to hire and the degree to which diversity is important.

The rhetoric on apprenticeship continues to focus on increasing starts and quality, with some emphasis on gender diversity but little on ethnic diversity. Preliminary findings from research by Olaleye (unpublished) indicate a mixed approach to diversity in apprenticeships by employers – the emphasis is on creating awareness and relying on diversity-related strategies in recruitment, mainly through attempting to attract a wider candidate pool. While some schemes target schools in deprived areas, or certain categories such as students who receive free school meals, others rely on organizations that work with the category of young people they hope to reach. Moreover, beyond attraction, there is an absence of radical action being taken to retain apprentices. The government's focus over the past ten years has been on increasing starts and numbers of apprentices; it is perhaps no surprise, therefore, that emphasis is placed on entry and not so much on progression.

There are also inconsistencies in the visible commitment of employers to apprenticeships. On one hand, the larger employers pay the apprenticeship levy, which they could then recoup to use towards training (not wages) of an apprentice. They also have the option to transfer to smaller businesses that do not pay the levy. But no diversity target is associated with the levy and this has a negative impact on employers' willingness to prioritize diversity in apprentice-hiring decisions.

On the other hand, some organizations seek to encourage employer action on diversity, such as the Apprenticeship Diversity Champions Network set up in 2017. The network's members must demonstrate their commitment to ensuring that people from under-represented groups (those with disabilities, women and minority ethnic individuals) consider apprenticeships (Whieldon, 2021). The members pledge to make measurable improvements to diversity, and must be willing to submit data on their progress and share best practice in order to ensure that they maintain the core ethos of being action-driven and employer-focused (National Apprenticeship Service, 2017, 2019). However, it would seem that this organization has made minimal contribution, judging by the number of progress reports published since its inception in 2018 (currently only one – the annual report for 2021/22). The IfA has stated it is working with employers to be as diverse as possible; but no explicit, tangible action other than using gender-neutral language has transpired (Institute for Apprenticeships and Technical Education, 2019). The 5 Cities Project, launched at the Department for Education to try to improve minority ethnic apprenticeship participation in London, Bristol, Manchester, Birmingham and Leicester, had its funding cut at the end of 2020, and had no new initiatives to be put in place or targets set (Whieldon, 2020).

Beyond government are advocacy organizations that attempt to encourage employer action towards diversity in apprenticeships. These include the Apprenticeship Diversity and Social Mobility Forum – set up in July 2020 by the Black Asian and Minority Ethnic (BAME) Apprenticeship Alliance (formally known as the Asian Apprenticeship Awards), to promote apprenticeship diversity through policy, advocacy and conversation – and the Apprenticeship Ambassador Network (AAN). The AAN consists of over 560 employer ambassadors (35 per cent representing SMEs) and around 400 apprentice ambassadors, who act as advocates and champions of apprenticeships (Education and Skills Funding Agency, 2021). While such organizations help, they are limited by the voluntarist approach to apprenticeships, under which employers decide the degree to which apprenticeship investment is vital to their organization and, more, where diversity fits.

Overall, therefore, action or commitment by the government towards the target it set in 2015 to improve ethnic and gender diversity in apprenticeships has not been 'strong', even in rhetorical terms, and the employer-led approach to apprenticeships leaves the power and decision making to employers. Although businesses are increasingly taking action to recruit from a diverse cohort, seeking to build their talent pipeline through apprenticeships and improve the degree of diversity in their organizations, the outcomes are still quite weak and fragmented.

Finally, the policy discourse appears to be shifting towards social mobility. The rhetoric around apprenticeship has historically been framed around skills development and tackling unemployment, while attempts or work on diversity are increasingly being described in terms of social mobility. The challenge of the emphasis on social mobility, which tends to focus on class more than ethnicity, is that it ignores complexities such as systemic discrimination and the position of people of minoritized ethnic groups behind their white counterparts. Ensuring that people from diverse backgrounds – diverse by gender, class and ability (to name a few) – can develop skills much needed by employers will no doubt significantly benefit the economy as a whole. A more systematic effort to address the complexities of inequalities in apprenticeships would further alleviate the skills shortage by widening and diversifying the talent pool.

In overall conclusion, therefore, the inconsistencies in the approach taken and the overall weak degree of commitment to diversity demonstrates yet more reflection of the effects produced by England's supposedly employer-led but ultimately atomized and individualistic approach to employer engagement. As Keep (2020, p 503) states, the English system is continually finding new carrots and few sticks, with the exception of the apprenticeship levy, which is not currently being used to its potential effect to incentivize greater diversity in apprenticeship recruitment and retention. Without a stronger approximation of a tripartite system of social partnership, employers in England look set to continue to play bit-parts as purchasers and volunteers, rather than commissioners or co-producers in the vocational education and training system on which they collectively rely.

Notes

[1] We use 'minority ethnic' or 'minoritized ethnic' in place of the acronym BAME (Black, Asian and minority ethnic), except in instances where BAME is used by the authors/publications referenced.

[2] General Certificate of Secondary Education: the school-leaving qualification in England and Wales at the end of secondary education.

[3] The Young Men's Christian Association; founded in 1844 to support young people in education, housing, training and health/wellbeing through advocacy and policy research.

References

Bredgaard, T. (2018). 'Employers and active labour market policies: Typologies and evidence', *Social Policy and Society* 17(3): 365–77.

Colahan, M. and Johnson, C. (2014). Apprenticeships evaluation 2014: Employer report, Research Paper No. 204, Department for Business, Innovation and Skills/Ipsos Mori: www.gov.uk/government/uploads/sys tem/uploads/attachment_data/file/387595/bis-14-1207-Apprenticesh ips-Evaluation-Employers-December-2014.pdf.

Croden, N. and Simmonds, L. (2008). *Employment and Skills Boards: Current and potential role*, Findings Paper, cfe.

DBIS (2012). The Richard review of apprenticeships, BIS/12/1323, Department for Business, Innovation and Skills: www.gov.uk/governm ent/publications/the-richard-review-of-apprenticeships.

DBIS (2013). Future of apprenticeships in England: Implementation plan, BIS/13/1175, Department for Business, Innovation and Skills: www.gov. uk/government/consultations/future-of-apprenticeships-in-england-rich ard-review-next-steps.

DBIS (2014). The future of apprenticeships in England guidance for trailblazers – from standards to starts, Department for Business, Innovation and Skills: www.gov.uk/government/publications/future-of-apprenticesh ips-in-england-guidance-for-trailblazers.

DBIS (2015a). Apprenticeships levy: Employer owned apprenticeships training, Consultation outcome, Department for Business, Innovation and Skills: www.gov.uk/government/consultations/apprenticeships-levy-emplo yer-owned-apprenticeships-training.

DBIS (2015b). English apprenticeships: Our 2020 vision, Corporate Report BIS/15/604, Department for Business, Innovation and Skills: www.gov. uk/government/publications/apprenticeships-in-england-vision-for-2020.

Delebarre, J. (2015). *Apprenticeships policy, England 2015*, Briefing Paper No. 03052, House of Commons Library.

Education and Skills Funding Agency (2021). 'New leadership appointments at the Apprenticeship Ambassador Network – GOV.UK', 25 November: www.gov.uk/government/news/new-leadership-appoi ntments-at-the-apprenticeship-ambassador-network.

Etherington, D. and Jones, M. (2016). 'The city-region chimera: The political economy of metagovernance failure in Britain', *Cambridge Journal of Regions, Economy and Society* 9(2): 371–89.

Foley, N. (2020). Apprenticeship statistics, Issue 06113, London: House of Commons Library.

Foley, N. (2021). Apprenticeship statistics, Commons Briefing Paper No. 06113, London: House of Commons Library: https://researchbriefings. files.parliament.uk/documents/SN06113/SN06113.pdf.

Fuller, A. and Unwin, L. (2007). 'What counts as good practice in contemporary apprenticeships? Evidence from two contrasting sectors in England', *Education + Training* 49(6): 447–58.

Garner, C. (2015). 'Advisory boards: bringing added value to business school-to-business (BS2B) collaborations', 30 June, Chartered Association of Business Schools: https://charteredabs.org/advisory-boards-bringing- added-value-to-business-school-to-business-bs2b-collaborations/

Gospel, H. (1998). 'The revival of apprenticeship training in Britain?' *British Journal of Industrial Relations* 36(3): 435–57.

Grugulis, I. (2007). *Skills, training and human resource development: A critical text*, Basingstoke: Palgrave Macmillan.

HM Revenue and Customs (2016). *Apprenticeship levy draft*, Legislation policy paper, HM Revenue and Customs: www.gov.uk/government/publicati ons/apprenticeship-levy.

HM Treasury (2015). Spending review and autumn statement 2015, Policy Paper, HM Government: www.gov.uk/government/publications/spend ing-review-and-autumn-statement-2015-documents/spending-review- and-autumn-statement-2015.

HM Treasury (2021). *Plan for jobs – progress update*, September, London: HM Government: www.gov.uk/government/publications/plan-for-jobs-progr ess-update

Huddleston, P. and Laczik, A. (2012). 'Successes and challenges of employer engagement: The new diploma qualification☆', *Journal of Education and Work* 25(4): 403–21.

Huddleston, P. and Laczik, A. (2018). '"In the driving seat", or reluctant passengers? Employer engagement in qualifications development: Some evidence from two recent 14–19 qualification reforms in England', *Journal of Education and Work*: 1–15.

Hunt, S.A. and Boliver, V. (2019). 'Private higher education in the United Kingdom', *International Higher Education* 98: 18–20.

Ingold, J. and Stuart, M. (2015). 'The demand-side of active labour market policies: A regional study of employer engagement in the work programme', *Journal of Social Policy* 44(03): 443–62.

Institute for Apprenticeships and Technical Education (2019). *Removing barriers to technical education and boosting quality*: www.instituteforapprenti ceships.org/about/newshub/news-events/removing-barriers-to-techni cal-education-and-boosting-quality/.

James Relly, S. and Laczik, A. (2022). 'Apprenticeship, employer engagement and vocational formation: A process of collaboration', *Journal of Education and Work* 35(1): 1–15.

Jones, M. (1997). *New institutional spaces: TECs and the remaking of economic governance*, Abingdon: Routledge.

Keep, E. (2012). 'Education and industry: Taking two steps back and reflecting', *Journal of Education and Work* 25(4): 357–79.

Keep, E. (2014). *What does skills policy look like now the money has run out?*, SKOPE Paper, Association of Colleges/University of Oxford.

Keep, E. (2020). 'Employers, the ghost at the feast', *Journal of Education and Work* 33(7–8): 500–6.

Keep, E. and James, S. (2011). 'Employer demand for apprenticeships.' In T. Dolphin and T. Lanning (eds) *Rethinking apprenticeships*, London: IPPR, pp 55–65.

Kirton, H. (2015). 'Employers divided over apprenticeships levy, finds CIPD survey', 10 February, People Management: www.cipd.co.uk/pm/peopl emanagement/b/weblog/archive/2015/10/02/employers-divided-over-apprenticeships-levy-finds-cipd-survey.aspx.

Martin, C.J. (2005). 'Corporatism from the firm perspective: Employers and social policy in Denmark and Britain', *British Journal of Political Science* 35(1): 127–48.

Martin, C.J. and Swank, D. (2012). *The political construction of business interests: Coordination, growth, and equality*, Cambridge: Cambridge University Press.

Mason, G. (2020). 'Higher education, initial vocational education and training and continuing education and training: Where should the balance lie?' *Journal of Education and Work* 33(7–8): 468–90.

McGurk, P. and Meredith, R. (2018). 'Local employer engagement or distant elites? Local enterprise partnerships and employment and skills in England', *Journal of Education and Work* 31(7–8): 692–714.

Mirza-Davies, J. (2015). Apprenticeship policy, England, Briefing Paper No. 03052, House of Commons Library: www.parliament.uk/briefing-papers/Sn03052.pdf.

National Apprenticeship Service (2017). *Membership information and application: Apprenticeship Diversity Champions Network*, pp 1–12.

National Apprenticeship Service (2019). *Championing diversity in apprenticeships*.

Newton, B. and Williams, J. (2013). Under-representation, by gender and race in apprenticeships: Research summary, Brighton: Institute for Employment Studies.

Ofsted (2015). Apprenticeships: Developing skills for future prosperity, No. 150129, Office for Standards in Education, Children's Services and Skills (Ofsted): www.gov.uk/government/uploads/system/uploads/attachme nt_data/file/469814/Apprenticeships_developing_skills_for_future_pro sperity.pdf.

Olaleye, O. (unpublished). *Apprenticeships: Breaking down barriers for Black, Asian and minority ethnic youth?*, PhD thesis, Queen Mary University of London.

Orton, M., Green, A., Atfield, G. and Barnes, S.-A. (2019). 'Employer participation in active labour market policy: From reactive gatekeepers to proactive strategic partners', *Journal of Social Policy* 48(03): 511–28.

Payne, J. (2008). 'Sector skills councils and employer engagement – delivering the "employer-led" skills agenda in England', *Journal of Education and Work* 21(2): 93–113.

Powell, A. (2020). Apprenticeships and skills policy in England, Commons Briefing Paper No. CBP03052, House of Commons Library: https://researchbriefings.files.parliament.uk/documents/SN03052/SN03052.pdf

Powell, A. (2021). *Coronavirus: Getting people back into work*, November, House of Commons Library: https://commonslibrary.parliament.uk/resea rch-briefings/cbp-8965/

Ryan, L. and Lőrinc, M. (2018). 'Perceptions, prejudices and possibilities: Young people narrating apprenticeship experiences', *British Journal of Sociology of Education* 39(6): 762–77.

Ryan, P. and Unwin, L. (2001). 'Apprenticeship in the British "training market"', *National Institute Economic Review* 178(1): 99–114.

SFA (2015). Trailblazer apprenticeship funding 2014 to 2015: Requirements for employers, Version 2, Skills Funding Agency: www.gov.uk/governm ent/uploads/system/uploads/attachment_data/file/412179/Trailblazer_ Apprenticeship_Funding_2014_to_2015_Requirements_for_Employ ers.pdf.

Snape, D. (1998). *Recruiting long-term unemployed people*, No. 76; Social Security Research, Department of Social Security.

Social Mobility and Child Poverty Commission (2016). Apprenticeships, young people, and social mobility.

Tiley, A., Morris, D. and Yusuf, H. (2021). *Generation COVID: The economic impact of COVID-19 on young people*, YMCA.

UK Government (2021). Autumn budget and spending review 2021, London: HM Government: www.gov.uk/government/publications/aut umn-budget-and-spending-review-2021-documents

van der Aa, P. and van Berkel, R. (2014). 'Innovating job activation by involving employers', *International Social Security Review* 67(2): 11–27.

Warner, P. and Gladding, C. (2019). Employers in the *driving seat?* New *thinking* for FE *leadership*, AELP Research, Further Education Trust for Leadership/Association of Employment and Learning Providers: https://fetl.org.uk/publications/employers-in-the-driving-seat-2/

Warrell, H. and Gordon, S. (2015). 'Summer Budget: Employers angry over plan for apprenticeships levy', *Financial Times*, 7 August: www.ft.com/cms/s/0/158dd0ce-257f-11e5-bd83-71cb60e8f08c.html#axzz3zve1I7vv.

Whieldon, F. (2020). 'Anger and dismay as BAME apprenticeship figures fall', *FE Week*, 23 October: https://feweek.co.uk/anger-and-dismay-as-bame-apprenticeship-figures-fall/

Whieldon, F. (2021). 'Former FE lecturer turned MP appointed new Apprenticeship Diversity Champions Network chair', *FE Week*, 11 February: https://feweek.co.uk/former-fe-lecturer-turned-mp-appoin ted-new-apprenticeship-diversity-champions-network-chair/

Wolf, A. (2015). Fixing a broken training-system: The case for an apprenticeship levy, Social Market Foundation: www.smf.co.uk/publicati ons/fixing-a-broken-training-system-the-case-for-an-apprenticeship-levy/

5

Practice Case Study: Programme Commissioning and Co-opetition in the UK and Australia

Orla Baker, Jo Ingold, Emma Crichton and Tony Carr

Introduction

The UK and Australia have similar employment service systems dominated by an outsourced model of service delivery.[1] In the UK, this began with private sector-led New Deals from 1998 and was further consolidated under the Work Programme 2011–17 and the Work and Health Programme from 2017. In Australia this occurred with the dismantling of the Commonwealth Employment Service in 1998 and the formation of a network of employment service providers – Job Network, then Job Services Australia and most recently jobactive and Workforce Australia. Collaboration between employment service providers has not been a feature of either model as the contracting regime and payment models have effectively discouraged this by encouraging intense competition between service providers (Ingold and Stuart, 2015). Also, commissioners do not account for employers as key stakeholders in either commissioning or contract management. Given the importance of employer engagement to the success of programmes, the commissioning landscape means that providers must 'retrofit' their delivery to efficiently and effectively service employers in a competitive environment comprising multiple programmes and providers in the same geographies with siloed caseloads all approaching the same employers (Ingold and Carr, 2020). This chapter compares approaches in the UK and Australia to improve the servicing of employers' needs through collaboration. In the UK, the ReAct Partnership, aligned to Restart from 2021, and in Australia the Magpies Next Generation Local Jobs Program are examined.

Paths to collaboration in the UK and Australia

Earlier developments in the UK

There have been two important bases for attempts at collaboration amongst the employment services sector in the UK. Firstly, the growing evidence that to service both jobseekers and employers as key customers of employment services requires collaboration between providers. Evidence suggests that if employers' requirements are greater than one provider can meet, there is a good case for collaboration, or providers risk losing immediate and future job opportunities from employers (Ingold and Stuart, 2014, p 8). In practical terms, providers can only place customers they have been assigned, meaning the available labour pool is spread across many providers. This means that an employer recruiting from one provider will not hear about all the available jobseekers in that area. Secondly, there is a good case for providers to share learning about 'what works' in employment services delivery for the benefit of commissioners, providers and service users. Between 2004 and 2010 under Labour there was unprecedented growth in programme evaluations by the Department for Work and Pensions (DWP) (Legrand, 2012, p 330). However, the introduction of the Work Programme saw both a reduction in DWP-commissioned evaluations and an implicit devolution of responsibility for sharing evidence to providers. To facilitate sharing of learning during the Work Programme the Centre for Economic and Social Inclusion (CESI – a research organization that undertook programme evaluations) convened a network of research leads from each 'Prime' (lead) provider in each contract package area (CPA – commissioning region) to share insights, labour market information and resources about what works for different customer groups. However, this was very limited in scale and unfunded, and for commercial reasons Primes were unable, unwilling and/or not incentivized to share. The Work Programme also pitted two Primes in the same geography against each other, with the biggest market share of caseloads being transferred to the highest performing provider. This mechanism clearly mitigated against both the sharing of vacancies and best practice. The *What Works Inclusion* initiative launched in 2016 by sector leaders Fran Parry and Tracy Fishwick aimed to encourage providers to share information about what works but was limited by similar challenges to those experienced by CESI (the initiative later morphed into the People's Powerhouse movement for change in the north of England). In addition, the DWP, as commissioner of services, began to explore with the research and academic communities how to better capture evaluation evidence for the benefit of all stakeholders. All of these initiatives were well-intentioned but unfortunately short-lived.

There were other provider-led attempts to foster collaboration in servicing employers. During the Work Programme the six Primes operating in London collaborated in order to better service Transport for London (TfL), an employer with large numbers of job vacancies. Together the Primes funded an Account Manager who sat within and was managed by TfL, who in turn cascaded job vacancies to all of the Primes, allowing TfL to access providers' caseloads of jobseekers across the six London delivery areas (CBI, 2012). Additionally, a bespoke, sector-based, training routeway was created for which sustainability of job outcomes was claimed to be 30 per cent higher than other placement outcomes. Under this model, competition amongst providers was hidden from employers but took place at the level of jobseeker service delivery, it being incumbent on providers wishing to service employers to better prepare candidates for vacancies.

A second example of collaboration to service employers was also during the Work Programme, when one of the first approaches to a 'National Employer Offer' was explored. In this case, Ingeus – the provider with the largest market share of Work Programme contracts (7 out of a total of 40 across the UK) – sought to offer UK-wide employers a single route into recruiting from the Programme as a whole. Ingeus worked with other Prime providers to offer a single recruitment service, regardless of which provider held the contract in a particular area. Operational innovations included a website map listing providers and their supply chain partners; this was shared across a working group of collaborating providers to assist them to navigate the complex employability delivery landscape. Providers also shared intelligence on how best to prepare jobseekers on their caseload, including shared training programmes where jobseekers on one provider's caseload could be referred to pre-employment training with a competing provider. The goal was to service employers better by operating outside the constraints of competitive and caseload structures. Employers involved benefited from a single Relationship Manager and broadly similar recruitment support across the UK.

One of the employers involved in the National Employer Offer initiative was the Cooperative chain of supermarkets and convenience stores. Through its Community Resourcing Programme, the Cooperative wanted to work with a supply chain of providers to support their priority of increasing workforce diversity and of hiring from local communities. Five providers and the Cooperative collaborated to co-design routes into employment, including developing guiding principles and a recruitment process. A structured framework for transitions into work was created, including presentations, tours of stores and undertaking work experience so that both employer and candidate could gain a realistic job preview of the candidate's capabilities and of the job and organization before the job commenced. This model was found to lead to better outcomes for both programme participants and Cooperative stores. There are similar examples of other such pathways, such as the Marks and Start programme run by Marks and Spencer in partnership with Gingerbread (lone parent charity), the Prince's Trust (charity for young people) and Remploy under the Work Programme, then Reed in Partnership under Work and Health (for disabled jobseekers).

A third example of collaboration was the Prime Provider Partnership during the Work and Health Programme (this succeeded the Work Programme) which offered a single point of contact for employers to reduce programme complexity, or 'hide the wiring'. The initiative involved a coordinated approach across five Primes delivering the programme across the UK. A lead from each Prime was appointed and all approaches from employers were coordinated through an Account Manager. There was a public web presence as a first point of contact, with opportunities being shared by the central account manager with the leads at the Primes. The focus was by definition predominantly on large employers with national coverage who had vacancies across a number of CPAs. Service level agreements were brokered between the lead provider and employers. However, there were challenges in relation to internal communications within the Primes and their supply chains and links with Jobcentre Plus/DWP were not as effective as they could have been (Mansour et al 2022).

The ReAct Partnership in the UK

A more recent example of provider collaboration is in relation to the UK government's Restart programme for the long-term unemployed launched in 2021. Primes who had succeeded in being placed on the DWP's framework (the Commercial Agreement for Employment and Health Related Services (CAEHRS)) were eligible to bid to deliver Restart. When the invitation to tender for Restart was published in late 2020 the funding available was significant (£2.9 billion) and for the first time in UK employment service commissioning, the assessment criteria required bidding Primes to state how they would cooperate with each other to share evidence. Tony Wilson at the Institute of Employment Studies (research organization) led an initiative to invite all Prime providers on CAEHRS to commit to setting aside 0.01 per cent of their income to fund a joint centre focused on sharing evidence amongst members and fostering collaboration. What became known as the ReAct Partnership was launched as a joint initiative between the Institute for Employment Studies, the Employment Related Services Association (the representative organization for employment service providers) and the Institute of Employability Professionals, the learning network for employability practitioners. All but two Prime providers agreed to participate, meaning that ReAct covered six out of eight Primes and ten out of a total of twelve CPAs.

The first project under the ReAct banner focused on employer engagement. Lower inflows into unemployment and lower long–term unemployment had led to predictions of an anticipated lower volume of jobseekers to meet employers' requirements, providing a clear rationale for collaboration amidst competition, or 'co-opetition' (Brandenburger and Nalebuff, 1996). Although it transpired that there were more vacancies across sectors than anticipated owing to a tight labour market, providers could offer added value to employers by assisting them in attracting, recruiting and retaining staff. A Prime Providers Network (PPN) was formed with account management service level agreements and shared commitments agreed in December 2021. At the time of writing, shared account management models were being drawn up with agreed minimum service standards that all ReAct providers would offer to employers, noting that providers had different service offers as standard in their organizations, for example guaranteed interviews. The standard offer could be modified if employers' needs required, but this needed to be agreed at PPN level even if not necessarily involving all providers. Restart encourages co-opetition as providers are not competing geographically as they were under the Work Programme.

Measurement of success under the ReAct Partnership will be based on the number of vacancies shared. Data is based on self-reporting by providers and will show who is sharing with whom and measure account management (types of employers and distribution across CPAs). It is a challenge to capture how many outcomes emanate from vacancy-sharing, first because it is difficult to separate these from other job outcomes, and second because all providers use different outcome measures. However, data can provide an indication of where to direct support for employers; for example if certain sectors have significant numbers of vacancies across CPAs, this could constitute a case for a national offer for a particular employer. Restart providers must demonstrate to the DWP as commissioner that they are collaborating, evidenced by how many vacancies they are sharing. Although providers cannot be sanctioned for not collaborating, they can be scored lower by the commissioner.

The Magpies Next Generation Project in Inner Melbourne, Australia

Similarly to the UK, the Australian employment services environment is characterized by intense competition and a focus on provider performance. One key difference from the UK was the jobactive Star Ratings system designed by the commissioner, the Department for Employment, Skills and Education (DESE). Under jobactive, the Star Ratings assessed the relative performance levels of providers against key performance indicator 1 (efficiency) and key performance indicator 2 (effectiveness) via six performance measures, the majority weighting being 26-week outcomes (Australian Government, 2021). This was intended to drive competition between providers for jobseekers, who could use Star Ratings as a guide to choose provider (in contrast, there is no choice for jobseekers in the UK employment services model). Against this backdrop and the challenges posed by COVID-19 economic recovery the Commonwealth government launched the Local Jobs Program (LJP) in April 2021, within ten employment regions that were considered to be the most disadvantaged. Following some success, the Program was extended in January 2021 to cover 26 regions and in July 2021 it was further expanded to all 51 employment regions. Each employment region has an Employment Facilitator who oversees the delivery of the LJP. The Employment Facilitator also chairs a Local Jobs and Skills Taskforce composed of representatives from local and state governments, employment and skills service providers, businesses and industry associations. The Local Jobs and Skills Taskforces aim to move as many people as possible into work and align the supply side with the demand side for jobseekers within the region including by connecting existing programmes. This provides potential to 'hide the wiring' for employers. Each employment region has an agreed Local Jobs Plan, which identifies the key priorities for each region, with a focus on creating employment opportunities, meeting local employer demands and improving local jobseekers' skills. The intention is to help people to find opportunities, employers to retrain staff and create opportunity through apprenticeships and traineeships, and grow the businesses, aligned with the challenges identified in the Local Jobs Plan.[2]

The Magpies Next Generation Project (Magpies) is an example of an LJP funded by DESE, designed to bring together expertise, resources and access to funding at the local level to support jobseekers and their communities in each region. Each LJP is competitively tendered and has a particular focus on reskilling, upskilling and employment pathways. In the inner metropolitan Melbourne employment region, the contract was awarded to Asuria, a for-profit provider that delivers a range of employment service contracts across Australia, with the Project being in partnership with Collingwood Sporting Club, known as the 'Magpies', hence the name. The project aimed to assist into sustainable employment up to 100 jobseekers who reside in the inner metropolitan Melbourne employment region and who were categorized as young people, migrants/refugees, culturally and linguistically diverse, Indigenous and/or women impacted by domestic violence. In addition to this core cohort, participants in the Magpies project were also selected based on additional circumstances, including being subject to family violence, criminal risk-taking activities, homelessness and social and economic disadvantage.

Unlike other employment service programmes, Magpies is uniquely centred on formal and informal partnerships amongst employment service providers and non-government organizations. Since at the time Asuria was delivering jobactive in regional Victoria but not in the inner metropolitan Melbourne region, it was therefore reliant on other providers to refer potential participants: in other words, 'collaborating with a competitor, because they're in the jobactive space'.[3] Although Asuria as project lead was not in direct competition with providers operating in inner Melbourne, several other providers were. Additionally, this was in the lead-up to the commissioning of the New Employment Services Model. This placed pressure on all providers to maintain performance and to demonstrate collaborative activities to the commissioner. In terms of fostering collaboration and co-opetition, the project's proposition was attractive to other providers in that it offered an additional intervention that could 'eliminate barriers to employment, whatever they may be'[4] and there were clear benefits to the providers holding the caseloads in terms of added value from an intervention administered by a third party: 'any programme that is available just to get our jobseekers employed. And of course this benefits the organization indirectly as well, because when you get a placement, then you get outcomes, so it all flows from that.'[5] In other words, all parties stood to win in some way.

The project had three stated priorities:

1. To create stronger supply chain management of jobseekers into significant job creation opportunities for growth industries by coordinating Federal, Victorian and inner metropolitan Melbourne councils' employment and training programmes, including those designed specifically as recovery programmes from COVID-19 impacts.
2. To work with partner organizations to broker opportunities for skills development/employment and mentoring for disadvantaged jobseekers.
3. To partner with Collingwood Sporting Club and registered training organizations to deliver the Magpies Next Generation Project to provide opportunity for the 100 jobseekers to be mentored and supported to complete activities including pre-employment foundation skills, industry skills training, mentoring and work experience to upskill and prepare them to meet the needs of employers.

The Magpies project offered an unprecedented opportunity to bridge the divide amongst providers within the sector and to create a new way of working, providing opportunity for collaboration and co-opetition. This is highly unusual in Australian employment services where providers are in general reluctant to share vacancies that may benefit other providers (Considine et al, 2021, p 132). Partnering to understand shared values and inter-agency obligations of respect has allowed the project to grow and provide opportunity for the project to develop into a sustainable financial model in the future. The project tested new approaches to assist highly marginalized jobseekers into sustainable employment pathways, including traineeships and apprenticeships. It aimed to reduce economic disadvantage for jobseekers by linking and supporting them into apprenticeships, training and job placements, and providing wrap-around services, i.e. services other than employment-related such as health, housing, and counselling. Individuals were referred by the partner agencies including jobactive providers and as participation was voluntary, jobseekers should not be financially penalized if they did not wish to attend.

The project involved a series of structured two-week programmes delivered to different cohorts. Each programme focused on personal development growth, goal setting and the development of soft skills. For example, participants examined the DESE's *Core Skills for Work Framework* and identified skills they wished to improve and develop into an action plan.[6] Participants were also encouraged to consider skills they had acquired from interests and hobbies, to engage in goal setting and a SWOT analysis of their skills (strengths, weakness, opportunities, threats), as well as to develop skills at self-reflection.

At the time of writing, each two-week programme had focused on a particular sector with demand for labour, for example warehousing or construction. Delivery partners had been engaged to run the programme. Frontline HR (a recruitment agency) delivered the first face-to-face programme. When the programme inevitably had to move online owing to lockdowns, One Wellbeing were engaged, a registered training organization that had begun life helping elite athletes to transition to life after sport and specialized in delivering online programmes to build confidence. Employers from Asuria's and the delivery partners' networks were closely involved in the project, particularly in the final day of the two-week programme, a graduation event in which participants delivered presentations and received feedback from project staff and from employers. The 'Project with Purpose' presentations were prepared over the days leading up to the graduation and included challenges set by employers, including the planning of an event or a training course within the workplace. Participants identified the roles that would be needed to complete their assigned project, devised a timescale and budgets and worked with designers for the presentations, offering good opportunities to build communication and team-working skills. The second week provided the opportunity to meet employers and gain insights into the organizations and the job roles available. At the time of writing, 51 individuals commenced the project, 34 completed and around 22 entered employment.

The outcome for jobseekers using the Magpie programme goes beyond being 'job ready' and there is a much greater need than simply attending a one-off pre-employment training course. The programme helped jobseekers to build their confidence and see their potential in the labour market. COVID-19 presented challenges for the project, including engaging hard-to-reach jobseekers with complex barriers such as speaking English as a second language; remote access proved difficult and further highlighted the need to pivot delivery methodologies in an inclusive and accessible way. Although it is too early to draw firm conclusions from the Magpies project, there are important emerging lessons about the benefits and challenges of collaboration amongst competing providers. In November 2021 Asuria subsequently launched a similar partnership with the Western Bulldogs football club through their Community Foundation.

Conclusion

The examples of collaboration in the UK and Australia presented here were driven by a desire for better job matching and greater sustainability of jobs by working directly with employers to service their needs and also through better preparation of candidates. Employment service providers as intermediaries are not merely 'information providers' who channel information about candidates to employers and about vacancies and employers to candidates (Autor, 2009). Instead, they are 'matchmakers', focused on appropriate matching of candidates to employers (and vice versa) (Ingold and Valizade, 2017). In the UK, an ongoing challenge is how to foster collaboration within Primes' supply chains. Additionally, within the Restart programme there has so far been no identified measure of employer satisfaction. It is critical that employer-facing services are needs-led rather than product-led (i.e. programme-led) and a key measure of success will be what providers do to increase conversion of vacancies to sustainable employment pathways.

In Australia it is too early to judge the success of the Local Jobs initiatives, including the Local Jobs Programs, the Employment Facilitator roles and the Taskforces. However, the case study demonstrates that it is possible to put structures in place to overcome barriers to employer engagement arising from commissioning models. The collaboration seen in the Magpies project to some extent echoes the Work Programme examples of collaboration of a decade earlier. This may suggest that the UK has travelled further along the path to collaboration than Australia and indicates that the journey is protracted. In the plans for the New Employment Services Model (Workforce Australia) due to commence in July 2022, collaboration and employer engagement both feature significantly (DESE, 2021). Currently Employment Facilitators are directed by DESE and it remains to be seen whether in future they will have more devolved control over their localized activities. Both country case studies highlight the need for government departments to work together, in order to meet employers' labour demands and to consider collaboration at the stage of policy and programme design, rather than expect providers to 'retrofit' their delivery within highly competitive commissioning models.

Notes

[1] The UK outsourced employment services model predominantly covers England and Wales (except for London and Greater Manchester) as Scotland and Northern Ireland both contract their services separately. However, there is some commonality in the models across all four nations and all have public employment services.

[2] Interview with local Employment Facilitator, July 2021.

[3] Interview with stakeholder, November 2021.

[4] Interview with provider, September 2021.

[5] Interview with provider, November 2021.

[6] www.dese.gov.au/skills-information-training-providers/core-skills-work-developmen tal-framework

References

Australian Government (2021). *Jobactive guideline: Performance framework*, Canberra: Commonwealth Government.

Autor, D. (2009). *Studies of labour market intermediation*, Chicago: University of Chicago Press.

Brandenburger, A.M. and Nalebuff, B.J. (1996). *Co-opetition*, New York: Doubleday.

Confederation of British Industry (2012). *Work in progress: Fulfilling the potential of the Work Programme*, London: CBI.

Department of Employment, Skills and Education (2021). *Request for proposal for the New Employment Services Model 2022*, Canberra: DESE.

Ingold, J. and Carr, T. (2020). 'How can we better integrate employer engagement in service delivery?' *Institute of Employability Professionals Journal 2*.

Ingold, J. and Stuart, M. (2014). *Employer engagement in the Work Programme*, CERIC Policy Report No. 5, Leeds: Centre for Employment Relations Innovation and Change.

Ingold, J. and Stuart, M. (2015). 'The demand-side of active labour market policies: A regional study of employer engagement in the Work Programme', *Journal of Social Policy* 44(3): 443–62.

Ingold, J. and Valizade, D. (2017). 'Employers' recruitment of disadvantaged groups: Exploring the effect of active labour market programme agencies as labour market intermediaries', *Human Resource Management Journal* 27(4): 530–47.

Legrand, T. (2012). Overseas and over here: Policy transfer and evidence-based policy-making, *Policy Studies* 33(4): 329–48.

Mansour, J., Allen, A., Cetera, R., Subosa, M. and Hammond, L. (2022). *Shared employer engagement models: What works*, Brighton: The ReAct Partnership.

O'Sullivan, S., McGann, M. and Considine, M. (2021). *Buying and selling the poor: Inside Australia's privatized welfare-to-work market*, Sydney: Sydney University Press.

PART II

The Meso Level: Programmes and Actors

6

The Weakest Link? Job Quality and Active Labour Market Policy in the UK

Anne Green and Paul Sissons

Introduction

For many years the labour market model in the UK was bound up with a predominant concern with job quantity, but with considerably less attention to job quality (Lauder, 1999). Recently however, there has been a shift in policymaking towards a greater concern with the idea of 'good work'. In active labour market policy (ALMP) the shift is most readily seen in a growing interest in labour market progression, and a process of policy searching for how employment services might support greater labour market mobility.

Within this context, this chapter explores ALMP approaches and practice in the UK alongside a wider national discourse about increasing good work. The chapter evaluates the extent to which ALMP is a weak link in seeking progress towards good work: firstly, as a result of the historically embedded nature of the employer engagement function within particular types of networks of employers with basic labour demand needs; and secondly how this has been supported by a work-first system in which jobseekers are encouraged, and can be mandated, to accept available opportunities. The argument is made that within this system there is only limited scope for public employment services to engage with a good work agenda, or to exert upward institutional pressure on job quality. However, the current context of labour and skills shortages offers ALMP an opportunity to capitalize on some upward pressures on job quality.

The chapter is structured as follows. The labour market context in the UK is described initially, followed by an appraisal of recent developments around the good work agenda and a discussion of the labour market trends which frame current opportunities. The following sections then provide a discussion of the evolution of ALMP in the UK, and the role of employer engagement within ALMP set against a changing policy context: but one in which work-first remains largely embedded. The final section provides a discussion of what this evidence suggests about the relationship between ALMP and job quality.

Context

Historically, the focus of employment policy in the UK has been on reducing unemployment. Hence, the quantity of jobs available has been a primary concern. However, over the last decade or so, as employment rates rose to record levels, concerns about in-work poverty have grown, with the proportion of working-age adults in working families who experience in-work poverty rising to more than one in seven (Innes, 2020). The relationship between employment and poverty is complex, but it is clear that in some sectors and occupations long working hours are not sufficient to protect individuals from poverty (Sissons et al, 2018).

Although the structure of employment has changed over time, evidence suggests that poor-quality jobs are a persistent feature of the UK labour market, with some workers experiencing limited wage progression and remaining in low-paid work for long periods (D'Arcy and Hurrell, 2014; Kumar et al, 2014; Lee et al, 2018). Several studies have traced a polarizing labour market, with jobs growth at the top and at the bottom of the wage distribution (Goos and Manning, 2007; Fernandez-Macias et al, 2012; McIntosh, 2013). Analyses over three decades (Salvatori, 2018) suggest that the polarization process is well established, with the employment growth in high-skill occupations always exceeding growth in low-skill occupations; the general increase in educational attainment contributes to this latter trend. The result is a 'hollowing-out' of the employment structure, with fewer jobs in the middle of the distribution. This, in turn, has implications for progression within employment and out of low pay.

Evidence suggests that low-paid workers are less likely than high-paid workers to work for employers that are willing to invest in their training and development (Lindsay et al, 2012; Devins et al, 2014; Sissons, 2020), which might help them progress in work. Literature on the low-skills equilibrium suggests that some firms are entrenched in low-skills, low-wage models of operating (Wilson and Hogarth, 2003; Green, 2016; Green et al, 2021a). In such a situation they face few labour or skills shortages and have a viable business model, so there is little incentive to participate in education and training and raise the qualification levels and aspirations of a predominantly low-paid workforce.

Firms with a low-skills, low-wage model will struggle to generate skills and productivity improvements without changing their product market or competitiveness strategies (and generally they face limited pressures to do either), or in the absence of external economic or regulatory factors (such as raising the minimum wage). Firms entrenched in a low-skills, low-wage model are likely to be part of the 'long tail' of least productive firms. While a gap between the most and least productive firms is not unique to the UK, concern about the UK's poor productivity performance relative to international competitors has risen up the policy agenda over the last decade. The financial crisis and recession of 2018 resulted in a marked downwards shock to productivity levels, and thereafter productivity growth rates were markedly lower than the pre-crisis trend. The UK's poor levels of productivity have been attributed to under-investment in technology, research and development, digitalization, skills training and management practices (McCann, 2018; Oliveira-Cunha et al, 2021).

Creating good work

Concerns about productivity, in-work poverty, employment precarity, labour market polarization and associated outcomes related to job quality are increasingly debated under a 'Good Work' label. Interest in good work in a UK and devolved nations context had been growing for some time, but it was the commissioning and publication of the independent Taylor Review of Modern Working Practices (Taylor et al, 2017) that really added impetus to growing policy interest in the topic. The Taylor Review looked at the implications of contemporary business practices, including the rise of flexible/atypical forms of working and the gig economy, for worker rights and responsibilities and employer freedoms and obligations. The Review's recommendations were based on the premise that all work in the UK economy should be fair and decent with realistic scope for development and fulfilment, and that the achievement of these goals matters for people's health and wellbeing and for tackling low productivity. In essence, the Review called on the government to pay closer attention to the quality of work alongside its quantity. The government responded to the Taylor Review with a Good Work Plan in 2018, placing equal importance on the quality and quantity of work and setting out the need for legislation and enforcement to address insecure and exploitative work.

The Good Work Plan (HM Government, 2018) noted that quality work means different things to different people. However, while good work is a broad concept with no universal meaning, it is generally related to an individual's wellbeing in employment and the factors which impact this. Recurring key components of good work are rate of pay, employment type, security of contracts, working conditions, opportunities for individual growth – including through opportunities for training and progression – wellbeing, freedom and support. These were reflected in a measurement framework for job quality developed by a Measuring Job Quality Working Group convened by the Carnegie UK Trust and the Royal Society of Arts in 2018, comprising 18 measures across 7 foundations: terms of employment, pay and benefits, job design and the nature of work, health, safety and psychosocial wellbeing, work–life balance, social support and cohesion, and voice and representation (Irvine et al, 2018). In practice, the relative weights that individuals place on different aspects of good work depend on their circumstances, personalities and expectations.

In Scotland and Wales concerns with Good Work have been advanced under the banner of Fair Work. According to the Fair Work Convention in Scotland, fair work is work that offers effective voice, opportunity, security, fulfilment and respect, that balances the rights and responsibilities of employers and workers and that can generate benefits for individuals, organizations and society. Likewise, according to the Fair Work Commission in Wales, fair work sees workers fairly rewarded, heard and represented, secure and able to grow and progress in a healthy, inclusive working environment and, importantly, respect and substantive effect for legal rights.

The latter represents a point of leverage to deliver good work. Prior to the COVID-19 pandemic, at which time there was a step change in state intervention in the economy, successive UK governments had tended to restrict their involvement in the market economy, with the exception of minimum wage policies and enforcement of employment regulations. Aside from the activities of the devolved nations in promoting fair work, some local authorities and metropolitan mayors have harnessed their soft power over their local economies, using informal measures to persuade local employers to implement decent work policies, including through living wage policies and employment charters (Johns et al, 2019). There are also examples of learning from co-designed programmes for boosting productivity, including in particular sectors characterized by low pay and limited progression opportunities. The short- and longer-term evaluation of the UK Futures Programme, in which between 2014 and 2016 the UK Commission for Employment and Skills brought together a series of co-investment projects supporting the development of innovative, employer-led solutions to workforce development challenges limiting business performance, emphasized a role for place-based initiatives here, utilizing local stakeholders from local anchor organizations to address common challenges through the development of a localized project ecology (Thom et al, 2016; Green et al, 2019). Examples include a hospitality-focused project in Cornwall which worked with local businesses to enable advancement within the sector through new professional development opportunities, and an initiative in St Helens in north-west England bringing together micro- and small firms to enhance management and entrepreneurial skills with a view to increasing their potential to grow and contribute to local economic development. Regionally and locally, there is some evidence that economic recovery strategies are embedding Good Work and job quality indicators in monitoring and performance frameworks (Green et al, 2021b).

Labour market trends

The Taylor Review (Taylor et al, 2017) set out key features of, and trends in, the UK labour market. It highlighted the greater flexibility of the UK labour market compared with the labour markets of many international competitors, characterized by a relatively high employment rate and a low unemployment rate. In terms of the profile of the workforce, it noted the faster increase in participation rates for women than for men and for older people (aged 50 years and over) than for younger people – among whom participation rates in education increased. Looking back over the previous 20 years, it reported that while full-time, permanent work as an employee continued to compose the majority of employment in the UK (63 per cent), there had been a shift towards more flexible forms of working, with changes in levels of self-employment and part-time working in particular, as well as agency and temporary work. Despite a relatively high employment rate it emphasized evidence of persistent under-employment, defined as workers wanting more hours. Going forward the Review identified under-employment, poor real wage growth, poor productivity performance, new business models, skills mismatch and increasing automation as challenges for the labour market.

Key medium-term trends in employment by sector and occupation include an increase in employment in business and other services and in non-marketed services, alongside a decline in employment in manufacturing despite a growth in output driven by continuing automation in the sector. Projections indicate that these broad trends are expected to continue in the future (Wilson et al, 2020). Changes in the occupational employment structure have been driven by changing sectoral employment patterns and technological and organizational trends influencing the patterns of occupational demand within sectors. Over the medium term, managers, professional and associate professional and technical occupations have seen significant increases in employment, as have caring, leisure and other service occupations. Administrative and secretarial occupations have seen declining employment as a result of technological innovations in the office environment, with skilled trade occupations also seeing long-term employment decline.

Against these medium-term trends, the pandemic represented a large shock to labour markets worldwide. The general impact across the developed world has been to accentuate existing trends and inequalities in the labour market. In particular, it has accelerated trends towards digitalization. In the UK it had uneven impacts sectorally, with the accommodation and food services sector and arts and entertainment amongst the sectors hardest hit. It resulted in lower labour force participation of particular groups, notably younger and older age groups. Between March and May 2020, the seasonally adjusted claimant count for unemployment benefits increased from 1.25 million to 2.68 million in the UK. The government sought to protect jobs through a number of schemes, notably the Coronavirus Job Retention Scheme which paid 80 per cent of employees' wages (up to £2,500 per month) in the first instance, and 'furloughed' 11.7 million people between March 2020 and September 2021 (Powell and Francis-Devine, 2021).

Although the economy has seen recovery since, many jobs hit by the pandemic have not (yet) returned. At the time of writing (November 2021) aggregate levels of vacancies have recovered to pre-pandemic levels, with some firms experiencing difficulties in filling vacancies in particular jobs, with heavy goods-vehicle drivers a prime example (Jung and Collings, 2021); but the broader picture across sectors is less favourable. Analyses by the Institute of Fiscal Studies (Costa Dias et al, 2021), taking account of individuals' current and recent occupations and their pre-pandemic pattern of movement between occupations, show that new opportunities are strongest in lowest-paying occupations, but a large share of workers still face reduced opportunities compared with before the COVID-19 pandemic. Groups more likely than average to see increased opportunities (based on pre-pandemic employment patterns) are those with the lowest levels of formal qualifications (especially compared with graduates who are more likely to see reduced opportunities). For 64 per cent of unemployed workers competition for relevant job openings is at least 10 per cent greater than before the pandemic. While this picture is likely to change over time, it emphasizes challenges in achieving full employment and good jobs for all.

ALMP in the UK

As has been detailed in the preceding sections, the interest in good work in the UK has grown over time, and particularly in recent years. In many respects, for much of this period good work conversations have developed in isolation from core approaches to employment as enacted through ALMP. This section now details the development of ALMP over time, before discussing the recent evolution of focus towards in-work progression, which provides an emerging link to the wider Good Work agenda.

The development of ALMP in the UK

The ALMP framework in the UK that has developed over the past 30 years has been characterized by two broad elements. The first is that the system has become increasingly based around ideas of conditionality. The second is that the process of 'activation' has been broadened to include a large number of groups – including single parents and disabled people – who have previously been largely outside this framework. It is worth noting also that, in a comparative context, ALMP in the UK has historically been characterized by an over-arching focus on 'work first', and speed of work entry and benefit exit, combined with relatively low levels of spending per head associated with human capital development and long-term opportunity (Berry, 2014).

Important changes to the UK ALMP framework include the establishment of Jobseekers' Allowance (JSA) and the roll-out of the New Deal programmes. JSA was introduced in 1996 and marked a significant watershed in UK social security, with new powers for benefit officers to enforce job-seeking among claimants (Novak, 1997). Building on this approach the Labour government of the day created a new framework for ALMP built on the idea of a New Deal. The New Deal programmes were an explicit extension of the move from a passive to an active benefits system, one which was organized around a 'work-first' principle (Finn, 2003). Beginning in 1997, a succession of New Deal programmes focused on different groups of benefit claimants, including mandatory programmes for young people and the long-term unemployed, and voluntary programmes for single parents, disabled people and partners of the unemployed (for an overview see Hasluck, 2000). These changes drew on experiences of programme design and emergent Workfare experiments in the USA (Peck and Theodore, 2001; Sunley et al, 2006).

Subsequently, with a change of government, a new over-arching employment programme, the Work Programme, was introduced in 2011. The Work Programme model was notable in two respects. Firstly, it extended previous trials and initiatives with private providers of employment services, and made these the main delivery vehicle for support to the long-term unemployed. Secondly, it embedded a payment-by-results model which gave greater weight to sustained employment outcomes than simply to job entry. The Work Programme was developed to provide more individually tailored support as a means to encourage sustainable employment outcomes. However, while there was considerable flexibility within the 'black box' of the programme, which did seem to increase work entry, evidence suggests these initial gains did not persist over the long term (Ray et al, 2014).

The most recent phase of ALMP development has been the introduction of a new benefit – Universal Credit (UC). UC has been introduced in a phased roll-out to replace six existing benefit streams and will cover around 8 million households (Millar and Bennett, 2017). The introduction of UC is a major change in the UK social security system, which redraws the boundaries of social security activation in relation to the distinction between work and non-work benefits. Individuals on UC who enter employment on a low income remain on UC as an in-work benefit, with a taper rate designed to incentivize taking on additional hours or employment. UC also develops an in-work support process for those who have moved into work. The in-work support is designed to encourage individuals on low wages to take on additional hours, additional jobs or to move to higher-paid work; controversially, it also includes provision for compulsion and mandation.

The introduction of UC has been the subject of a range of criticisms. These include linking the introduction of UC to impacts on health and wellbeing (Wickham et al, 2020) and critiques of the gender and dependence implications of the benefit (Millar and Bennett, 2017; Andersen, 2020). Critiques have also focused on the elements of conditionality and sanctions associated with UC (Wright and Dwyer, 2020). UC extends work requirements into the workplace, to those in employment and on low pay – generating what Wright and Dwyer have termed a 'relentless coercion towards "more work"' (p 11), and the 'deepening and widening control of claimants' lives' (Millar and Bennett, 2017, p 169). In this sense UC is argued to be not just about work, but about economic independence from state support (Dwyer and Wright, 2014; Reeves and Loopstra, 2017).

Employment sustainability and progression within ALMP

As ALMP programmes have become embedded in the UK, the focus on the outcomes of these programmes has also begun to evolve. In particular, in recent years there has been a greater concern to 'design in' an emphasis on employment sustainability and, most recently, wage progression.

A major development demonstrating the shift in thinking towards the sustainability of employment outcomes was the roll-out of the Employment, Retention and Advancement (ERA) pilot in 2003. Drawing in large part on a delivery approach developed in the USA, ERA had two target groups – the long-term unemployed and single parents. The programme provided several different types of support – including access to job coaching, services, financial support for training (up to £1,000) and employment/career guidance (Hendra et al, 2011). The programme also included a financial incentive for participants in the form of a work retention bonus of £400 which was paid every 17 weeks for those remaining in work and meeting a minimum hours threshold (up to a maximum of £2,400). The large-scale, randomized evaluation of ERA demonstrated positive outcomes, although these faded over time for the single parent group (Hendra et al, 2011). The training provision appeared less successful in securing earnings gains; although the reasons for this are not well understood (Ray et al, 2014).

Greater emphasis on the sustainability of employment outcomes was subsequently designed into the (largely) private-provider-led Work Programme. The Work Programme's payment-by-results model included a relatively small attachment fee with performance-based payments on job outcomes (at either three or six months after entry), and particularly what is referred to as 'sustaining employment' (payable every four additional weeks the individual remained in work [although not necessarily in the same job], for either 12, 18 or 24 months depending on the group). However, evidence suggested that this change largely did not spur significant transformation in delivery practice (Ray et al, 2014), and that harder-to-help groups did not benefit from the potential for tailored support in ways in which the programme design had envisaged (Rees et al, 2014).

Most recently, UC has sharpened the focus again on not just the sustainability of employment but also issues of progression once in work. One important aspect which UC changes is the nature of the relationship between worker and employer – creating, in effect, a tripartite relationship between individual, employer and government. This focus on in-work progression is examined in greater detail in the following section.

New directions for employment progression

UC represents, at least in part, a new direction in ALMP in the UK. It effectively opens up a new frontier of activation. The introduction of UC therefore reworks in some respects the way in which the public employment service – Jobcentre Plus (JCP) – engages with benefit claimants. In addition to the established JCP advisor role, which is oriented towards work entry, 'work coaches' seek to play a role in encouraging individuals on UC and in work (on a low income) to pursue opportunities for wage progression.

While the pandemic has altered elements of UC and appears to have slowed down the practical delivery of the framework, there is recent evidence that the focus on progression is becoming embedded. The DWP has established an In-work Progression Commission tasked with developing ideas and recommendations around progression policy. The report of the Commission provides an outline of the dimensions of the policy, which are likely to be taken up as a focus (In-Work Progression Commission, 2021). This includes an evolution of the role of JCP, moving towards the delivery of a series of progression-focused 'career conversations'. Some early experimental evidence suggests that the intensity of support provided by work coaches can be associated with higher earnings (although it was also associated with more sanctions) (Department for Work and Pensions, 2018). Additionally, the Commission highlights the possibilities of better embedding information and access to wider learning and skills opportunities, and sector-focused 'bridging courses' (including access to apprenticeships). In a departure from the predominant concerns with the supply side which have typified much of ALMP in the UK, the In-Work Progression Commission sets out the need for more action on the employer side to develop more transparent and accessible progression pathways, as well as suggesting a new registration body for care workers (a major low-paid sector) in England to support with development and progression. Finally, the Commission highlights opportunities to do more using the opportunities that government procurement offers, and the need to address wider transport and childcare barriers to in-work progression.

Through this work the In-Work Progression Commission is beginning to move beyond the established supply-side focus, and to situate the ALMP framework within the wider Good Work policy framework (as discussed in the previous section). However, the scale of the ambition, for example around skills and training, is relatively limited, and suggests a modest evolution of role rather than a wholesale shift from work-first to career-first. The employer-focused suggestions are voluntary rather than mandatory, and the means of influencing employer practices are unclear. For example, there is no clear sense of how ALMPs might be developed to seek to change or challenge employer behaviours. We discuss the issues around the progression agenda and its wider links, including constraints in delivering a Good Work agenda, starting with the employer engagement function in ALMP.

Employer engagement in ALMP

The employer engagement function in ALMP

The employer engagement function has been an important element of the development of the ALMP framework. JCP acts as a matching agent – hosting employer vacancies through the Find a Job site (previously known as Universal Job Match), and using this as one mechanism for matching claimants with jobs. Employers have been engaged in a variety of ways as part of employment programmes; in particular this has been encouraged through the development of employment programmes more focused on being demand-led (and often sector-demand-led). However, overall the ALMP system in the UK has developed around a predominant model characterized by a reliance on employers who depend on a large supply of low-paid labour (Martin and Swank, 2004; McGurk, 2014).

The New Deal Innovation Fund, introduced in 1999, developed a 'demand-led' approach in a number of sectors aimed at improving engagement with employers to better understand their needs (Fletcher, 2001). However, although understandings of employer needs were improved through the programme, there was less progress on influencing employer recruitment practices, and encouraging recruitment from more disadvantaged groups, or support for employee retention (Fletcher, 2004). Such approaches to employer engagement were taken forward in the Fair Cities Pilot (2004–8), which designed pre-employment training to match the vacancy needs of large local employers, and supported disadvantaged ethnic-minority residents to access these opportunities (Atkinson et al, 2008). Local Employment Partnerships (2007–10) also used this pre-employment model, alongside a recruitment subsidy (in response to the 2008 recession), and prioritized employer engagement. The programme evaluation found some evidence that closer employer engagement did provide a means for 'Jobcentre Plus staff to challenge employers' recruitment practices ... thus opening doors for disadvantaged jobseekers to apply for vacancies' (Bellis et al, 2011, p 17). However, it is unclear how widespread such changes were, or whether such conversations extended into other aspects of Good Work.

These approaches to employer engagement, focused on opening up employment entry, continued with the Work Programme, with providers developing their own employer engagement functions (Ingold and Stuart, 2015). However, as noted by Ingold (2018), employers firmly held the power in this relationship, with little scope for providers to influence employer practices in a way that might support improved employment quality, and with the emphasis on the individual needing to fit the job rather than vice versa. Employer engagement has also been a major strand of the public employment services administered sector-based work academies (SBWAs) (introduced in 2011), now known as the sector-based work academy programme, which developed a pre-employment training and work experience model, alongside a significant employer engagement function and an overall sector focus typically driven by a large number of sector vacancies locally. SBWAs have operated in sectors including retail, hospitality, care, teaching, manufacturing, logistics, food and administration (Department for Work and Pensions, 2016).

Overall, the types of sector and employer that employer engagement models have focused on appear to have yielded relatively little change to the quality of jobs made available through the ALMP system, with little evidence to suggest any significant application of upward institutional pressure on the practices of employers and the quality of the employment offer to those looking for work. In short, while employer engagement functions within ALMP in the UK appear to have been relatively successful in understanding and meeting employer needs, and potentially have opened up entry-level vacancies to disadvantaged groups, there is less evidence to suggest they have effectively functioned as a 'disruptive strategy' to 'expand the pool of better jobs' (O'Regan, 2015, p 17).

Employer engagement and job quality – developing a more productive partnership?

To date, where ALMP has focused around job quality, it has been almost exclusively aligned to the idea of in-work progression. However, even within this partial view of job quality there remain significant unanswered questions. The first is around the balance between the extent to which progression is pursued via either the internal or the external labour market. This raises a whole set of issues for policy design and for employer engagement. If targeting progression through the internal labour market, this has important implications for the initial placement in jobs of those moving into employment, as rates of wage progression have distinct sectoral patterns and are comparatively slow in many low-paid sectors that employ many of those entering work – such as retail, hospitality and care (Lee et al, 2018). Furthermore, where the logics of employer engagement are driven by short-term labour demand needs, this raises important questions about the ability of employment service providers to engage employers with a progression agenda (Sissons and Green, 2017). While a progression approach focused on the external labour market potentially exacerbates a high-turnover ALMP model, it also opens up potentially difficult conversations with employers about encouraging staff to move to different job opportunities. From a policy perspective, relatively little is known about how to design individual support for progression: when should interventions occur, where are the critical junctures and over what period is the process viewed?

While recent developments provide some initial progress around linking ALMP to employment progression, there are a range of challenges to establishing a wider link between ALMP and a Good Work agenda. There is little evidence from UK ALMP that public employment services can exert a strong influence on employer practices. Fundamentally, the relationship has tended to be rooted in the need for JCP to serve employer needs. In doing this the work-first system, with its emphasis on applying to, and accepting, available opportunities (which may or may not be a good match and/or offer opportunities for advancement), provides a steady flow of available labour. With employers finding few barriers to recruiting and meeting labour supply needs, there is often little impetus for them to develop good working practices in order to secure engagement and recruitment from ALMP.

Recent evidence has demonstrated the tensions which exist within JCP advisory roles between an agenda which purports to seek to engender personalization and progression, and one that remains fundamentally rooted in 'work-first', basic employability and prioritizes the speed of job entry, which reinforces the historical patterns of matching into low-wage jobs (Berry, 2014; Johnson et al, 2021). This takes us to the core of the issue in seeking to link ALMP more successfully with improved job-quality outcomes. Firstly, within a system where the 'work-first' approach is embedded, the employer engagement function tends to remain a relationship with large employers of low-paid workers and, although the supply-side emphasis may shift to sustainability and progression, actions on the demand side remain muted. This can be seen in the recent In-Work Progression Commission report, which – although encouraging in some respects around the identification of wider barriers – does not resolve the issue of how the unemployed may access better jobs. The question remains, then, whether a more career-first focus is needed to align ALMP and job quality more closely (Fuertes et al, 2021). The second major issue is the isolation of ALMP from wider debates on good work. ALMP is largely developed and implemented in a way that is not well integrated with other important policy domains (such as skills and economic development). One area where there is some early indication that ALMP is being more integrated is in the context of actions taking place at city and regional level: some cities have taken a wider approach to good work and sought to connect this to devolved activities (such as pilot programmes) which function as part of the ALMP framework (Green et al, 2022). An example of this is work in Manchester, which includes both devolved elements of ALMP and a wider Good Work agenda focused on a Good Employment Charter for the city. There are also somewhat different developments in the devolved nations (as discussed in connection with Good Work), perhaps particularly Scotland, where issues of good work or fair work have tended to come more to the fore. However, all these activities remain somewhat experimental, and for the most part there is still a lack of clarity about how ALMP might be better integrated to a good jobs agenda.

Assessment and discussion

This chapter has examined the development of ALMP in the UK in the context of a growing interest in the idea of good work. Until relatively recently, the predominant focus of UK employment policy was bound up with a concern for employment quantity (with less consideration of the quality of work). ALMP has developed around a more active approach to out-of-work benefit claimants, increasing use of mandation and an over-arching work-first emphasis. This was aligned with the wider national focus on employment quantity; and the availability of jobseekers to meet entry-level needs was associated with little upwards pressure on job quality. Employer engagement with JCP has been typically characterized by employers seeking a large and steady supply of low-paid labour.

More recently there has been a noticeable shift in ALMP of relevance to job quality. This shift is towards an increasing emphasis on issues of employment sustainability and in-work progression. Successive ALMP approaches have moved towards this, with the UC having a specific progression aim for the first time (while at the same time opening up a new frontier in activation). This shift can also be seen in the launch of a new In-Work Progression Commission, which is beginning to consider approaches to wider barriers to progression. However, this new approach remains rooted in work-first and links to the demand side are at present under-developed. As such, although the delivery intention is that individuals are able to access in-work progression, the ALMP framework remains to a large extent disconnected from wider policy debates about good work.

While the question of how ALMP might support improved job quality largely has not featured in policy debates in the UK, there is growing scope to ask how elements of the current context might allow ALMP to capitalize on some upwards pressures on job quality. In particular, recent data demonstrate significant and growing labour and skills shortages in parts of the UK economy, which may encourage employers to improve aspects of terms and conditions in order to fill these. This is set alongside other shortages in some economic sectors induced by labour changes resulting from the Brexit referendum and the shock of the COVID-19 pandemic (Costa Dias et al, 2020). There are also a number of other regional and local factors, which are opening up new directions around job quality, including in entry-level roles. Some examples of these opportunities are now discussed.

A specific example of how the prevailing labour market situation opens up opportunities for policy is provided by the role of anchor institutions in the employment policy domain. The term 'anchor institution' describes an organization that has an important presence in a local area. This is usually through a combination of firstly (and of foremost importance here) scale – providing a range of job roles in an area – and secondly being a large-scale purchaser of goods and services. Importantly from a place-based perspective, anchor institutions tend to be spatially immobile. Examples of anchor institutions include local authorities, universities, hospitals, large local businesses and housing associations. All of these organizations have a stake in the local economy. Universities, for example, are placing greater emphasis on their civic role (UPP Foundation Civic University Commission, 2019), while hospitals are exploring how they can use their financial, employment and other assets to support local economies and tackle social determinants of health (Vize, 2019). From an employment and workforce development perspective, hospitals are increasingly active in a range of anchor institution workforce strategies. Reed et al (2019) note that such strategies typically fall into one of three categories: first, targeting positions for local people – including through creating pre-employment programmes, work placements and volunteering opportunities; second, building the future workforce, notably through apprenticeships; and third, Good Work initiatives, including fair pay and employment conditions and professional development and career progression. The content of these three categories chimes with the issues of employer engagement in ALMP, in-work progression and Good Work discussed in this chapter.

In practice, successful implementation of such workforce strategies requires good knowledge of the local area and the characteristics of the local labour force, together with strong local partnership working. An example of how these ingredients can combine in practice comes from the 'Hospitality to

Health' project run by Birmingham Anchor Network (composed of seven anchor institutions in Birmingham, UK). This pilot project brought two of these institutions together to combine their expertise and work on a specific action. In this case, the Pioneer Housing Group was concerned about residents in deprived neighbourhoods losing jobs in the hospitality sector during the COVID-19 pandemic. Although there was an awareness of job opportunities in the National Health Service (NHS), prior to working together on the project staff at Pioneer had been unfamiliar with the language, processes and pathways into the NHS. Likewise, before working with Pioneer on the project, the local NHS Trust had been unfamiliar with delivering recruitment initiatives targeted at particular neighbourhoods (Parke, 2021). As a result of this pilot project, the NHS Trust is reviewing its employment processes to make them more accessible to people outside the NHS, while the Pioneer Housing Group have started working with other major employers.

This project shows what can be done to open up employment opportunities in a large internal labour market with prospects for progression by organizations working in partnership. Although the public employment services (that is, JCP) were not an active partner in this particular project, some of the beneficiaries were benefit claimants. This shows that local stakeholders other than public employment services can take the initiative in developing new projects and programmes without direct PES involvement. However, it is important that JCP and other employment advisors have knowledge of such initiatives and, where applicable, offer support to similar ones. There is a window of opportunity to capitalize on the activities of anchor institutions and local recovery partnerships. Moreover, it is notable that in the light of the spotlight shone during the pandemic on many relatively low-paid but essential jobs, many recovery strategies include an imperative to create and/or promote quality jobs alongside tackling unemployment (Green et al, 2021b).

References

Andersen, K. (2020). 'Universal Credit, gender and unpaid childcare: Mothers' accounts of the new welfare conditionality regime', *Critical Social Policy* 40(3): 430–49.

Atkinson, J., Dewson, S., Fern, H., Page, R., Pillai, R. and Tackey, N.D. (2008). *Evaluation of the Fair Cities Pilots 2007*, Department for Work and Pensions Research Report 495. London: Department for Work and Pensions.

Bellis A., Sigala, M. and Dewson, S. (2011). *Employer engagement and Jobcentre Plus*, Department for Work and Pensions Research Report 742. London: Department for Work and Pensions.

Berry, C. (2014). 'Quantity over quality: A political economy of "active labour market policy" in the UK', *Policy Studies* 35(6): 592–610.

Costa Dias, M., Joyce, R., Postel-Vinay, F. and Xu, X. (2020). 'The challenges for labour market policy during the COVID-19 pandemic', Observation, Institute for Fiscal Studies: https://ifs.org.uk/publications/14767#

Costa Dias, M., Johnson-Watts, E., Joyce, R., Postel-Vinay, F., Spittal, P. and Xu, X. (2021). 'Job opportunities during the pandemic', IFS Briefing Note BN335, Institute for Fiscal Studies.

D'Arcy, C. and Hurrell, A. (2014). *Escape plan: Understanding who progresses from low pay and who gets stuck*, London: Resolution Foundation.

Department for Work and Pensions (2016). *Sector-based work academies: A quantitative impact assessment*, Department for Work and Pensions Research Report No 918: https://assets.publishing.service.gov.uk/government/uploads/system/uploads/attachment_data/file/508175/rr918-sector-based-work-academies.pdf

Department for Work and Pensions (2018). *Universal Credit: In-work progression randomized controlled trial: Impact assessment*, London: Department for Work and Pensions.

Devins, D., Bickerstaffe, T., Mitchell, B. and Halliday, S. (2014). *Improving progression in low-paid, low-skilled retail, catering and care jobs*, York: Joseph Rowntree Foundation.

Dwyer, P. and Wright, S. (2014). 'Universal Credit, ubiquitous conditionality and its implications for social citizenship', *Journal of Poverty and Social Justice* 22(1): 27–35.

Fernandez-Macias, E., Hurley, J. and Storrie, D. (2012). *Transformation of the Employment Structure in the EU and USA, 1995–2007*, Basingstoke: Palgrave Macmillan.

Finn, D., 2003. 'The "employment-first" welfare state: Lessons from the New Deal for young people', *Social Policy & Administration* 37(7): 709–24.

Fletcher, D. (2001). *Evaluation of the New Deal Innovation Fund – Rounds One and Two*, Employment Service Research Report ESR86. London: Employment Service.

Fletcher, D. (2004). 'Demand-led programmes: Challenging labour-market inequalities or reinforcing them?' *Environment and Planning C: Government and Policy* 22(1): 115–28.

Fuertes, V., McQuaid, R. and Robertson, P.J. (2021). 'Career-first: An approach to sustainable labour market integration', *International Journal of Education & Vocational Guidance* 21: 429–46.

Goos, M. and Manning, A. (2007). 'Lousy and lovely jobs: The rising polarization of work in Britain', *Review of Economics & Statistics* 89(1): 118–33.

Green, A. (2016). *Low skill traps in sectors and geographies: underlying factors and means of escape*, London: Government Office for Science.

Green, A., Stanfield, C. and Bramley, G. (2019). *Evaluation of co-designed programmes for boosting productivity: a follow-up of selected UK Futures Programme projects*, Productivity Insights Network.

Green, A., Sissons, P., Broughton, K. and Qamar, A. (2021a). 'Public policy for addressing the low-skills low-wage trap: Insights from business case studies in Birmingham city-region, UK', *Regional Studies* 55(2): 333–44.

Green, A., Rossiter, W., Taylor, A., Hoole, C., Riley, R., Karagounis, K. and Pugh, A. (2021b). *Mapping the architecture of economic development policy and strategy across the Midlands Engine pan-region*, Midlands Engine.

Green, A., Hughes, C., Sissons, P. and Taylor, A. (2022). 'Localising employment policy: Opportunities and challenges', in A. Jolly, R. Cefalo and M. Pomati (eds) *Social policy review 34: Analysis and debate in social policy, 2022*, Bristol: Bristol University Press, pp 24–47.

Hasluck, C (2000). 'Early lessons from the evaluation of New Deal programmes', Paper prepared for the Employment Service: https://warwick.ac.uk/fac/soc/ier/publications/2000/hasluck_2000_esr49rep.pdf

HM Government (2018). *Good work plan*.

In-Work Progression Commission (2021). *Supporting progression out of low pay: A call to action*, London: In-Work Progression Commission.

Ingold, J. (2018). 'Employer engagement in active labour market programmes: The role of boundary spanners', *Public Administration* 96: 707–20.

Ingold, J. and Stuart, M. (2015). 'The demand-side of active labour market policies: A regional study of employer engagement in the Work Programme', *Journal of Social Policy* 44(3): 443–62. doi: 10.1017/S0047279414000890.

Innes, D. (2020). *What has driven the rise of in-work poverty?* York: Joseph Rowntree Foundation.

Irvine, G., White, D. and Diffley, M. (2018). *Measuring good work: The final report of the Job Quality Working Group*, Carnegie UK Trust and Royal Society of Arts.

Johns, M., Raikes, L. and Hunter, J. (2019). *Decent work: Harnessing the power of local government*, Institute for Public Policy Research North.

Johnson, M., Martinez Lucio, M., Grimshaw, D. and Watt, L. (2021). 'Swimming against the tide? Street-level bureaucrats and the limits to inclusive active labour market programmes in the UK', *Human Relations*: 1–26.

Jung, C. and Collings, F. (2021). *Full employment and good jobs for all: Why the UK is seeing a lopsided jobs recovery and what to do about it*, Institute for Public Policy Research.

Kumar, A., Rotik, M. and Ussher, K. (2014). *Pay progression: Understanding the barriers for the lowest paid – CIPD policy report*, London: John Lewis Partnership and CIPD.

Lauder, H. (1999). 'Competitiveness and the problem of the Low Skill Equilibria: A comparative analysis', *Journal of Education and Work* 12(3): 281–94.

Lee, N., Green, A. and Sissons, P. (2018). 'Low-pay sectors, earnings mobility and economic policy in the UK', *Politics & Policy* 46(3): 347–69.

Lindsay, C., Canduela, J. and Raeside, R. (2012). 'Polarization in access to work-related training in Great Britain', *Economic and Industrial Democracy* 34(2): 205–25.

Martin, C. and Swank, D. (2004). 'Does the organization of capital matter? Employers and active labor market policy at the national and firm levels', *American Political Science Review* 98(4): 593–611.

McCann, P. (2018). *Productivity perspectives synthesis*, Productivity Insights Network.

McGurk, P. (2014). *Employer engagement: A human resource management perspective*, University of Greenwich Business School Working Paper No. 17. London: Greenwich University.

McIntosh, S. (2013). 'Hollowing out and the future of the labour market', BIS Research Paper 134.

Millar, J. and Bennett, F. (2017). 'Universal Credit: Assumptions, contradictions and virtual reality', *Social Policy and Society* 16(2): 169–82.

Novak, T. (1997). 'Hounding delinquents: The introduction of the Jobseeker's Allowance', *Critical Social Policy* 17(50): 99–109.

O'Regan, F. (2015). *Sector workforce intermediaries: Next generation employer–engagement strategies*, Washington, DC: The Aspen Institute.

Oliveira-Cunha, J., Kozler, J., Shah, P., Thwaites, G. and Valero, A. (2021). *Business time: How ready are UK firms for the decisive decade?* London: Resolution Foundation.

Parke, C. (2021). 'Anchor networks in practice: "Why?" to "how?"', City-REDI blog, University of Birmingham.

Peck, J. and Theodore, N. (2001). 'Exporting workfare/importing welfare-to-work: Exploring the politics of Third Way policy transfer', *Political Geography* 20: 427–60.

Powell, A. and Francis-Devine, B. (2021). 'Coronavirus: Impact on the labour market', House of Commons Library CBP8898.

Ray, K., Sissons, P., Jones, K. and Vegeris, S. (2014). *Employment, pay and poverty. Evidence and policy review*, York: Joseph Rowntree Foundation.

Reed, S., Gopfert, A., Wood, S., Allwood, D. and Warburton, W. (2019). *Building healthier communities: The role of the NHS as an anchor institution*, London: Health Foundation.

Rees, J., Whitworth, A. and Carter, E. (2014). 'Support for all in the UK Work Programme? Differential payments, same old problem', *Social Policy & Administration* 48: 221–39.

Reeves, A. and Loopstra, R. (2017). '"Set up to fail"? How welfare conditionality undermines citizenship for vulnerable groups', *Social Policy and Society* 16(2): 327–38.

Salvatori, A. (2018). 'The anatomy of job polarisation in the UK', *Journal for Labour Market Research* 52(8).

Sissons, P. (2020). *Making progress? The challenges and opportunities for increasing wage and career progression*, Work Foundation.

Sissons, P. and Green, A. (2017). 'More than a match? Assessing the HRM challenge of engaging employers to support retention and progression', *Human Resource Management Journal* 27(4): 565–80.

Sissons, P., Green, A. and Lee, N. (2018). 'Linking the sectoral employment structure and household poverty in the United Kingdom', *Work, Employment and Society* 32(6): 1078–98.

Sunley, P., Martin, R. and Nativel, C. (2006). *Putting workfare in place*, Oxford: Blackwell.

Taylor, M., Marsh, G., Nicol, D. and Broadbent, P. (2017). *Good work: The Taylor review of modern working practices*, London: The Stationery Office.

Thom, G., Agur, M., Mackay, S., Chipato, F., MacLeod, K., Hope, H. and Stanfield, C. (2016). *Evaluation of the UK Futures Programme: Conclusions and guidance*, UK Commission for Employment and Skills.

UPP Foundation Civic University Commission (2019). *Truly civic: Strengthening the connection between universities and their places*, UPP Foundation.

Vize, R. (2019). 'Hospitals as anchor institutions: How the NHS can act beyond healthcare to support communities', *British Medical Journal* 361(k2101): 1–2.

Wickham, Sophie, Bentley, Lee, Rose, Tanith, Whitehead, Margaret, Taylor-Robinson, David and Barr, Ben (2020). 'Effects on mental health of a UK welfare reform, Universal Credit: A longitudinal controlled study', *Lancet Public Health* 5(3): E157–E164.

Wilson, R. and Hogarth, T. (2003). *Tackling the low skills equilibrium: A review of issues and some new evidence*, London: DTI.

Wilson, R., Barnes, S-A., May-Gillings, M., Patel, S. and Bui, H. (2020). *Working Futures 2017–2027: Long-run labour market and skills projections for the UK: Main report*, Department for Education.

Wright, S. and Dwyer, P. (2020). 'In-work Universal Credit: Claimant experiences of conditionality mismatches and counterproductive benefit sanctions', *Journal of Social Policy*, 51(1): 1–19.

7

Opening the Black Box: Promoting Employer Engagement at the Street Level of Employment Services

Tanja Dall, Flemming Larsen and Mikkel Bo Madsen

Introduction

In recent years, employer engagement in employment and social services has received increasing attention from both researchers and policymakers, especially regarding how this can provide disadvantaged groups of unemployed individuals with relevant training and subsequent employment. The discussion focuses largely on either conceptualizing and mapping employers' willingness to engage in employment services for disadvantaged groups (Idowu et al, 2015; Bredgaard, 2018) or examining how employers can be made more socially responsible for broader social or environmental issues (for an overview, see Aguinis and Glavas, 2012; Barnett et al, 2020; see also the literature on corporate social responsibility (CSR)). However, as pointed out in some of recent studies on CSR, less attention has been paid to the micro-processes of how to make employers socially responsible (Barnett et al, 2020), which also seems to be the case in the literature on employer engagement in employment and social services.

In this chapter, we intend to open up this black box of employer engagement by examining the day-to-day work of the staff in public employment services (PES) working in the area of employer engagement. The point of departure for this analysis is Danish employment policies and their implementation in municipal jobcentres. We examine how employer engagement is created, developed and maintained at the street level of local employment services. We set out with an understanding of employer engagement as 'the active involvement of employers in addressing the societal challenge of promoting the labour-market participation of vulnerable groups' (van Berkel et al,

2017, p 505). Employer engagement not only entails employers being socially responsible on paper; it involves the employing organizations as a whole: managers on all levels, supervisors, HR staff, union representatives, employees and others.

In particular, we analyse how the public authorities involve employers in the work of helping those unemployed individuals who have social, mental and physical challenges interact with employers and their organizations. In doing so, we elaborate on existing conceptualizations of employer engagement and link employer engagement to the aims of strengthening the ability of the disadvantaged unemployed to work. Empirically, our analysis is based on a diverse, qualitative dataset consisting of interviews with job consultants, ethnographic observations of municipal employer engagement staff, interviews with unemployed individuals and, to a lesser extent, observations at actual workplaces in real companies.

The rest of the chapter is structured as follows. The second section introduces employer engagement and workplace training in the context of Danish active labour market programmes (ALMP). The third section presents and discusses a conceptual framework for analysing processes and results from employer-based workplace training. The fourth section analyses our research question, grounded in targeted empirical analyses. The fifth section discusses the conceptual implications of our analytical findings before offering our conclusion.

Employer engagement and workplace training in Danish ALMPs

Our study examines Danish employment services, where policymakers in recent decades have tried to promote employer engagement as a preferred course of action for bringing more people into employment. Denmark constitutes a typical case, following the path of many other countries in the Western world. The increasing focus on employer-based activities has been prioritized politically, with reference to Danish and international evidence documenting how employer-based policies raise employment probabilities more than other active labour market policy measures (Card et al, 2018; STAR, 2018). Increasingly, also, this strategy has been expanded to include still more disadvantaged groups of unemployed individuals, following a trend of replacing 'train then place' approaches with 'place then train' approaches, which move the training and personal development of unemployed individuals who have social, mental and physical challenges from public training grounds into local workplaces. Several studies have shown such approaches to be especially effective for disadvantaged groups, as documented in individual placement and support and supported employment (SE) (for an overview, see Bond and Drake, 2014). One result of these concurrent trends is that the annual number of work placements in Danish ALMPs has increased from 54,000 in 2007 to 197,000 in 2019 (before COVID-19). As in many other Western welfare states, these developments have been followed by increased levels of conditionality, still more active measures aimed at bringing the unemployed into employment and more restricted access to benefits and the permanent disability pension.

The Nordic welfare state model (Esping-Andersen, 1990) adopted by Denmark also differs from other cases in several ways. Denmark is one of the highest-spending countries in the world in terms of both active and passive labour market measures (Lauringson and Lüske, 2021). The Danish PES make a huge (and costly) effort to integrate unemployed people into the labour market. However, Denmark differs from the typical Nordic welfare state by having very low regulation of job security and employer obligations in the labour market. The combination of this flexible and unregulated labour market (or, rather, self-regulated by market participants) and the generous and active welfare state is often referred to as the Danish flexicurity model. Flexicurity combines flexibility for labour market actors to hire and fire workers with security for citizens who are in between jobs (Bredgaard et al, 2006, 2008). As such, there are no labour market laws stipulating an obligation for employers to participate in ALMPs, and municipal efforts to engage employers, therefore, have to be based on their voluntary participation.

The Danish case thus offers an example of how employer engagement and participation in integrating unemployed individuals with social, mental and physical challenges into the labour market can take place when it is politically prioritized yet voluntary for employers. Following Vedung's (1997) typology, Danish PES make use of 'sermons' to encourage employers to share responsibility for developing the workforce and, to some extent, 'carrots' by offering to cover the costs to employers of providing unemployed individuals with training placements. In other words, persuasion and negotiation become the main instruments the PES use to engage employers and make them participate in integrating the disadvantaged unemployed into the labour market.

Since 2009, Danish municipalities have been responsible for employment services, including the engagement of employers around ALMPs. The shift in political focus to employer engagement and workplace training as the main active labour market measure has resulted in a strong prioritization of employer-oriented work in the municipalities (Andersen and Larsen, 2018). New units have been created with new types of professionals, and the more traditional social work units in the employment services have been asked to develop a more employer-oriented approach. This intensification of employer-oriented work for unemployed individuals who have social, mental and physical challenges puts pressure on making this group able to do some kind of 'real work' in unpaid work placements, while at the same time making employers engage in both training activities and recruitment for subsequently ordinary or subsidized work. As argued throughout this chapter, the match between the unemployed individual and the workplace in question becomes crucial. However, the Danish case, with its new focus on 'place then train' approaches, illustrates an obvious challenge: namely, not only to create openings for work-training placement but also to transition individuals from these placements into real jobs. Working with employers does not end with establishing a single placement; it also involves issues of how and when unemployed individuals transition into paid employment.

In general, the Danish case illustrates how employer engagement can be achieved through political, economic and organizational prioritization, with very low regulation of, and obligations for, the employers. This case allows us to study the processes of preparing and processing unemployed people before, during and after placements, particularly how employers engage and participate in these processes. The Danish case exemplifies the extent to which persuasion and negotiation can promote employer engagement when it comes to disadvantaged groups of unemployed individuals.

Data

Our analysis builds on a unique type of dataset. Through two projects based on a partnership between Aalborg University and five municipalities between 2016 and 2020 (LISES, funded by Innovation Fund Denmark), and four municipalities from 2020 to 2024 (CUBB, funded by the Maersk Foundation and the participating municipalities), we have had full and open access to all types of activity involved in employer engagement. Both projects are mutual innovation projects between researchers and practitioners, with the overall purpose of finding ways to co-create further and identify barriers for this development. Engaging the practice field as co-producers of knowledge in this way creates a less hierarchical relationship between science and practice. The level of trust in this interaction has helped researchers access all parts of the municipal employment services – from jobcentre manager to the individual jobseeker – thereby making it possible to shed light on processes and connections that researchers would otherwise seldom see. This privileged access to the inner workings of jobcentres has made it possible to study the dilemmas and trade-offs in the work done to promote employer engagement and participation in the services for the disadvantaged unemployed. We are thus dealing with an atypical research project that nevertheless involves traditional data collection, and this chapter builds on comprehensive data. In addition to ethnographic observations in these organizations – gained by shadowing, interviews and informal talks with managers and staff – the data consist of recorded and transcribed observations and interviews with job consultants who have a role in employer engagement and interviews with unemployed individuals with experience from work placements.

Employers' role in active labour market programmes

Research on ALMPs often distinguishes between supply-side policies and demand-side policies (Ingold and Stuart, 2014; Bredgaard and Halkjær, 2016). Supply-side policies are oriented towards the individual jobseeker, aiming to encourage individuals to take a job they would not have taken or obtained by themselves. Demand-side policies are oriented towards employers, seeking to stimulate them into hiring people they would not have hired or found by themselves if the hiring process were purely market-led.

Since the 1990s, active labour market policies in most Western welfare states have mainly focused on supply-side measures (Peck and Theodore, 2000), although countries vary widely in the general scale and scope of ALMPs and in the use of measures based on enabling and disciplinary logics (Bonoli, 2013; Immervoll and Scarpetta, 2012; van Berkel et al, 2017). Similarly, studies have focused on supply-side measures, with extensive research examining which interventions produce the best employment results for different groups of unemployed people (Card et al, 2010, 2018; Kluve, 2010; OECD, 2020). Related studies analyse, compare and classify different approaches and measures in ALMPs (Bonoli, 2010, 2013; Brodkin and Marston, 2013; Lødemel and Moreira, 2014; Filges and Hansen, 2015; Lødemel and Trickey, 2000; van Berkel et al, 2017).

There are still relatively few studies on demand-side policies and programmes, though research on the importance of employer engagement for the character and outcomes of ALMPs is gradually growing (van Berkel and van der Aa, 2012; Halkjær, 2014; van der Aa and van Berkel, 2014; Ingold, 2015, 2018, 2020; Ingold and Stuart, 2014; McGurk, 2014; Bredgaard and Halkjær, 2016; Ingold and Valizade, 2017; Bredgaard, 2018). Within management research, the focus is on employers' practices and attitudes towards CSR (Moura-Leite and Padgett, 2011; Idowu et al, 2013; Idowu et al, 2015).

While this research has produced important insights into the overall uses, approaches and effects of supply-side ALMP interventions, as well as into general employer attitudes and perspectives on the demand side, they tend to have two different but interrelated shortcomings. First, they tend to overlook or downplay how labour market activities typically take place in dynamic interactions between the supply and demand sides (Frøyland et al, 2019). Second, they tend to represent and analyse dynamic and contextual processes as relations between static variables, either for methodological or conceptual reasons. These issues are interrelated, and we will try to address them accordingly.

Integrated approaches in ALMP research

There are examples of acknowledging combined or integrated approaches in research on ALMP. For instance, Ingold and Valizade (2017) adopted a combined demand-side and supply-side orientation in their analysis of how ALMP agencies act as labour market intermediaries affecting employers' recruitment of people from disadvantaged groups. In our study, we discuss how ALMP agencies can act as 'information providers' or 'matchmakers' (Bonet et al, 2013) in the process of furthering employment for people with social, mental and physical challenges. The concept of labour market intermediaries and their acting as information providers or matchmakers makes visible how ALMP agencies do engage in processes of engagement between employers and unemployed individuals. In the same vein, Bredgaard (2018) outlines a 'match approach' as a supplement to supply-side and demand-side policy approaches (pp 366–7). The match approach targets both jobseekers and employers by addressing information asymmetries and insufficiencies; Bredgaard thus treats information providers and matchmakers as two sides of the same coin. The information asymmetries between jobseekers and employers are well known from classic sociological studies of labour market functioning (Akerlof, 1970; Granovetter, 1973, 1995; Larsen and Vesan, 2012), and the matching approach may make a match possible that probably would not occur in an unassisted market process. Ingold (2018) expanded on the role of ALMP agencies to demonstrate how 'employer engagement staff' in street-level organizations in the UK Work Programme act as 'boundary spanners', traversing the boundaries between employers and those organizations in the attempt to connect employers and jobseekers. As boundary spanners, employer engagement staff take on roles and functions well known from private sector recruitment agencies (Ingold, 2018, p 708).

These studies support the need to approach employer engagement from an integrated approach, examining the interrelations between employment agencies, unemployed individuals and employers. However, as evidenced in the research on SE presented, employment engagement work is more complex than simply providing information.

Supported employment approaches

A separate field of research examines disability policy and vocational or occupational rehabilitation. In this context, extensive integrated approaches to bring persons with disabilities into the competitive labour market have been developed and tested. These approaches are often given the overall label 'supported employment' (Bond et al, 2001; EUSE, 2010; Spjelkavik, 2012; Wehman, 2012; Gustafsson et al, 2018).

In general, SE approaches are characterized by using workplaces as arenas of inclusion; they recommend addressing workplaces early in the process to utilize their capacities for practice learning, resource building and recovery in a 'place then train' approach (Wehman, 2012). SE approaches generally compare favourably with other ALMPs when tested for employment impact on different disadvantaged groups (the literature is vast, but see especially Heffernan and Pilkington, 2011; Kinoshita et al, 2010; Modini et al, 2016).

Support in SE approaches can take different forms, but they generally focus on pragmatic collaboration and negotiations with employers and jobseekers about finding the right ways to make a sustainable employment relation possible (Frøyland, 2019; Frøyland et al, 2019). In this way, support interventions in SE are more similar to co-creation processes than simple service provision (see the distinction in van der Aa and van Berkel, 2014). Support interventions in SE can include (often task-specific) training for the jobseeker and training in inclusive capacities for employers and co-workers. The combined supply-side and demand-side approach is visible in that supportive activities can address challenges for both the jobseeker and the employer. These efforts are sometimes presented as 'carving out' or 'creating' a suitable job in a specific workplace for a specific disadvantaged jobseeker (Griffin et al, 2008; Riesen et al, 2015; Scoppetta et al, 2019). Whereas supply-side ALMP approaches try to make an individual person fit into or accept an existing vacancy, the 'fitting' in SE approaches is directed at both employee and employer – the supply side and the demand side.

In general, SE approaches originate from disability policies and diverge from typical ALMPs in being based on values, insisting on building in individual choice (Drake et al, 2012) and a right-to-work perspective (Peck, 2001; Wehman et al, 2018). However, in our research on Danish employer engagement efforts, we recognize many of the insights from the SE literature in an ALMP context characterized by conditionality and an obligation to work if at all possible (Patrick, 2017; Ingold, 2020; Larsen and Caswell, 2020). We present our findings in the next section.

Developing employer engagement at the street level

Our analysis focuses on how employer engagement is developed at the street level of Danish public employment services. In Denmark, the jobcentres in the 98 municipalities are responsible for delivering ALMPs, although the state still maintains some control through detailed national regulation. Every unemployed person is assigned a *personal caseworker* who is responsible for the overall case process and carries legal authority. In many municipalities, the personal caseworkers are not directly involved in collaboration with employers. Most often, *job consultants* take care of the ongoing, day-to-day processes of establishing and maintaining internships and wage subsidies for

Figure 7.1: Simplified model of activities and purposes in the employer engagement process

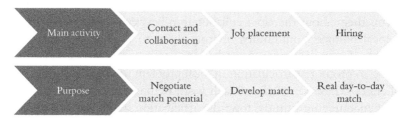

individuals in specific workplaces. Municipalities can choose to outsource this function to private contractors, and many municipalities do so in combination with an in-house division that takes care of some subset of the unemployed population. The municipalities in our study have all prioritized their in-house delivery of ALMPs set in the labour market, and all of our data concern these efforts. In many municipalities, there is a further specialization in *business consultants* working to build and service a network of employers to collaborate with and assist companies with recruitment. Business consultants typically do not have a caseload of unemployed people to manage.

Within this basic structure, employer engagement is produced in the day-to-day work of job and business consultants. By examining how employer engagement staff collaborate with employers and unemployed individuals who have social, mental and physical challenges, this section aims to clarify how employer engagement is produced and interwoven with processes of developing the capacities of both employers and unemployed individuals.

The section is structured around the general process of first identifying and motivating local employers to engage with ALMPs and then developing jobseekers' work ability alongside capacities for inclusion in local workplaces (Figure 7.1).

Establishing contact with employers

The very first step and a basic precondition for founding and maintaining employer-based ALMPs is establishing contact with employers who could be interested in taking on unemployed individuals in work placements, subsidized employment or paid employment.

In the municipalities, special groups of business consultants contact local employers to promote and register motivation for participation in ALMPs. These consultants inform employers about the main categories of ALMPs and the supportive measures offered by the centre. For instance, employers engaged with ALMPs in one of the municipalities get special access to a hotline via which they can ask about any dealing with the municipality (for example, building permits, rules for serving food outdoors, and so on) and have their application or question fast-tracked. Newly established companies in the municipality are welcomed with a mayoral letter that informs them about the close collaboration between the municipality and the local business community, inviting them to engage. Furthermore, a selection of new companies is marked for a visit from a business consultant seeking to promote participation in local problem solving, including social challenges. These kinds of outreach work by business consultants are one way of encouraging attitudes towards participation, and business consultants primarily engage with employers as clients (van der Aa and van Berkel, 2014), trying to provide employers with attractive recruitment services while also registering their motivation to take on more involvement.

Job consultants who work directly with the unemployed are asked to use these registrations and 'open doors'. The work of the job consultants, however, shows that employers' engagement or motivation to participate is neither static nor a binary variable, with employers being interested or not. Rather, employers' engagement is produced, formed and articulated in collaboration with employment specialists; in the job consultants' reports, employers are engaged as co-producers of ALMPs (van der Aa and van Berkel, 2014).

Creating engagement and motivation to participate

Job consultants have a caseload of unemployed individuals whom they seek to introduce to local workplaces in order to promote employment. Most often, the caseload of job consultants is divided according to whether their clients are 'ready for work' – that is, aiming for ordinary employment – or have 'challenges beside unemployment' that qualify them for more intensive programmes. Our data focus on the groups of unemployed people who have social, mental and physical challenges and who often require extra effort by employers to engage in ALMPs. This often means that business consultants' first registration of employers' attitude becomes questionable in the eyes of the job consultants. One job consultant described how he prioritizes 'canvassing' local companies himself, even though his business consultant colleagues contact companies and register their engagement and vacancies.

'To me, it is also important to get out there [visiting employers], because often I have to be at the company and tour it, in order to find these small jobs; because I do not have any clients that can go out for 37 hours a week, not even 30 hours, you know. We are talking 10 hours a week for most of them. Therefore, I have to go out there and find these jobs, which are not apparent to the employers themselves, and talk [them] into whether this could maybe be a thing. "Don't you need someone to fix the mess in the corner over there?" – Whatever it may be.' (Job consultant 1, municipality B)

This job consultant will show up at an employer without calling in advance to set up a future meeting. Cold-calling on employers in this way, whether in person or by phone, is a way to build a personal network of local employers, creating a need and motivation to include the unemployed in less than full positions, as well as a way to source openings for unemployed individuals with specific needs of their own. The job consultants in our study typically have between 25 and 50 unemployed clients each, which allows them to know and remember all of their clients fairly well.

Contacting employers without previous agreement reflects an understanding among job consultants that employers' engagement with ALMPs is not a static phenomenon that can be taken for granted based on an initial mapping. Rather, employers' motivation is treated as something that is dynamic and capable of being created in specific interactions with job consultants and unemployed individuals. For instance, one job consultant stated that they do not pay much attention to the database of motivated local employers because an employer may have rejected collaboration over one jobseeker but might engage in collaboration over another. In this way, they indicate that the employer's engagement is created in the shared process of collaborating around a specific unemployed person.

The mutual relational engagement between consultants and employers becomes even clearer when job consultants start challenging employers on their engagement with ALMPs, based on their shared history of collaboration:

'In the beginning, when you are establishing a new relation within a company, then you are very focused on securing a good match [between unemployed individuals and employers], and it just has to be a success story. Because if I am going to get a collaboration up and running, then I have to prove my worth, as someone from the jobcentre, and prove this candidate's worth. You are very focused on making sure it is a success. And then when you've had that [success] a couple of times, you can take the liberty of calling the company and say "you know what, I have given you some really good candidates, a lot of times, and I actually found you a good employee, that you hired" and stuff like that. After some time, I can say "you know what, now you have to help me out. I have someone who needs immediate activation, and all I can tell you is, I do not know what I am bringing you. But can't you help me out here?" And often you do help each other out in these situations. It is about having these good relations and collaborations. They can solve some of our challenges sometimes.' (Job consultant 2, municipality B)

This quote illustrates how job consultants actively try to move 'instrumentally engaged employers', focused on one-off activities centred around their own recruitment, towards a more relationally engaged position, where engagement is deeper, repeated and more sustained (Ingold and Valizade, 2015). The history and quality of the collaboration and the personal relations between consultants and employers leverage engagement as co-production around unemployed people with more challenges who are furthest from the labour market. Ingold (2018, p 718) illustrates how staff in a UK context prioritize 'the best' unemployed individuals to send to employers in order to secure ongoing engagement. Notably, the staff in our study also seem to use good experiences with more promising individuals to leverage engagement with the more disadvantaged individuals whose short-term contribution may be more uncertain.

Establishing a match

The respondents in our data widely agree that, in order for a work placement or trial to be successful, the 'match' between employers and unemployed people is crucial. The match is made over practical issues, such as how far unemployed individuals' physical or mental disabilities can accommodate the requirements of a given function, but it is also a matter of the personality and social abilities of both the unemployed and the employers. One job consultant says:

> 'For instance, I may know that this employer is very calm and quiet and then I have this young guy with ADHD who wants to be a carpenter, and he should definitely go out to this [other] employer who can keep him on a tight leash, activate him but also give him boundaries ...
>
> You learn along the way what the different employers are good at, what type of unemployed they are good at. And that is not something that is written down anywhere, that is just something we know.' (Job consultant 3, municipality C)

The very first meeting between employers and unemployed individuals is, to some extent, a test of the personal match between them, that is, a test of the potential for starting a work placement. Many job consultants talk about 'personal chemistry' and 'connection' between the unemployed and employers, and how to know whether the basic match is right as a matter of 'gut feeling'/'fingerspitzengefühl'. However, while a lack of chemistry may be mentioned as a reason for cancelling a potential placement after the initial meeting, the presence of chemistry is not necessarily a guarantee that the placement will develop successfully.

At the most practical level, for the most challenged unemployed, a work placement with an employer can be a training ground to develop specific skills and the capacity for working more hours. However, a recurrent theme in interviews with job consultants and the unemployed themselves is the personal development of confidence and social skills. Another frequently recurrent theme in our interviews with both job consultants and the unemployed is that a good relationship between employer and potential employee, as well as time to develop this relationship, can provide the foundation for the substantial development of the unemployed individual's work abilities. The relational character of developing the ability to work has also been examined and documented in other studies (for example, Baum and Christiansen, 2005; Frøyland et al, 2019).

When work abilities develop and become valuable – even profitable – for the employer, the engagement in the process becomes increasingly meaningful and potentially sustainable even from a business perspective. The match develops from potentiality to day-to-day reality and provides a basis for considering transition to paid work. As such, the development of the capacity for inclusion in the workplace often entwines closely with the development of work abilities in the employee-to-be.

Developing the capacity for inclusion

Working with employers over an extended period not only potentially allows job consultants to move employers from an instrumental engagement towards a more co-creating engagement, as illustrated in the previous subsection, but it also lays the foundation for developing an increased capacity for inclusion, understood as the collective resources and competencies of a workplace for supporting the development of the ability to work and employability of the disadvantaged unemployed. The aim is the development of productive labour specifically adapted to the needs of the workplace, which entails mutual adjustments by both the potential employee and the workplace. However, this result sometimes requires a lengthy process of development. One job consultant offered the following interpretation of why a recent engagement around a young woman with severe social anxiety ended up with her being a valued and independent employee at a veterinary clinic:

'I think it was their shared interest; they just had a shared interest for [the work at the wildlife station]. And I think being met in your illness matters a great deal, that [the employer] had thoroughly acquainted himself [with the unemployed person's situation]. I think his interest came from participating in our mentorship course, where someone did a talk about some diagnosis, and I think he just found that so interesting that he spent a lot of his spare time reading about this.

Then when he meets Sara for the first time and learns what diagnoses she has, he acquaints himself 100 per cent with why she reacts the ways she does, and what can I do to help her, and I must say, that is not something we expect of our mentors or employers at all.' (Job consultant 3, municipality C)

While the employer in this example is highlighted as going above and beyond what is usually expected from employers, it is a recurrent theme in our data that employers and/or co-workers show personal interest in, and motivation to understand, the situations and difficulties of the unemployed person, and adjust their behaviour to accommodate that person. Sometimes, this can be rooted in an interest in certain diagnoses, personal experience from family members with similar challenges or simply a wish 'to make a difference' for a person in need. Frøyland and Kvåle (2014) introduced the notion of 'natural support' in the workplace, which refers to the capacities for inclusion that exist in workplaces among co-workers and employers without any specific support intervention or knowledge about certain diagnoses or experiences when dealing with unemployed individuals who have social, mental and physical challenges. In our study examining employment services, we also see municipalities involved in supporting the development of capacities for inclusion in workplaces.

In our study, knowledge seems to play a central role in these efforts. In municipality C, the employment services support the development of a capacity for inclusion by offering mentorship courses for employers alongside sustained collaboration with the jobcentre. Topics at these courses may cover intercultural communication, conflict management and basic knowledge of 'common' psychiatric diagnoses. At a two-hour session, one of the authors observed how eight local employers were introduced to the general features of borderline personality disorder and discussed how to talk with unemployed individuals or employees about poor personal hygiene and suspected intoxication. In our interviews, job consultants in all municipalities talked of offering employers feedback on how to manage particular challenges of the unemployed individuals in their day-to-day work. This does not necessarily involve detailed knowledge on a given diagnosis but may be simpler strategies such as making agreements between colleagues not to talk to the trainee when they put on their headphones. Such strategies suggest that the capacity for inclusion is collective, which means that both employers and the 'colleagues' of a person in a placement are motivated to include people with social, mental and physical challenges and capable of doing so. Inclusion capacity is further developed over the course of a given placement, and while the development of the unemployed individual's ability at work will necessitate a capacity to keep an atypical employee for some period of time, job consultants are very aware that the aim of developing sustainable employment must be present at all times. That is, employers do not engage in developing work ability for CSR reasons alone. Rather, there must be a possibility that the individual will develop into a productive worker over time – even if it will not be possible to offer them paid employment at this specific workplace.

Transitions into employment

Transitions into employment present an ongoing challenge for municipal efforts to engage employers. Work placements essentially constitute free labour for employers, and not all employers are interested in engaging in sustained collaboration towards developing individuals' work ability and the inclusive capacity of the workplace. Municipalities are not allowed to formally deny or blacklist employers. However, job consultants in all municipalities that took part in these studies talk of having informal (and unwritten) lists of local workplaces that have a history of taking on unemployed individuals in unpaid work placements without engaging in the sustained development of their work ability and/or without ever turning placements into paid employment. Job consultants will avoid establishing placements at these workplaces, and they continually discuss how they can identify employers looking to 'exploit' the system. It goes beyond the scope of this chapter to further explore the challenge of transitioning employer engagement in unpaid or subsidized work placements into paid employment, but the existence of the challenge itself nuances the otherwise 'ideal' process we have outlined so far. Our focus has mostly been on the processes that take place when sustained employer engagement *does* take place. Hence, our analysis contributes detailed insights into how employer engagement develops at the street level – municipal employment services – as well as a more nuanced understanding of the concept of employer engagement. We discuss these contributions in the concluding section.

Conclusion

We set out to explore how employer engagement is created, developed and maintained at the street level – municipal employment services. We did so by examining the day-to-day efforts of employer engagement staff in a Danish setting, characterized by a) high expenditures on public ALMP efforts and a policy and organizational prioritization of ALMPs set in local workplaces, and b) a system based on voluntary arrangements between employers and municipalities.

By examining the processes of how employer engagement is developed, our analysis demonstrates how employer engagement as 'the active involvement of employers in addressing the societal challenge of promoting the labour market participation of vulnerable groups' (van Berkel et al, 2017, p 505) is an ongoing process. Hence, establishing contact with 'motivated' employers is only a first step in the processual work of developing collaborative relations that engage employers in the development of both the ability of the unemployed to work and the inclusive capacity of workplaces.

As such, employer engagement is a dynamic phenomenon that takes place at the intersection between supply-side and demand-side policies. Existing studies have cast this intersection as a matter of providing information and/ or matchmaking (for example, Ingold and Valizade, 2017; Bredgaard, 2018). Our analysis nuances these understandings further by demonstrating how employer engagement is developed relationally over time in negotiated collaborations between employer engagement staff, employers and unemployed individuals, and contextually in the specific circumstances of the unemployed, the workplace and the active labour market policies.

This also implies that establishing work placements and/or temporary subsidized employment for specific individuals cannot be an end goal of employer engagement if the aim is to promote the labour market participation of unemployed individuals who have social, mental and physical challenges. Our analysis, supported by research on supported employment, suggests that such employer engagement extends beyond 'opening the door' for less 'attractive' jobseekers. Rather, employer engagement aimed at promoting labour market participation for disadvantaged groups includes sustained involvement in the development of individuals' ability and the capacity of the workplace to be inclusive, or, in other words, developing the potential for a match into an actual day-to-day match in a specific workplace setting. In this sense, employer engagement is a backdrop against which to develop the capacities of unemployed clients and workplaces alike, and these capacities simultaneously influence the character of engagement in a given situation.

One implication from such an understanding is that employer engagement is not something that can easily be produced through standard policies and implementation models. Local autonomy and flexibility in the applied solutions become important preconditions for such types of broker processes. This further poses certain demands on the efforts of employer engagement staff. For example, there is considerable difference between understanding employer engagement work as establishing contacts and making agreements about certain clients, on one hand, and seeing work as centred around building relations and supporting development in workplaces as well as for unemployed individuals, on the other. In our study, we see this indicated by the local differentiation between business consultants, who look to engage employers in initial contact around potential ALMPs, and job consultants, who look to develop ongoing relationships that can carry a more sustained, reciprocal collaboration. In general, the relational and contextual processes in creating employer engagement place high demands on the employment services' organizational capacity for collaborative work and the qualifications needed by the frontline staff who work with employer engagement.

Our analysis of two specific Danish cases implies that it is possible to create employer engagement even in a context of voluntary engagement and with the use of only 'sermons' and 'carrots' by the employment services. However, it also shows that employers who are mainly motivated by short-term goals – productive (or free) labour – might be less motivated for relational and reciprocal engagement over a prolonged period. We see this indicated in the attention that job consultants pay to identifying employers looking for free labour or who are otherwise not motivated to participate in the necessary mutual development, and so far as possible avoid collaboration with them. This touches upon the delicate balance between regulatory requirements and the voluntary participation of the employers. Our analysis raises the question whether employer engagement in the development of work ability and inclusive capacity can actually be created with the 'stick' approach of regulation. However, it may be the case that employer engagement created through the relational processes presented in our data is only possible precisely because, in the Danish context, employer engagement is based on voluntary participation. Paradoxically, this could also relate to the extent of voluntary participation by unemployed persons. ALMPs based on conditionality assume that the unemployed lack motivation and incentives to work, which is why work (or work placement) must be requirements for them. However, this can create problems for the generation of employer engagement, as we have described throughout this chapter, since unemployed individuals who are forced into placements are often not highly motivated or easy for the employers to work with. This insight chimes with the present focus on New Public Governance (NPG), with the use of co-production and co-creation in public service organizations. The introduction of such new forms of governance is highly visible in Danish municipal employment services. These organizations currently work more intensively, with user involvement part of their services – although they are still based in part on a conditional approach – and deeper cooperation with employers than using them only as providers of a high number of placements (Larsen and Caswell, 2020). More research is needed on how these developments evolve and, not least, how they relate to other welfare state contexts.

In general, there seems to be a lack of research on the processes of employer engagement in the existing literature. We are aware that the perspectives and research presented are in their initial phase, but we hope that this chapter can inspire others to initiate more research into those processes.

References

Aguinis, H. and Glavas, A. (2012). 'What we know and don't know about corporate social responsibility: A review and research agenda', *Journal of Management* 38(4): 932–68.

Akerlof, G.A. (1970). 'The market for "lemons": Quality uncertainty and the market mechanism', *The Quarterly Journal of Economics* 84(3): 488–500.

Andersen, N.A. and Larsen, F. (2018). *Beskæftigelse for alle? Den kommunale beskæftigelsespolitik på kontanthjælpsområdet siden 2000*, Aarhus: Frydenlund Academic.

Barnett, M.L., Henriques, I. and Husted, B.W. (2020). 'Beyond good intentions: Designing CSR initiatives for greater social impact', *Journal of Management* 46(6): 937–64.

Baum, C.M. and Christiansen, C.H. (2005). 'Person-environment-occupation-performance: An occupation-based framework for practice.' In C.H. Christiansen, C.M. Baum and J. Bass-Haugen (eds) *Occupational therapy: Performance, participation, and well-being*, 3rd edn, Thorofare, NJ: SLACK, pp 243–66.

Bond, G.R. and Drake, R.E. (2014). 'Making the case for IPS supported employment', *Administration and Policy in Mental Health and Mental Health Services Research* 41(1): 69–73.

Bond, G.R., Becker, D.R., Drake, R.E., Rapp, C.A, Meisler, N., Lehman, A.F., Bell, M.D. and Blyler, C.R. (2001). 'Implementing supported employment as an evidence-based practice', *Psychiatric Services* 52(3): 313–22.

Bonet, R., Cappelli, P. and Hamori, M. (2013). 'Labor market intermediaries and the new paradigm for human resources', *The Academy of Management Annals* 7(1): 341–92.

Bonoli, G. (2010). 'The political economy of active labor-market policy', *Politics & Society* 38(4): 435–57.

Bonoli, G. (2013). *The origins of active social policy: Labour market and childcare policies in comparative perspective*, Oxford: Oxford University Press.

Bredgaard, T. (2018). 'Employers and active labour market policies: Typologies and evidence', *Social Policy and Society* 17(3): 365–77.

Bredgaard, T. and Halkjær, J.L. (2016). 'Employers and the implementation of active labor market policies', *Nordic Journal of Working Life Studies* 6(1): 47–59.

Bredgaard, T., Larsen, F. and Madsen, P.K. (2006). 'Opportunities and challenges for flexicurity: The Danish example', *Transfer: European Review of Labour and Research* 12(1): 61–82.

Bredgaard, T., Larsen, F. and Madsen, P.K. (2008). 'Flexicurity: In pursuit of a moving target', *European Journal of Social Security* 10(4): 305–23.

Brodkin, E.Z. and Marston, G. (eds) (2013). *Work and the welfare state*, Copenhagen: DJØF Publishing.

Card, D., Kluve, J. and Weber, A. (2010). 'Active labour market policy evaluations: A meta-analysis', *Economic Journal* 120(548): F452–77.

Card, D., Kluve, J. and Weber, A. (2018). 'What works? A meta analysis of recent active labor market program evaluations', *Journal of the European Economic Association* 16(3): 894–931.

Drake, R.E., Bond, G.R. and Becker, D.R. (2012). *Individual placement and support: An evidence-based approach to supported employment*, Oxford: Oxford University Press.

Esping-Andersen, G. (1990). *The three worlds of welfare capitalism*, Cambridge: Polity Press.

EUSE (2010). *European Union of Supported Employment toolkit*. European Union of Supported Employment.

Filges, T. and Hansen, A.T. (2015). 'The threat effect of active labor market programs: A systematic review', *Journal of Economic Surveys* 31(1): 58–78.

Frøyland, K. (2019). 'Vital tasks and roles of frontline workers facilitating job inclusion of vulnerable youth', *European Journal of Social Work* 22(4): 563–74.

Frøyland, K. and Kvåle, L.S. (2014). 'Utvikling av naturlig bistand på arbeidsplassen.' In K. Frøyland and Ø. Spjelkavik (eds) *Inkluderingskompetanse. Ordinært arbeid som mål og middel*, Oslo: Gyldendal Akademisk, pp 93–106.

Frøyland, K., Andreassen, T.A. and Innvær, S. (2019). 'Contrasting supply-side, demand-side and combined approaches to labour market integration', *Journal of Social Policy* 48(2): 311–28.

Granovetter, M.S. (1973). 'The strength of weak ties', *American Journal of Sociology* 78(6): 1360–80.

Granovetter, M.S. (1995). *Getting a job: A study of contacts and careers*, 2nd edn, Chicago, IL: The University of Chicago Press.

Griffin, C., Hammis, D., Geary, T. and Sullivan, M. (2008). 'Customized employment: Where we are; where we're headed', *Journal of Vocational Rehabilitation* 28(3): 135–9.

Gustafsson, J., Peralta, J. and Danermark, B. (2018). 'Supported employment and social inclusion: Experiences of workers with disabilities in wage subsidized employment in Sweden', *Scandinavian Journal of Disability Research* 20(1): 26–36.

Halkjær, J.L. (2014). *Firms and active labour market policies*, Copenhagen: Department of Political Science, University of Aalborg.

Heffernan, J. and Pilkington, P. (2011). 'Supported employment for persons with mental illness: Systematic review of the effectiveness of individual placement and support in the UK', *Journal of Mental Health* 20(4): 368–80.

Idowu, S.O., Capaldi, N., Zu, L. and Das Gupta, A. (eds) (2013). *Encyclopedia of corporate social responsibility*, Berlin: Springer Verlag.

Idowu, S.O., Schmidpeter, R. and Fifka, M.S. (eds) (2015). *Corporate social responsibility in Europe: United in sustainable diversity*, Berlin: Springer.

Immervoll, H. and Scarpetta, S. (2012). 'Activation and employment support policies in OECD countries: An overview of current approaches', *IZA Journal of Labor Policy* 1(1): 1–20.

Ingold, J. (2015). 'Street-level organisations and employer engagement in the UK Work Programme', The Interplay between Policy Reforms, Governance and Street-Level Practices and the Implications for the Assistance-Seeking Citizens, 18–19 November, Aalborg University, Copenhagen.

Ingold, J. (2018). 'Employer engagement in active labour market programmes: The role of boundary spanners', *Public Administration* 96(4): 707–20.

Ingold, J. (2020). 'Employers' perspectives on benefit conditionality in the UK and Denmark', *Social Policy and Administration* 54(2): 236–49.

Ingold, J. and Stuart, M. (2014). 'The demand-side of active labour market policies: A regional study of employer engagement in the work programme', *Journal of Social Policy* 44(3): 443–62.

Ingold, J. and Valizade, D. (2015). *Employer engagement in active labour market policies in the UK and Denmark: A survey of employers*, Policy Report no. 6, Centre for Employment Relations, Innovation and Change (CERIC), Leeds: Leeds University Business School.

Ingold, J. and Valizade, D. (2017). 'Employers' recruitment of disadvantaged groups: Exploring the effect of active labour market programme agencies as labour market intermediaries', *Human Resource Management Journal* 27(4): 530–47.

Kinoshita, Y., Furukawa, T.A., Omori, I.M., Watanabe, N., Marshall, M., Bond, G.R., Huxley, P. and Kingdon, D. (2010). 'Supported employment for adults with severe mental illness', *Cochrane Database of Systematic Reviews 9*.

Kluve, J. (2010). 'The effectiveness of European active labor market programs', *Labour Economics* 17(6): 904–18.

Larsen, C.A. and Vesan, P. (2012). 'Why public employment services always fail. Double-sided asymmetric information and the placement of low-skill workers in six European countries', *Public Administration* 90(2): 466–79.

Larsen, F. and Caswell, D. (2020). 'Co-creation in an era of welfare conditionality – Lessons from Denmark', *Journal of Social Policy*: 1–19.

Lauringson, A. and Lüske, M. (2021). Institutional set-up of active labour market policy provision in OECD and EU countries: Organisational set-up, regulation and capacity, No. 262; OECD Social, Employment and Migration Working Papers, Paris: Organisation for Economic Co-operation and Development.

Lødemel, I. and Moreira, A. (eds) (2014). *Activation or workfare? Governance and the neo-liberal convergence*, Oxford: Oxford University Press.

Lødemel, I. and Trickey, H. (eds) (2000). *'An offer you can't refuse': Workfare in international perspective*, Bristol: Policy Press.

McGurk, P. (2014). *Employer Engagement: A human resource management perspective*, No. 7; WERU Working Paper.

Modini, M., Tan, L., Brinchmann, B., Wang, M.J., Killackey, E., Glozier, N., Mykletun, A. and Harvey, S.B. (2016). 'Supported employment for people with severe mental illness: Systematic review and meta-analysis of the international evidence', *British Journal of Psychiatry* 209(1): 14–22.

Moura-Leite, R.C. and Padgett, R.C. (2011). 'Historical background of corporate social responsibility', *Social Responsibility Journal* 7(4): 528–39.

OECD (2020). Impact evaluation of labour market policies through the use of linked administrative data. Final report, Paris: Organisation for Economic Co-operation and Development.

Patrick, R. (2017). 'Wither social citizenship? Lived experiences of citizenship in/exclusion for recipients of out-of-work benefits', *Social Policy and Society* 16(2): 293–304.

Peck, J. (2001). *Workfare states*, New York: The Guilford Press.

Peck, J. and Theodore, N. (2000). '"Work first": Workfare and the regulation of contingent labour markets', *Cambridge Journal of Economics* 24(1): 119–38.

Riesen, T., Morgan, R.L. and Griffin, C. (2015). 'Customized employment: A review of the literature', *Journal of Vocational Rehabilitation* 43(3): 183–93.

Scoppetta, A., Davern, E. and Geyer, L. (2019). '*Job carving and job crafting. A review of practices*', Directorate-General for Employment, Social Affairs and Inclusion, European Commission: https://doi.org/10.2767/95966

Spjelkavik, Ø. (2012). 'Supported employment in Norway and in the other Nordic countries', *Journal of Vocational Rehabilitation* 37(3): 163–72.

STAR (2018). *Viden om effekter af indsatser for ledige og andre personer på overførselsindkomster*, Copenhagen: Styrelsen for Arbejdsmarked og Rekruttering.

van Berkel, R. and van der Aa, P. (2012). 'Activation work: Policy programme administration or professional service provision?' *Journal of Social Policy* 41(3): 493–510.

van Berkel, R., Caswell, D., Kupka, P. and Larsen, F. (eds) (2017). *Frontline delivery of welfare-to-work policies in Europe: Activating the unemployed*, Abingdon: Routledge.

van der Aa, P. and van Berkel, R. (2014). 'Innovating job activation by involving employers', *International Social Security Review* 67(2): 11–27.

Vedung, E. (1997). *Public policy and program evaluation*, New Brunswick, NJ: Transaction Publishers.

Wehman, P. (2012). 'Supported employment: What is it?' *Journal of Vocational Rehabilitation* 37: 139–42.

Wehman, P., Taylor, J., Brooke, V., Avellone, L., Whittenburg, H., Ham, W., Brooke, A.M. and Carr, S. (2018). 'Toward competitive employment for persons with intellectual and developmental disabilities: What progress have we made and where do we need to go', *Research and Practice for Persons with Severe Disabilities* 43(3): 131–44.

8

Active Labour Market Programmes and Employer Engagement in the UK and Germany

Jay Wiggan and Matthias Knuth

Introduction

If active labour market policies are to mean more than disciplining and nudging claiming working-age benefits, the questions of how and under what circumstances employers are more or less willing to hire non-employed benefit claimants of working age, and how this is affected by claimants' ascribed social characteristics, are crucial ones. Over the last decade a growing body of work has provided fruitful insights into employer preferences and behaviour with respect to engagement in employment services (Ingold and Stuart, 2015; Ingold and Valizade, 2017; Bredgaard, 2018). This chapter considers and compares employer engagement in national-level active labour market programmes (ALMP) in the UK and Germany through examination of a selection of government-commissioned research into public programmes intended to integrate a variety of claimant groups (long-term and short-term unemployed; lone parents; sick and disabled people; older jobseekers; newly arrived refugees) into the labour market. The chapter is organized as follows. The first section provides a brief overview of the organization of the public employment service (PES)[1] and changing patterns of employment participation during the last 40 years. The second section considers employers' views of benefit claimants and the PES. The third section outlines the types of policy tools used to activate claimants into the labour market and foster employer engagement. The fourth section explores the integrative capacity of employers, namely whether they are willing and/ or able to recruit benefit claimants and/or participate in the services offered by the PES to facilitate this.

Labour market trends and employment service institutions

Over the last 40 years the size of the labour force aged 16–64 in employment in the UK has expanded considerably, rising from a low point of around 23.2 million in 1983 to 31.6 million by the end of 2019 (ONS, 2021b). The overall growth in employment has been mirrored by an increase in the employment rate for people aged 16–64, albeit subject to fluctuation with recessionary periods and their aftermath. Prior to the emergence of the COVID-19 pandemic in 2020/21, the UK economy had experienced three recessions during this period – 1980–81; 1990–91 and 2008–09. From the 1983 dip in the employment rate to around 65 per cent, participation recovered in waves to the highest level recorded since the 1970s, reaching 76 per cent during 2019, before the impact of the pandemic made itself felt (ONS, 2021b).

Although each recession occasioned a rise in people unable to find or keep jobs, the headline rate of unemployment was greater during the 1980s and 1990s than that which followed the financial crisis and 2008–10 recession (Jenkins, 2010). In the 1980s and again in 1993, the number of unemployed people peaked at 3 million, while unemployment following the 2008–10 recession hit 2.7 million in 2011. By the final quarter of 2019, however, unemployment had dropped to around 1.3 million (ONS, 2021a). Concurrent with this was a decline in long-term unemployment after the 1990s, that is, being without paid work for longer than 12 months. In 1985/ 86, and again in the recession of the early 1990s, the numbers of long-term unemployed people reached 1.2 million, but after the 2008 financial crisis it peaked at around 900,000 in 2012/13, before falling to under 300,000 in late 2019 (CSO, 1990, p 80; ONS, 2021a).

Similarly, Germany experienced a decline in employment in the early 1980s, in the first half of the 1990s,[2] and again in the first half of the 2000s, but survived the 2008 financial crisis without a net loss of employment. From 2006 to 2020, employment numbers grew from 40 million to 45 million. Simultaneously, the working-age population diminished until 2012 and would have continued to shrink if increasing migration had not provided some balance. Nevertheless, the working-age population of 2020 is only 98 per cent that of 2005 (Destatis online databank, retrieved on 26 October 2021). The unemployment rate (administrative count)[3] halved from 11.8 per cent (2005) to 5.2 per cent (2019). Moreover, among the working-age population without vocational degrees, it went down from 26 per cent to only 17 per cent (Röttger et al, 2020). The share of those unemployed for three years plus reduced from 16 to 12 per cent (Bundesagentur für Arbeit – Statistik, 2021b; own calculations). In other words, neither employers' demand nor demographics have solved the unemployment problem for those at the margins of the labour market. This is where employer engagement comes into play, with governments seeking to incorporate mechanisms to drive this into the activity of the PES and programme content/structure of ALMP. It is to a brief discussion of the nature of the PES and ALMP in each welfare state that we now turn.

Whether overall favourable developments in employment and unemployment since the 1980s (or, in the German case, since 1998) are attributable to more vigorous ALMP, as some contend (Wells, 2001; Fahr and Sunde, 2009; Walwei, 2017; critical: Knuth, 2014b), we cannot say. Lower levels of unemployment, though, may explain the enthusiasm of successive British governments to expand ALMP to encompass recipients of social assistance benefits paid on grounds of ill health, disability or lone parenthood (that is, 'economic inactivity') (Griggs et al, 2014). By the late 1990s working-age recipients of benefits paid on grounds of disability or ill-health, for example, had overtaken the numbers of people claiming unemployment benefits, and since 2000 the total has remained above 2 million people (Crossfield et al, 2021, p 25). Though work-related conditions attached to social assistance benefits for 'economically inactive' claimants are less demanding than for unemployed claimants, greater levels of work-oriented activity have increasingly been required. In Germany, permanent withdrawal from the labour market, exemption from activation and non-inclusion in the unemployment count for health reasons have always been more restricted so that unemployment rates may not be directly compared cross-nationally for periods and countries where poor health opened up major ways out of the labour market (Erlinghagen and Knuth, 2010).

The key institutions of the British employment service and social security administration were reconfigured 20 years ago under the then Labour government,[4] which created Jobcentre Plus (JCP) as a semi-autonomous agency under a new 'work-focused' department – the Department for Work and Pensions (DWP) (Wiggan, 2007). The succeeding Conservative–Liberal coalition government then subsumed JCP into the DWP, which remains the lead organization for ALMP in Britain,[5] though delivery of employment programmes is generally contracted out to third and private sector organizations (Greer et al, 2017, pp 32ff). Employers may consequently find themselves approached by national, regional or local PES contacts as well as organizations under contract to deliver employment schemes, creating a complex patterning of employer engagement activity.

In Germany, an important move towards a universal 'activating' approach entailed transfer of responsibilities for former claimants of social assistance from the municipalities to the central state. However, since the municipalities – backed by the Christian Democrats, then in parliamentary opposition but dominating the federal states – were unwilling to withdraw completely, a delicate construct was found under which municipalities are partners of the Federal Employment Agency in jointly running local jobcentres.[6] This resulted in a two-tier PES with 'employment agencies' serving those claiming contribution-based benefits plus the general public of employers and the labour force, and 'jobcentres' serving those of working age claiming minimum income benefits (see Knuth, 2009). These claimants have either exhausted their entitlements to contribution-based benefits through the duration of their unemployment, or have never acquired any (which category includes newcomers on the German labour market like refugees). Accordingly, we encounter particular endeavours to engage employers only within this second tier of the PES. As in Britain, working with groups of claimants is contracted out to providers for a period, either via competitive tendering or by issuing vouchers to clients (Greer et al, 2017, pp 36*ff*).

In a sense, in both countries the PES remains a hierarchical, centralized benefit system that manages and coordinates a relatively decentralized system of employment service delivery. As noted later in this article, this has fostered an approach to employer engagement that assumes that improvements in employer awareness, alignment of schemes with employer interests and sifting candidates to fit employer needs will stimulate employer programme participation and increase the placement of claimants.

Employer recruitment practices and perceptions of claimants

Employer use of the PES as a recruitment channel seems to have declined during the last decade. The 2013 DWP employer survey indicated that just under one third (30 per cent) of surveyed employers who had recruited in the preceding 12 months used the PES, while just under one in ten also reported making use of the then new online portal 'Universal Jobmatch' (DWP, 2014, p 43). In comparison, the 2018 survey indicated that amongst those employers recruiting during the preceding 12 months only 13 per cent reported using the PES, while just over one in ten reported using the Universal Jobmatch service (DWP, 2019a, p 14).[7] There is a striking variation by employer size, however, with almost half (48 per cent) of the very largest businesses reporting use of the PES for recruitment in the 2018 survey compared to under one in ten of the smallest (8 per cent) and around one fifth of medium-sized (18 per cent) companies (DWP, 2019b, table 3.5).[8] We will return to employer size, but businesses' limited use of the PES for recruitment exacerbates a tension the PES faces between serving employers and serving the needs of its (most excluded) non-employed benefit claimants.

As Fletcher (2004) noted with respect to the New Deal Innovation Fund pilots that sought to improve employer recruitment from 'disadvantaged' claimant groups, this presents the PES and contracted provider organizations with a dilemma. If services align closely to employer preferences, then claimants perceived as 'less job-ready' will be deprioritized, but if they do not then they risk the continuing participation of the very employers the PES seeks to engage (Fletcher, 2004, pp 122–5). Indeed, lack of 'suitable' candidates is often identified as a source of employer disaffection with the PES (Stafford et al, 2007, pp 81–2). This is not to say there is a fixed group of 'unemployable' people, as employer attitudes and recruitment practice vary, and shift with the economic cycle (Gore, 2005, p 351). Claimants participating in employment programmes, but identified as on the 'periphery' of employment relative to other participants, are better placed to transition into employment during periods of high labour demand as indicated in findings from the New Deals of the early 2000s (Bunt et al, 2001, p 29; Burniston and Rodger, 2003, pp 81–4).

Conversely, when employers have a wider pool of labour to select from, the PES or contracted providers may be more circumspect in who they put forward to employers for consideration. The analysis of the Employer Engagement strategy of Jobcentre Plus between 2007 and 2010 by Bellis et al (2011, pp 9 and 16), for example, identified that the initial focus on lone parents and claimants of incapacity related benefits had been deprioritized following the 2008/09 financial crisis as attention turned to placing claimants who had been unemployed for six months or more. Such practices indicate how overcoming existing patterns of labour market segmentation through employer engagement is sensitive to broader economic changes and its interaction with employer calculation of costs and benefits of recruitment.

It is important to note, however, that employer views and practices are neither homogeneous nor static. DWP employer surveys during the last decade suggest growing employer recognition of the business value of a diverse workforce, albeit hedged with concerns about recruitment of people with particular ascribed social characteristics. The 2013 DWP survey of employers, for example, indicated that two thirds of respondent employers agreed that a diverse workforce was of benefit to a company, but a majority (52 per cent) also agreed that accommodating individuals with impairments or health conditions was difficult (DWP, 2014, p 38). This indicates a potential gap between the positive aspiration of some employers and employer practice, also noted in other research (Bredgaard, 2018). In addition, the proportion of surveyed employers indicating that a mental health condition does not affect their hiring practice rose from 54 per cent in 2015 to 64 per cent in the 2018 survey (DWP, 2019a, p 48). Conversely, over four in ten employers responding to a question as to whether various interventions could encourage them to recruit from those the PES term 'disadvantaged groups'[9] indicated that, irrespective of any PES assistance, or clarification of the benefits of such recruitment, they would not hire from this group of claimants (DWP, 2019a, p 40).

Similarly, according to a 2011 survey of German employers, only one third of respondents indicated that they would consider long-term unemployed applicants as candidates *at all,* while 16 per cent said they would not consider *any* unemployed candidate, irrespective of unemployment duration (Moertel and Rebien, 2013). Since 2007, however, employers' perception of skills shortages has grown and, in 2016, passed demand shortages as a factor constraining business activities (Bossler et al, 2018). Employers' professed willingness to hire long-term unemployed candidates peaked with 44 per cent of respondents in 2016 and fell again to 39 per cent in 2018, while the percentage of those excluding any unemployed candidate fell to 8 per cent but then grew to 17 per cent again (Pohlan and Rothe, 2020). While employers' professed attitudes fluctuated, actual hiring from the unemployed workforce declined from 43 per cent in 2005 to 21 per cent in 2016 (Bossler et al, 2018) because there were simply fewer unemployed candidates around. Annual flows from unemployment to employment in relation to the average annual stock of unemployed persons have remained relatively stable around a rate of 0.8.[10] However, flow rates are extremely stratified, depending on preceding unemployment durations (Künkler, 2018).

In this era of online job search and recruitment, with the PES operating their own platforms and with companies recruiting via their own homepages, the role of the PES in supporting or bringing about placements in the labour market is difficult to assess. Firms and jobseekers use several search channels simultaneously, and personal networks, including the networks of a firm's employees, have always been the most important. This explains the disadvantages of jobseekers with weak personal networks or whose networks do not extend into the world of work. According to a German 2016 employer survey, employers used the PES directly in 34 per cent of their recruitment processes, but in only 5 per cent of the cases attributed actual hires to this channel. The PES online platform figures are about the same, with 34 per cent usage and a 7 per cent success rate (Bossler et al, 2017). The relative importance of the PES as a means of recruitment is much higher for unemployed – and, in particular, long-term unemployed – than for recruiting from the employed. However, unemployed jobseekers achieve higher wages and a more stable employment perspective when they find a job via unsolicited applications, online platforms, firms' homepages or private placement services rather than through placement by the PES (Pohlan and Rothe, 2020). The principal structural disadvantage of the PES in placing disadvantaged jobseekers has been generalized by Albrekt Larsen and Vesan (2012). This particular study explains why more than the standard placement procedure is needed in order to engage employers in hiring from this group.

Integrative capacity of employers and PES policy instruments

In terms of the overall distribution of jobs amongst 'small' (1–49 employees), 'medium' (50–249) and 'large' (over 250) companies, the two countries appear to differ: the German distribution is more even and leans more towards smaller employers (small: 36 per cent UK, 43 per cent DE; medium: 16 per cent UK, 27 per cent DE; large: 48 per cent UK, 30 per cent DE; Bossler et al, 2017; DBEIS, 2020, p 4). However, these figures are not exactly comparable since UK statistics refer to 'companies' as legal entities, whereas German statistics refer to 'establishments' or 'sites' as organizational units, and large companies tend to have more than one such unit. On the other hand, unlike UK statistics, German statistics include public employers, which should somewhat counteract a bias towards 'small' units. For Germany, it is also known that labour turnover is lower in large companies so that their share in overall hiring (24 per cent) is lower than their share in employment stocks (30 per cent) (Bossler et al, 2017).

It appears reasonable to assume that company characteristics, of which size is the easiest to observe, make a difference to general capacity to integrate applicants from the margins of the labour market. However, it is not at all obvious in which direction this effect works. Should the PES and labour market intermediaries (that is, organizations that link jobseekers with employers; Ingold and Valizade, 2017, p 531) focus on smaller or on larger companies when trying to engage employers for disadvantaged workers? In the UK, larger employers have long been reported as having better awareness of activation initiatives, greater capacity to engage with PES/ contracted organizations and to offer more intense engagement (for example internships, involvement in training design and selection processes) (Fletcher, 2001, 2004; Burniston and Rodger, 2003, pp 51–4; Stafford et al, 2007, p 58). The size of the labour force within small companies also makes each additional hire a greater investment risk than in large companies. Conversely, small employers disproportionately benefit from PES schemes that offer additional labour resource at little cost, and may be more flexible in taking on 'non-traditional' recruits.

How the PES organizes its activity and delivery of ALMP is likely to affect which employers do or do not engage in a given programme and how they engage with it. There are of course a variety of instruments at the disposal of the PES to foster employer engagement. These include: greater support in screening claimants for interview; delivery of pre-employment training oriented to employer needs; and (unpaid) work experience schemes that place claimants with employers. Similarly, public subsidies may be offered to employers who hire (and potentially pay) claimants with particular ascribed characteristics (that is, lone parent; disabled person; young unemployed).

Financial or practical assistance to help with 'additional costs' and/or challenges associated with recruitment of less 'job-ready' claimants may be provided (Bredgaard, 2018, p 367).

Previous analysis of the UK system indicates that the approach of successive UK governments has been dominated by supply-side instruments which concentrate on matching PES and claimant activity to the needs or preferences of employers (Ingold and Stuart, 2015; Orton et al, 2019). That is, successive flagship British ALMPs for long-term unemployed and economically inactive benefit claimants (Fletcher, 2001, 2004; Burniston and Rodger, 2003; Stafford et al, 2007; Bellis et al, 2011; Ingold and Stuart, 2015) have tended to position employers as somewhat passive participants rather than 'proactive' shapers of provision and claimant capabilities (Orton et al, 2019, pp 525–7). We will consider employer engagement with two employment schemes intended to foster demand for shorter-term unemployed claimants – the Work Experience scheme (WE) and Sector-Based Work Academy (SBWA) (the latter building in an element of employer 'co-production' of training provision). We then consider recent findings from an initiative to specifically engage small business and raise employer demand for recruitment of disabled people – the Small Employer Offer (SEO).

The WE and SBWA schemes were introduced by the Conservative–Liberal Democrat coalition government in 2011/12 and focused on recently unemployed claimants with an orientation to those under 25 years old (Coleman et al, 2013). The WE scheme involved an unpaid placement with an organization for a period of up to eight weeks with the presumption that claimants with a weak record of paid employment would gain acculturation to employer expectations, serve as an example of 'gainful' activity and potentially give the participant a referee for future jobs. For employers, the attraction was: additional labour at low cost; the opportunity to preview potential recruits in the work environment; and/or an opportunity to contribute to community cohesion or CSR commitments. In contrast to the WE, the duration of the SBWA was six weeks and involved pre-employment training provided by an employer or other organization, a short, unpaid placement with an employer and then a post-placement guarantee of a job interview with that employer. As such, the WE scheme leant towards promotion of labour discipline and more closely positioned employers as passive, reactive participants to the PES 'offer'. Conversely, the SBWA, with its albeit limited co-production to channel candidates to sectors with high vacancies (Coleman et al, 2013, pp 24–5), was underpinned by presumption (and fostering) of the type of 'proactive' employer participants identified by Orton et al (2019).

In the SBWA, around six in ten employers surveyed (59 per cent) were large companies compared to around four in ten (38 per cent) for those participating in the WE scheme. Strikingly, of the companies engaged with the WE scheme over one half (54 per cent) employed fewer than 50 people, whereas surveyed companies engaged in the SBWA employing fewer than 50 people accounted for around one fifth (21 per cent) of employers (Coleman et al, 2013, p 34). Given the fewer resource commitments involved in offering unpaid WE placements it is perhaps not surprising that micro- and small (and public and third sector) employers were more represented in the WE and large (and private sector) employers in the SBWA (57 per cent private sector WE vs 70 per cent private sector SBWA). In part this appears related to PES activity, with the authors noting almost six in ten (58 per cent) of surveyed large employers involved with the SBWA reporting that the PES had contacted them directly about becoming involved in the scheme. Conversely, amongst companies with fewer than 250 employees this was under four in ten (36 per cent) (Coleman et al, 2013, p 40). This is perhaps indicative of PES attempts to source employers best placed to offer a greater number of claimants the combination of sector-related pre-employment training, unpaid work placements and guaranteed job interviews that marked the SBWA.

The broader literature on employer involvement has noted varying motivations for employer involvement in employment programmes including CSR; opportunism; altruism; and instrumentality (Bredgaard, 2018, p 368). We find a mix of this present in the WE/SBWA with some variation between schemes. A majority of employers, for example, indicated that their involvement in each scheme was the somewhat altruistic notion 'to give young people a chance', with 57 per cent citing this for the WE and 43 per cent for the SBWA. Between a fifth and a quarter of employers (WE 22 per cent; SBWA 23 per cent) reported engagement for instrumental reasons, gaining '[e]xtra resource at low cost' and a quarter of SBWA employers indicated participation was to '[t]ry before you buy' (25 per cent) with a slightly lower figure for the WE employers (21 per cent) (Coleman et al, 2013, pp 43–5). It is unclear whether there was systematic variation in employer motivation by sector, industry or size for each scheme and this seems a potentially fruitful avenue for future research more broadly.

In contrast to the WE and SBWA target group, the SEO (2017–19) focused on people receiving out-of-work benefits on grounds of disability or ill health, and sought to improve the understanding/engagement of small businesses. The SEO included a dedicated Small Employer Advisor role in participating JCP offices and a £500 payment made available in half the participating districts to employers willing to offer a 12-week (16-hour minimum) placement to participants. The latter was to test whether such a payment might incentivize employer participation (Crossfield et al, 2021). The SEO subsidy is redolent of what Cronert (2019) terms an 'outsider' integration subsidy, intended to foster recruitment of candidates deemed to be on the periphery of the labour market. The general orientation of the SEO, though, is consistent with the last twenty years of employer engagement in ALMP in the UK, which orients towards a 'job matching' model (Bredgaard, 2018, p 366). This emphasizes improving the flow of information between the PES, employers and claimants (hence the Small Employer Advisor) and training up claimants to better match employer preferences/vacancies. Given the low value of the SEO subsidy however it is perhaps not surprising that participating employers did not generally regard it as inducement to participate. Instead, employers tended to foreground previous experience with JCP, particularly good job matching of candidates (or not), although smaller organizations were keenest on the financial support (Crossfield et al, 2021, pp 50–53). That employer sensitivity to subsidies may link to employer size echoes the earlier findings from the coalition government's Youth Contract employer subsidy to hire young unemployed people, under which the majority of recipient organizations were small employers (Coleman et al, 2014, p 31). With respect to employer attitudes, the review of the SEO by Crossfield et al (2021) found that more socially inclusive perspectives were associated with employers who had personal experience of ill health/disability, or where the organization had a history of diverse recruitment, or professed commitments to equality and diversity. Employers without such experience or organizational orientation indicated greater wariness of the cost of more diverse recruitment, which implicitly supports the logic of interventions such as SEO that aim to improve support to employers and enhance knowledge and trust in the value of such recruitment (Crossfield et al, 2021, pp 44–5).

Turning to employer engagement in German ALMP we consider here three schemes that variously targeted older claimants and refugees. The first, 'Perspective 50plus'[11] was a programme for claimants of minimum income benefits aged 50 and over; it operated from 2005 to 2015. Although there was no formal minimum unemployment duration, participants' median unemployment during the ten years before entering the programme was five years, and the average age of the participants was 54 (data only available for 2010). The programme attracted up to 200,000 new participants per year and reached more than a third of the theoretical target group. Despite focusing, in practice, on jobseekers with a twofold stigma – age and long-term unemployment – employer engagement in hiring was not framed in terms of 'giving them a chance', but rather in terms of 'preparing enterprises for demographic change' – i.e. instrumental innovation rather than altruism. The implementation of the programme was anchored in local politics, where every year some particularly active employers were honoured in a public event as 'employers with vision'.

The programme lacked any prescribed 'standard treatment' but was flexible and open to experimental approaches. Employers valued services, such as introducing suitable candidates or targeted training for the job, higher than recruitment subsidies. Where monetary incentives were used, lump sum payments tied to certain milestones (for example recruitment, remaining in employment for six months, conversion of a fixed-term contract into a permanent one) were preferred over percentage shares of wage costs. In some jobcentre areas, soliciting latent labour demand (jobs 'carved' by analysing a client's potential and the employer's needs) played some role. A slight majority of hirings occurred in establishments with fewer than 50 employees (around 25 per cent each in size categories 1–9 and 10–49); recruitment by establishments with more than 500 represented 10 per cent overall (Knuth et al, 2012; Knuth, 2014a).

In 2015, the Federal ESF Programme for the Placement of Long-Term Unemployed Claimants of Minimum Income Benefits succeeded 'Perspective 50plus' and lasted until 2020.[12] The programme addressed jobseekers aged 35 or more who had been unemployed for at least two years. Company canvassers endeavoured to place clients with private employers for a minimum of two years using initially high but regressive wage subsidies. Mentoring clients *vis-à-vis* potential employers involved a kind of stigma management, as clients were stigmatized by the programme's defined entry criteria and by its title, which emphasized long-term unemployment and benefit dependency. Besides the canvassers, there were job coaches who accompanied participants once they had started work and supported them to persevere in the job. The role of the job coaches *vis-à-vis* the employers was ambivalent, as many employers objected to an outsider looking into their company. There was no formal restriction or focus on the type of employers that could or should participate. Empirically, private for-profit employers dominated at 71 per cent (three quarters of these were owner-led companies), followed by associations and cooperatives at 17 per cent and public employers at 12 per cent. One quarter (25 per cent) of the participants were employed by micro-businesses with no more than 5 employees, 23 per cent were employed in companies employing between 6 and 19, 31 per cent were in the category between 20 and 99, and only 20 per cent were employed by companies with 100 or more. Of the private employers who participated in the programme 64 per cent were positive or very positive about the fit or match; public employers and associations were slightly more positive (Boockmann et al, 2021).

Finally, Germany has introduced labour market integration measures for refugees, which emerged in response to the increased arrival of refugees in Germany in 2015 and 2016. After some special programmes of smaller scale (Knuth, 2016), the jobcentres came to rely on the range of standard schemes always at their disposal. Potential participants were all asylum seekers who could be allowed to work, which covers a range of different residence status too complex to explain here. The high political priority of the target group gave rise to a special evaluation (Bonin et al, 2021; Brussig et al, 2022) which, after a long tradition of separate evaluations of instruments in different periods, for the first time undertook a cross-sectional evaluation of the effectiveness of different instruments when applied to a discrete target group under identical labour market conditions and with a uniform methodology. The quantitative evaluation used data from around 150,000 refugees who had arrived in Germany after 2014, were at least 18 years old in September 2018 and entered one of the five mainstream German ALMP between 1 August 2017 and 11 September 2018, plus a control group of around 280,000 refugees with similar statistical properties who could have entered a programme but did not.[13] Programmes involving a relationship with an employer figured best in terms of employment outcomes observed over 40 months, in this order: hiring subsidies, subsidized preparatory stages for an apprenticeship, and unpaid internships with employers where participants continue to receive their benefits (Bonin et al, 2021, p 221). Since the PES uses its mainstream programmes for refugees rather than operating refugee integration as an integrated programme of its own, data about the sizes of companies involved are not available.

Among the strategies pursued by the PES in order to integrate refugees in employment, cooperation with employers ranks top (Bonin et al, 2021, p 79). Internships with employers – one of the three most effective instruments – were slightly more frequent where the local PES had a special focus on refugees in its approach to employers (Bonin et al, 2021, p 116). Employers see this kind of effort as an investment that they are reluctant to make if an asylum seeker's expectation of being allowed to stay is still uncertain or of too short a remaining duration.[14] Furthermore, employers expressed confusion about the variety of ALMP and wanted a single contact person with the PES (Brussig et al, 2022). In order to connect the PES with employers, an ancillary programme funding 'welcome pilots' to be employed by economic chambers was launched. Employer engagement in the labour market integration of refugees is primarily driven by current and expected skills shortages. Two decades of public discourse have made it clear to employers what demographic ageing means for them. Immigration promises some compensation here. An in-depth investigation of refugees' employment and vocational training during the pandemic showed no widening of the initial gap, which means that the burden of adjustment was not passed on to refugees (Knuth, 2022). However, there also remains variation in employer practice regarding recruitment of refugees. Again, small and medium-sized companies are over-represented in employing recent refugees. While accounting for 31 per cent of total employment, companies employing 250 people or more account for only 12 per cent of refugee employment in 2017 (Kubis and Röttger, 2019). In Germany, then, the smaller companies are the more promising target for engaging employers in employment programmes.

Conclusions

As the PES endeavours to engage employers in ALMP, it faces a fundamental paradox that a focus on jobseekers deemed to have limited employment opportunities risks signalling to potential employers that the job capabilities of this group are somehow flawed. As the examples of 'Perspective 50plus' and integrating refugees in the German labour market demonstrate, this can be mitigated by framing the issue in a wider perspective beyond ALMP, such as 'managing demographic change' or 'integrating refugees? Yes, we can' ('wir schaffen das' – Angela Merkel in 2015). In the German context, framing employer engagement as an issue of national importance also reactivates corporatist mechanisms of mutual responsibility. By contrast, this is not the case when the target group is framed as marginal or 'outsiders'. As indicated in the UK, the willingness of some employers to recruit those the PES deem 'disadvantaged' appears limited, while PES staff perceive employer openness to inclusion to vary with the economic cycle, which in turn constrains the scope to challenge exclusionary beliefs/practices. Nevertheless, offering subsidies and extensive support services to employers does encourage some level of engagement, though whether this is a passive or proactive form (Orton et al, 2019) may vary with the specific policy instrument used (and hence the employer target group).

In the two countries different-sized companies seemed most inclined to consider disadvantaged applicants. In Germany, owner-managed small and micro-enterprises are more willing to take on applicants who are unusual in some respect. A tentative explanation would be that the German labour market is more structured by formal and documented vocational qualifications and professionally structured career paths than the UK market. This indicates perhaps the continued salience of the distinction in the 'varieties of capitalism' literature (Menz, 2011, p 537) between training and employment provision and employer preferences in Germany (as a coordinated market economy) and the UK (as a liberal market economy). In Germany HR departments usually do not have sufficient discretion to deviate from this pattern. It takes the owner's decision-making power to take such a risk, and therefore the employer's commitment is easier to gain in companies where the owner assumes the HR function. Conversely, despite identifying the potential of small employers to recruit non-employed claimants of working age, the GB PES and ALMP seem more oriented to engagement of large employers, perhaps reflecting a drive to maximize vacancies/placements per employer engaged.

More broadly, it is notable that the same (narrow) types of instruments for activating claimants and engaging employers are turned to time and again, though often under different labels. We might consider here that this reflects a contradiction between the mechanisms of political and economic business. Political and electoral pressure generates an incentive for politicians to frequently adjust, discontinue and reinvent programmes, to address the recurrent issue of unemployment and economic inactivity. Arguably, employers, on the other hand, seek simplicity, transparency and continuity, which aid development of a base of knowledge of what services/ supports are available, reduce transaction and hiring costs. The lack of fit between these two approaches means continually directing resources to making employers aware of the (changing) PES 'offer'. As is noted in the case of the UK where demand-led employer engagement approaches seems to revolve mainly around 'job matching', much is not new and this perhaps reflects how the UK approach to employer engagement is the obverse of a 'supply-side' fundamentalist approach to activating claimants by raising their 'employability' (Ingold and Stuart, 2015; Orton et al, 2019). By implying that (flawed) employer perceptions of claimant capabilities and/ or perceived costs of hiring 'non-traditional' candidates are the reasons for claimant exclusion, the PES is enjoined in a continual search to tailor services to suit employers better. Yet, what an employer deems suitable is neither fixed, nor divorced from (shifting patterns of) labour market stratification, segmentation and demand.

Notes

[1] The state employment service rather than the broader ecology of public, private and community organizations involved with various employability services.

[2] This period was marked by reunification and the disruptive transformation in the east (Bosch and Knuth, 1993).

[3] The German administrative count differs from the internationally comparable count based on labour force surveys.

[4] The DWP does not operate in Northern Ireland (see Wiggan, 2015).

[5] ALMPs for long-term unemployed people and disabled people are partly devolved (Wiggan, 2017; Orton et al, 2019).

[6] The English word is actually the official German term.

[7] Since replaced by the 'Find a job' service.

[8] Largest here refers to businesses with 500 employees or more, while smallest refers to those with 2–9 employees and medium-sized to those with 50–249 employees (DWP, 2019b, table 3.5).

[9] This included care leavers, ex-offenders, people with very long-term absence from the labour market, people experiencing homelessness and people with drug and/or alcohol issues (DWP, 2019a, p 39).

[10] A flow rate of 0.8 means that the number of previously unemployed people starting work during the year is 80 per cent of the annual average of unemployed people in the stock. This includes individuals who shift from unemployed to employed status more than once (Bundesagentur für Arbeit – Statistik, 2021a; own calculations).

[11] In the UK an equivalent scheme for unemployed people aged 50 and over, albeit oriented more to the supply side, was the New Deal 50 plus, which was introduced in 2000 and discontinued in 2011.

[12] The European Social Fund co-funded the programme.

[13] This was not a randomized controlled trial, which is not an acceptable approach in Germany on ethical grounds: The chance to participate should not be determined by a secondary purpose like the design of a study.

[14] Refugees may be allowed to work after waiting for nine months for a decision on asylum (six months if accompanied by their children); residence permits issued after recognition of refugee status are limited to three years and subject to revision; applicants whose claim for asylum is denied may still receive a short-term toleration permit and be allowed to work; all this creates opportunities for work but also an abundance of uncertainties, not the least of these being the uncertainty whether the immigration office will manage to prolong one's permit in time, even where prolongation should be legally routine.

References

Albrekt Larsen, C. and Vesan, P. (2012). 'Why public employment services always fail. Double-sided asymmetric information and the placement of low-skill workers in six European countries', *Public Administration* 90(2): 466–479.

Bellis A., Sigala, M. and Dewson, S. (2011). *Employer Engagement and Jobcentre Plus*, Department for Work and Pensions Research Report 742. London: Department for Work and Pensions.

Bonin, H., Boockmann, B., Brändle, T., Bredtmann, J., Brussig, M., Demir, G. et al (2021). *Begleitevaluation der arbeitsmarktpolitischen Integrationsmaßnahmen für Geflüchtete*, Bonn: Bundesministeriums für Arbeit und Soziales.

Boockmann, B., Brändle, T., Fuchs, P., Klee, G., Kugler, P., Laub, N. et al (2021). *Evaluation des ESF-Bundesprogramms zur Eingliederung langzeitarbeitsloser Leistungsberechtigter nach dem SGB II auf dem allgemeinen Arbeitsmarkt*, Bonn: Bundesministeriums für Arbeit und Soziales.

Bosch, G. and Knuth, M. (1993). 'The labour market in East Germany', *Cambridge Journal of Economics* 17(3): 295–308.

Bossler, M., Kubis, A. and Moczall, A. (2017). 'Neueinstellungen im Jahr 2016: Große Betriebe haben im Wettbewerb um Fachkräfte oft die Nase vorn.', *IAB-Kurzbericht* 18: http://doku.iab.de/kurzber/2017/kb1817.pdf

Bossler, M., Gürtzgen, N., Kubis, A. and Moczall, A. (2018). 'IAB-Stellenerhebung von 1992 bis 2017. So wenige Arbeitslose pro offene Stelle wie nie in den vergangenen 25 Jahren', *IAB-Kurzbericht* 23: http://doku.iab.de/kurzber/2018/kb2318.pdf

Bredgaard, T. (2018). 'Employers and active labour market policies: Typologies and evidence', *Social Policy & Society* 17(3): 365–77.

Brussig, M., Kirchmann, A., Kirsch, J., Klee, G., Kusche, M., Maier, A. et al (2022). *Arbeitsförderung von Geflüchteten. Instrumente, Herausforderungen, Erfahrungen*, Baden-Baden: Nomos.

Bundesagentur für Arbeit – Statistik (2021a). *Abgang und Verbleib von Arbeitslosen in Beschäftigung*. Deutschland, Länder, Kreise, Regionaldirektionen und Agenturen, Monats-/Jahreszahlen.

Bundesagentur für Arbeit – Statistik (2021b). *Langzeitarbeitslosigkeit (Monatszahlen)*. Deutschland, Länder, Kreise und Jobcenter.

Bunt, K., Shury, J., Vivian, D. and Allard, F. (2001). *Recruiting benefit claimants: A survey of employers in ONE pilot areas*, Research Report No 139, Department for Work and Pensions.

Burniston, S. and Rodger, J. (2003). *New deal for lone parents: An evaluation of the Innovation Fund 2001–2002*, Research Report No. 156, Department for Work and Pensions.

Central Statistical Office (1990). *Social trends 20*, London: HMSO.

Coleman, N., McGinigal, S. and Hingley, S. (2013). *Employer perceptions of work experience and sector-based work academies*, Research Report No. 842, Department for Work and Pensions.

Coleman, N., McGinigal, S., Thomas, A., Fu, E. and Hingley, S. (2014). *Evaluation of the youth contract wage incentive: Wave two research*, Research Report No. 864, Department for Work and Pensions.

Cronert, A. (2019). 'Varieties of employment subsidy design: Theory and evidence from across Europe', *Journal of Social Policy* 48(4): 839–59.

Crossfield, J., Finnerty, K., Hughes, K., Beatty, C., Gore, T. and Harris C. (2021). *Small employer offer evaluation*, Research Report No. 1003, Department for Work and Pensions.

Department for Business, Energy and Industrial Strategy (2020). 'Business population estimates for the UK and the regions 2020', Statistical Release, 8 October.

Department for Work and Pensions (2014). DWP Employer Engagement and Experience Survey 2013, Research Report No 856, Department for Work and Pensions.

Department for Work and Pensions (2019a). Employer Engagement Survey 2018, DWP Report 977, Department for Work and Pensions.

Department for Work and Pensions (2019b). Employer Engagement Survey 2018, Data tables, Department for Work and Pensions.

Erlinghagen, M. and Knuth, M. (2010). 'Unemployment as an institutional construct? Structural differences in non-employment in Europe and the United States', *Journal of Social Policy* 39(1): 71–94.

Fahr, R. and Sunde, U. (2009). 'Did the Hartz reforms speed up the matching process? A macro-evaluation using empirical matching functions', *German Economic Review* 10(3): 284–316.

Fletcher, D.-R. (2001). New Deal Innovation Fund Round 1 and 2, Report for Employment Service, ESR86, Working age research and analysis publications 2001, Department for Work and Pensions.

Fletcher, D.-R. (2004). 'Demand-led programmes: Challenging labour-market inequalities or reinforcing them?' *Environment and Planning C: Government and Policy* 22: 115–28.

Gore, T. (2005). 'Extending employability or solving employers' recruitment problems? Demand-led approaches as an instrument of labour market policy', *Urban Studies* 42(2): 341–53.

Gospel, H. and Edwards, T. (2012). 'Strategic transformation and muddling through: Industrial relations and industrial training in the UK', *Journal of European Public Policy*, 19(8): 1229–48.

Greer, I., Breidahl, K., Knuth, M., Larsen, F. and Breidahl, K.N. (2017). *The marketization of employment services: The dilemmas of Europe's work-first welfare states*, Oxford: Oxford University Press.

Griggs, J., Hammond, A. and Walker, R. (2014). 'Activation for all: Welfare reform in the United Kingdom, 1995–2009.' In I. Lodemel and A. Moreira (eds) *Activation or workfare? Governance and the neo-liberal convergence*, Oxford: Oxford University Press, pp 73–100.

Ingold, J. and Stuart, M. (2015). 'The demand side of active labour market policies: A regional study of employer engagement in the Work Programme', *Journal of Social Policy* 44(3): 443–62.

Ingold, J. and Valizade, D. (2017). 'Employers' recruitment of disadvantaged groups: Exploring the effect of active labour market programme agencies as labour market intermediaries', *Human Resource Management Journal* 27(4): 530–47.

Jenkins, J. (2010). 'The labour market in the 1980s, 1990s and 2008/09 recessions', *Economic & Labour Market Review*, 4: 29–36.

Knuth, M. (2009). 'Path shifting and path dependence: Labour market policy reforms under German federalism', *International Journal of Public Administration* 32(12): 1048–69.

Knuth, M. (2014a). 'Broken hierarchies, quasi-markets, and supported networks: A governance experiment in the second tier of Germany's public employment service', *Social Policy & Administration* 48(2): 240–61.

Knuth, M. (2014b). '"The impossible gets done at once; the miraculous takes a little longer." Labour market reforms and the "jobs miracle" in Germany', European Economic and Social Committee – Workers' Group, European Economic and Social Committee: www.eesc.europa.eu/resources/docs/germany_xl_en.pdf

Knuth, M. (2016). Arbeitsmarktintegration von Flüchtlingen. Arbeitsmarktpolitik reformieren, Qualifikationen vermitteln, WISO Diskurs, Bonn: Friedrich-Ebert-Stiftung: http://library.fes. de/pdf-files/a-p-b/18824.pdf

Knuth, M. (2022). *Der Corona-Effekt: Was wissen wir über die Arbeitsmarktsituation von Migrant_innen und Geflüchteten in der Pandemie?* Bonn: Friedrich-Ebert-Stiftung.

Knuth, M., Niewerth, C., Stegmann, T., Zink, L., Boockmann, B., Brändle, T. et al (2012). *Evaluation der Zweiten Phase des Bundesprogramms 'Perspektive 50plus – Beschäftigungspakte für Ältere in den Regionen' (2008–2010)*, Abschlussbericht: Duisburg, Tübingen.

Kubis, A. and Röttger, C. (2019). 'Der Löwenanteil der Geflüchteten wird in kleinen und mittleren Betrieben eingestellt', 6 December, IAB-Forum: www.iab-forum.de/der-loewenanteil-der-gefluechteten-wird-in-kleinen-und-mittleren-betrieben-eingestellt/?pdf=13933

Künkler, M. (2018). 'Langzeitarbeitslosigkeit als Kernproblem des Arbeitsmarktes', *Soziale Sicherheit* 67(7): 261–68.

Menz, G. (2011). 'Employer preferences for labour migration: Exploring *Varieties of Capitalism*-based contextual conditionality in Germany and the United Kingdom', *British Journal of Politics and International Relations* 13(4): 534–55.

Moertel, J. and Rebien, M. (2013). 'Wie Langzeitarbeitslose bei den Betrieben ankommen', *IAB-Kurzbericht* 9: http://doku.iab.de/kurzber/2013/kb0913.pdf

Office for National Statistics (2021a). 'Table UNEM01: Unemployment by age and duration: People (seasonally adjusted)', People not in work: unemployment, Dataset UNEM01 SA.

Office for National Statistics (2021b). 'Table A02: Labour Force Survey Summary: People by economic activity for those aged 16 and over and those aged from 16 to 64 (seasonally adjusted)'.

Orton, M., Green, A., Atfield, G. and Barnes, S.-A. (2019). 'Employer participation in Active Labour Market Policy: From reactive gatekeepers to proactive strategic partners', *Journal of Social Policy* 48(3): 511–28.

Pohlan, L. and Rothe, T. (2020). 'Personalrekrutierung von Beschäftigten, Kurz- und Langzeitarbeitslosen: Unterschiede bei Besetzungswegen und Beschäftigungsqualität', *IAB-Kurzbericht* 6: http://doku.iab.de/kurzber/2020/kb0620.pdf

Röttger, C., Weber, B. and Weber, E. (2020). 'Qualifikationsspezifische Arbeitslosenquoten', Aktuelle Daten und Indikatoren, IAB: https://doku.iab.de/arbeitsmarktdaten/Qualo_2020.pdf

Stafford, B. with Bell, S. Kornfield, R. Lam, K. Orr, L., Ashworth, K., Adelman, L., Davis, A., Hartfree, Y., Hill, K. and Greenberg, D. (2007). *New Deal for Disabled People: Third synthesis report – key findings from the evaluation*, DWP Research Report No. 430, Department for Work and Pensions.

Walwei, U. (2017). 'Agenda 2010 und Arbeitsmarkt: eine Bilanz', *Aus Politik und Zeitgeschichte* 67(26): 25–33.

Wells, B. (2001). 'From Restart to the New Deal in the United Kingdom', in *OECD Labour market policies and the public employment service: Lessons from recent experience and the directions for the future*, Proceedings of the Prague Conference, July, Paris: OECD, pp 241–62.

Wiggan, J. (2007). 'Reforming the United Kingdom's public employment and social security agencies', *International Review of Administrative Sciences* 73(3): 409–24.

Wiggan, J. (2015). 'Varieties of marketisation in the UK: Examining divergence in activation markets between Great Britain and Northern Ireland 2008–2014', *Policy Studies* 36(2): 115–32.

Wiggan, J. (2017). 'Contesting the austerity and "welfare reform" narrative of the UK Government: Forging a social democratic imaginary in Scotland', *International Journal of Sociology and Social Policy* 37(11/12): 639–54.

9

Practice Case Study: Reconnecting Employee and Employer Engagement through Continuous Improvement of Policy

Andrew Hamilton

Introduction

This chapter explores the intentions behind, progress made towards and practical barriers faced by the Australian government in its bid to help more people with disabilities gain meaningful employment. Insights into these issues along with some key recommendations are illustrated through a case study of Holy Cross Services in their adherence to new government policy. The chapter thereby provides insights into the general policy issues along with some specific recommendations.

Four key dimensions are explored, based on a continuous improvement approach to supporting people with different abilities in achieving their career goals. Firstly, we provide an overview of the Australian employment market for people with a disability and recent changes. Secondly, we present a case study reviewing the design and implementation of a supported employment (SE) service delivery model designed to empower people in achieving their career ambitions. Thirdly, we offer an introduction to the challenges encountered by people with different abilities as they progress through their career opportunities. Finally, we discuss the learnings and principles informed by these initiatives and case study to support future employment models for empowering the individual to achieve their career goals and enabling employers to employ more people with different abilities.

Australian disability employment policy

National Disability Insurance Scheme

The National Disability Insurance Scheme (NDIS) provides support for Australians with disability, their families and carers. The NDIS is designed to provide approximately 460,000 Australians under the age of 65 who have a permanent or a significant disability, reasonable and necessary support to live an ordinary life. As an insurance scheme, the NDIS takes a lifetime approach, investing in people with disability early to improve their outcomes later in life. The NDIS supports people with disability to build skills and capability so they can participate in the community and employment. Participants are provided with an NDIS package which allows them to receive support from service providers of their choice, and when they choose it, giving the participant 'choice and control' over where and what support they receive. This model of providing services to people with their own funding is referred to as individualized funding. Previously, participants could only access services that the providers were funded by the government to provide. The NDIS aims to give choice and control to people with disability, with a core objective of supporting, encouraging and helping them achieve employment goals. This objective will ultimately help the NDIS gain some level of financial certainty – as a significant percentage of people with a disability enter the workforce and, ultimately, become taxpayers.

Some people with disability are unable to obtain work at full wage rates owing to the impact of their disability on their level of work productivity. For these individuals some employers calculate their wages using wage assessment tools under the Supported Employment Services Award 2020. This includes Australian Disability Enterprises (ADEs) that operate as intermediate labour markets (not as open employment/mainstream employers) where employers have historically paid supported employees a lower wage than those working in mainstream employment to reflect competency and productivity. As detailed further in the chapter, the wage assessment is currently under review.[1]

Supported employment

Supported employment (SE) in Australia is mainly provided through ADEs. The ADE sector has been operating for around 70 years, and consists generally of not-for-profit (NFP) organizations that play an important role in providing SE opportunities to people with moderate to severe disability across Australia.

ADEs offer similar working conditions to other employers and an opportunity for people with disability to contribute to and connect with their local community. They provide a wide range of employment opportunities in areas including packaging, assembly, production, recycling, screen-printing, plant nursery, garden maintenance and landscaping, cleaning services, laundry services and food services. The workers in ADEs are often people with intellectual disability, who are usually paid much less than the national minimum wage. Within all ADEs nationally, a supported wage assessment is made to determine an individual's productivity on tasks. This has amounted to some people being paid a very low wage per hour (for example $AU2 per hour). Over a number of years this model was scrutinized, investigated and reported on, and ultimately it was agreed by all stakeholders that the methodology of wage assessment was flawed and discriminatory.

The Australian government previously funded ADEs directly, but they are now funded through the NDIS. Some recently introduced NDIS rules about how ADEs can provide more flexible support to people who might be interested in finding a job in open employment mean a person can now receive frequent and ongoing on-the-job employment supports from any workplace using funding from their NDIS plan. With the introduction of the NDIS in 2016, a person with disability who has employment as a goal within their plan can receive reasonable and necessary employment mentoring, guidance and support from their employer paid from their NDIS plan.

According to the NDIS, in order to be considered reasonable and necessary, a support or service:

• must be related to a participant's disability;
• must not cover day-to-day living costs not related to disability support needs;
• should represent value for money;
• must be likely to be effective and work for the participant; and
• should take into account support given to the participant by other government services, their family, carers, networks and the community.

As long as the employer provides the necessary support ratios for people with disability (for example one support worker to five supported employees), and the additional support enables the person to achieve their job and career goals, the employer can be either a 'pathway' or a 'destination' for people with disability. In other words, the person with disability could obtain skills and qualifications that will enable them to work at another employer (a pathway), or remain employed by the ADE for their working life (a destination).

A challenge for the NDIS and funded participants in the scheme is the interplay between the employment objectives of the scheme and other associated government programmes. Because the NDIS rollout is working alongside legacy funded employment programmes, it has introduced complexity and there now remains insufficient clarity on how to navigate the multiple systems. This has resulted in key employment outcomes falling behind the aims of the NDIS. The employment goal of the NDIS is to have

30 per cent of participants of a working age in meaningful employment by 30 June 2023. In recognition of this and with considerable feedback from participants and advocates there have been a number of adaptations and improvements during the five-year rollout of the scheme resulting in greater choice of employment pathways and more control for NDIS participants. This principle of 'choice and control' represents an important set of changes and opportunities for people with disability, the legacy disability employment providers (for example ADEs) and for all employers.

Furthermore, the funding for businesses operated by disability service providers has undergone significant change. Service providers were traditionally funded by state governments through block funding (government grants received in advance), but now many service providers will be funded in a commercial manner: the participant (person who receives the service) chooses where they obtain the service and thereby determines who receives the funding. In addition, under the NDIS funds are paid in arrears based on use (for example, after the service is provided). Providers of services are competing in a participant-driven environment, and therefore it is essential that they move to a customer-service-focused delivery model. Fundamentally, it is the change to a market-driven, commercial, supply-and-demand scheme that will dictate how the sector will operate and this creates new risks for organizations that need to be addressed. Also, many opportunities are being created for agile organizations seeking to establish themselves as employers of choice, or to increase their market share.

The NDIS is a complex social and economic reform and the magnitude of change to a business specializing in disability services and employment should not be under-estimated. The potential change in market dynamics in Australia will impact strategy, cash flow and staff retention for NFP organizations reliant on NDIS-funded participants. Additional complexities and risks that will impact a service provider include the increase in the number of participants, the higher expectations of participants under NDIS funding, workforce, strategy, culture and mergers and partnerships. In the next section we will review a case study of how these complexities have been confronted and resolved by one employer.

Policy implementation: case study

Further changes to ADEs' funding have had implications for organizations' abilities to continue to employ people with disability and specifically target a high ratio of supported employees, now required by legislation. This case study reviews the implications of these changes in government policy and identifies ways forward for organizations to employ more supported employees and the opportunities for both employees and employers.

Holy Cross Services (HCS) is a business unit of the Mater (a Catholic not-for-profit ministry of Mercy Partners) in Queensland, Australia, that has run a commercial laundry for over 30 years. The commercial laundry moved premises and expanded capacity in 2015, and the business became a separate commercial entity of the Mater with a focus on growth. The mission of the laundry was to employ people facing barriers to employment, including people with disability. Historically, the Australian government imposed a cap on the number of people with a disability who could be employed by ADEs. This cap limited the laundry to 35 'supported employees'. The new legislation lifted this cap in 2018, meaning that as HCS grew, it could employ more people with a disability. The aspirational goal of the organization was to employ more than 100 people, making up close to a third of total employees.

HCS provides linen, ironing and folding services for Brisbane-based hospitals and restaurants, specializing in providing high-grade industrial cleaning for hospitals and sterilizing. In addition to the laundry, it provides catering and food services and recently expanded into cleaning services, thus offering a greater variety of employment options for people. Its service model involves stocking linen, transporting linen and replacing linen on site. The laundry industry in Brisbane is characterized by a small number of high-volume providers and HCS is the only laundry that employs people facing barriers to employment, including disability. As an employer of people with disability HCS has been an exemplar, as evidenced by the consistently high numbers of people they have employed at any one point in time, as well as the tenure of a significant number of people.

HCS provides a supported employment environment for people with disability who haven an NDIS package, through employment opportunities, pathways and a destination, in addition to a choice of work roles across their three business units – laundry, food services and cleaning. The support HCS provide for people with disability includes transport support, healthy eating guidance and flexibility in rostering and start and finish times. As an employer they focus on being flexible to enable their employees to perform at their best. When an ADE became able to claim funding from the NDIS participant plans, by employing people with a disability and providing the right and necessary support, employers such as HCS could then become cost-neutral, and in some instances cash-positive, whereas historically there would have been a cost overhead for HCS in the majority of cases. So the introduction of NDIS became a positive experience for HCS, both allowing it to employ people with diverse skills and abilities and experiences, and being good for business.

The changes in government funding have meant that persons with disability seeking employment can now exercise choice and control. They have control over how they spend the funding allocated to them, and choice as to who it is spent with. Previously the government funding model limited choice and control, meaning that a person with disability might have had to accept employment by an employer that was not the best fit for their support needs or their career goals. Similarly, a person might have been employed for several years by an employer that offered suitable support, but in a job that may not have suited their career aspirations and goals. Now, a person with disability and an NDIS package can seek employment in an area in which they are interested, where the employer provides suitable supports to meet their needs and career goals.

Previously, government funding provided employment models that ostensibly suited the employer and employee but limited choice. Typical ADE employment models consisted of highly manual tasks with the work environment suited to the individual performing these manual tasks. The choice of meaningful employment beyond this highly structured and modified work environment was minimal. Now, in theory, a person with a disability seeking employment can gain employment with any employer, because the person with a disability can bring their own supports, to enable them to thrive in any work environment.

This funding change, enabling choice and control and any employer to be matched to an employee, has enabled greater competition across employers, with more employers focusing on employing people with different abilities. This has been of significant benefit for people with disability. People with different abilities are now in demand by some employers – one only needs to take a look at the significant demand for the unique skills and abilities that people on the autism spectrum can offer to business. Three programmes specializing in hiring people on the autism spectrum are: Xceptional, The DXC Technology Dandelion Program and Specialisterne Australia.[2]

Social Scaffolding was engaged by HCS to help it employ more people facing barriers to employment. Social Scaffolding is a technical consulting firm located in Brisbane. The team have been working together for more than six years enabling NFP organizations to focus on opportunities and implement strategies to succeed in competitive environments. The NDIS has forced NFP organizations to transition from predominantly government-funded entities into transaction-focused commercial providers. Much of the work of Social Scaffolding involves working with employers of people with different abilities, and they could see consistent and recurring issues for both employers and employees when employing such people. To gain a deeper understanding of these issues, and wishing to use this understanding to improve the outcomes for its clients, Social Scaffolding facilitated a significant number of conversations, meetings and forums. The learnings from a forum in November 2020 are briefly summarized in the next section of this chapter. Social Scaffolding designed a career guidance service – Equalising Employment Opportunities – to address a specific gap in the market for people with disability seeking meaningful careers. The learnings were also used in a project for HCS.

The objective of the Social Scaffolding project was to prepare HCS for the transition to the new NDIS pricing for supported employees – changing from a weekly to an hourly model, commencing in December 2021. These changes in pricing would have major implications for operating model design, processes, policies and the systems required to efficiently support HCS's disability employment strategy. The changes across these operating parameters also had the potential to impact HCS retention of supported employees, so consideration needed to be given to the recruitment process and activities that will support growth ambitions.

Implementation challenges and learnings: case study

With the major changes occurring in NDIS funding, a number of recurring issues were encountered by the team at Social Scaffolding, prompting proactive engagement with people of different abilities. These issues included the following challenges:

- multiple and legacy employment programmes competing for 'the client' whilst facing a decline in employees, as NDIS-funded participants exercised their 'choice' for different employment options that met their individualized needs and goals;
- lobbying government to prop up ADEs that might prove financially unviable;
- people with disability experiencing strong disincentives to enter the employment market stemming from the complexity of existing funding programmes, the policies underpinning the programmes, funding packages lacking incentives to enter the employment market and corresponding lack of support workers to enable the incentives to be enacted; and
- a lack of genuine, solution-focused 'co-design' between participants, employers and government agencies.

With the intention of better understanding these issues with a solution-focused design, Social Scaffolding curated co-design activities including multiagency, round-table discussions facilitated by people with different abilities to determine both barriers and solutions for individuals.

The topics discussed during the forum included:

- employment, jobs and career pathways – the importance of all three for people with disability;
- shared exchange of value between people with disability and employers – the benefits to the employer of people with different abilities on their team, and the value of a job for a person with different abilities;

- understanding employers and employees' legal obligations and rights – including 'reasonable adjustments' to the workplace and adhering to non-discriminatory practices in hiring people; and
- job creation and innovation – this included discussion of hiring for skills and talent, not as a disability quota, developing heightened understanding of diversity in the workplace from the top down, the need to review and adjust approachs to screening and interviewing potential candidates to get the best out of each individual and ultimately hire the best candidate for the job, and supporting recruitment agencies that advocate, educate, 'upskill', inform and use strength-based approaches to represent people with different abilities.

For detailed analysis of the process and recommendations, see Social Scaffolding (2020). Two key initiatives stemmed from this work.

Equalising Employment Opportunities (EEO): an evidence-based and co-designed methodology to increase sustainable employment for people with different abilities. Through this methodology Social Scaffolding offered focus and resources on four areas of specialization – career profiling, career planning, industry networking and building disability confidence – providing an innovative approach to delivering supports for both people with different abilities and businesses.

Inclusive Employment Movement (2020): a multistakeholder campaign with the aim to build momentum across the employment landscape for people with different abilities, so that whenever there is a recruitment process they are unreservedly engaged, considered and employed. The movement maintains a focus on people with diverse abilities to consistently have equal opportunities for enriching, fulfilling jobs and supported career progression, doing whatever sets their heart on fire.

The main learnings and principles coming out of these initiatives is summarized in three points.

1. *The importance of innovative thinking*: People of different abilities are solving problems innovatively every day, seeing and doing things in a different way. People with diverse abilities bring a different perspective to the workplace and their teams. Some may have experienced challenges and hurdles that develop resilience, determination and courage – these are essential skills for innovation, solving problems and overcoming challenges, all skills beneficial to today's employers.
2. *The importance of a more diverse talent pool*: One in five people in Australia live with a disability (AIHW, 2019). A more inclusive approach means a larger pool of prospective talent. By investing in inclusive people and culture strategies, businesses can access to up to 20 per cent more candidates. Employing people with diverse abilities also makes good

business sense. They bring a wealth of new ideas, talents and experiences, help to build organizational resilience and improve the businesses' ability to connect with customers in a meaningful way.

3. *The importance of reflecting on your community and creating a positive customer perception*: It is in the best interests of a business to reflect the community they serve. Companies that recruit from a wide range of backgrounds and are known for embracing differences build a reputation as an employer of choice. Having a more representative workforce helps to connect with customers, understand their needs and develop more creative ways to engage. Being inclusive can generate goodwill which delivers competitive advantages, builds brand reputation and provides a point of difference from the competition.

Overcoming challenges: implementation of the learnings

The intent of the IEM and EEO initiatives is to identify collective interest, intent and ambition in progressing real and meaningful employment for people with disability. These initiatives have subsequently informed strategies and pathways for people with different abilities to assist in their career opportunities as well as learnings and strategies for employers to adopt. This work has informed the transformation of HCS in its efforts to employ more people with disability in more meaningful career opportunities.

Within this context, the deliverables for Social Scaffolding's project with HCS included the following:

1. workforce scheduling models for the three HCS business units (food services, cleaning and laundry);
2. a communications plan for supported and mainstream employees;
3. updates to HCS procedures to support the new models;
4. supported employee transition and recruitment planning;
5. a training programme for facilitators and supported employees; and
6. automation of key supported employee processes.

The supported employee transition programme that Social Scaffolding developed consisted of a threefold approach to gather and analyse the supported employee's current and future employment situations, to support HCS transition to the new NDIS pricing model. This involved:

1. investigating the supported employee's work situation, delving into questions of where, how many hours, and what assistance is received at work, based on HCS records;

2. interviewing the supported employees about their future goals and aspirations for work at HCS, current NDIS funding and future training needs and goals; and

3. developing a Supported Employee profile report outlining their needs and wants, including future NDIS supports in employment funding requirements for work at HCS (which will also assist with the supported employees' next NDIS plan review).

The project also included in-depth training for all staff. Whilst the HCS disability training was primarily targeted at supported employees, the involving of all staff enabled cohesion and inclusiveness across all employees. Some of the characteristics of the training programme included:

1. delivering training across the employee journey – joining, growing and exploring;

2. expanding upon traditional workplace training to provide options in areas of interest under the exploring phase;

3. introducing an 'outcomes-focused' reporting tool to support the six-monthly SE reviews; and

4. creating a revenue stream to complement employment services.

With the opportunity for HCS to employ more people and implement the learnings from Social Scaffolding's IEM and EEO initiatives, the stage was set to develop a strategic plan that would enable Holy Cross Services to employ more people with disability. The planning process looked at the current number of supported employees, the necessary support worker ratios, the skill sets required to perform job tasks, the available and potential training on offer to 'upskill' individuals to perform existing tasks and the opportunity for career progression within the organization. This plan was multifaceted and involved the majority of people in the organization. Training was offered to all employees, as was the review and updating of policies and procedures including streamlining recruitment, interviewing and 'onboarding' processes. A campaign promoting to supported employees the skills training on offer in the organization, friendships available and the all-important salary was used through existing employee recruitment channels as well as friends, family, networks and peak bodies relating to the sector.

Not only did HCS experience a reduction in staff turnover attributed to the positive training and work culture, but they also started to hit the employment targets set for the new environment. Those targets had gained little traction owing to the complexities and barriers identified in the case study. Now the targets are being met and more and more people are experiencing employment, and the joy and benefits resulting from ongoing, stable, meaningful employment.

Implications for employer engagement in the future

From a broad perspective, some of the key learnings from this project have been the importance of ongoing review and improvement of an organization's commitment to, and ability to engage with, people of different abilities. The recruitment and selection processes must take into account the needs of, and the benefits offered by, a person with different abilities, and this can often mean improved, accessible and user-friendly information and resources.

A commitment to diversity and inclusion from the top down was also a clear requirement to provide the necessary process, people and clarity on what is expected by an organization and the people working there. This can come from highlighting the unique skills on offer that are beneficial to today's and future employers.

Lessons for all employers to consider and adopt include the following:

1. Employers should develop increased awareness, understanding and knowledge about engagement with and employment of people with disability.
2. Employment should be re-contextualized to be about a skills match between an individual and the employer, rather than about filling diversity quotas.
3. Recruitment and career processes within the organization should be reviewed to ensure they enable people of all abilities to succeed.
4. People with disability must have access to peer supports and champions to increase their knowledge and capacity to engage with employers in meaningful and progressive career opportunities (IEM, 2021).

The opportunities for employment currently in Australia are extremely positive. As a result of COVID limiting overseas arrivals, and the Australian government's unfortunate policy of restricting immigration and support for people seeking asylum, Australia now has a significant demand for workers. The country's unemployment rates are low, and it has growing and emerging industries seeking a workforce; for example an ageing population is seeking aged care, and there is a substantial growth in demand for disability support as a result of the NDIS. Current estimates are that 130,000 to 150,000 new workers will be required over the next few years across the aged care, veterans and disability sectors (ABC News, 2021).

This is good news for people seeking employment. Demand is high, and the federal government has consistently provided necessary skills development and training (either heavily subsidized or free). This means the opportunity for a person with different abilities to gain employment with ANY employer is now greater than ever before. This includes the opportunities for persons of different abilities to be support workers in these high-demand sectors.

The learnings and challenges for the potential employee (a person with different abilities) are to understand this demand from the employer's perspective, matching their unique skills and abilities to the needs of the employer, and then navigating the existing recruitment and onboarding processes into an employer.

The opportunity for the employer is to research and understand that people with different abilities are valuable assets and, in many respects, an untapped market of potential employees. Employers need to understand the unique skills and attributes of a person with different abilities and, if necessary, make suitable efforts to enable the person to thrive within their work environment. Many organizations are providing this level of expertise and upskilling – the opportunity is now for all employers to make this transition.

Notes

[1] Information about the review-of-assessment tools, discriminatory practices and wage assessment guidelines can be found in Australian Government (2018) and DSS: www.dss. gov.au/disability-and-carers/programmes-services/for-people-with-disability/bswat-paym ent-scheme

[2] See Useful links under References at the end of the chapter.

References

ABC News (2021). 'The national campaign tackling a critical support worker shortage', 15 August: www.abc.net.au/news/2021-08-15/disability-minis ter-linda-reynolds-on-new-support-work-campaign/100372022

Australian Government (2018). *Supported wage system under the Supported Employment Services Award (2010): Assessment guidelines V 1.0*, Canberra: Commonwealth Government.

Australian Institute of Health and Welfare (2019). *People with disability in Australia 2019: In brief, How many people have disability?* Canberra: AIHW.

Inclusive Employment Movement (2020). *Inclusive employment: A comprehensive guide to creating a culture of inclusion for people with disability in your organisation*, Brisbane: LeapIn!/IEM.

Social Scaffolding (2020). *EEO_Forum Learnings 19 November 2020*, Brisbane: Social Scaffolding: www.socialscaffolding.com.au/_files/ugd/ a8a967_2560833efdca47689b91862469270e92.pdf?index=true

Useful Links
DXA Technology Dandelion Program: https://dxc.com/au/en/cp/social-impact-practice/dxc-dandelion-program
Holy Cross Services: www.hcl.org.au/our-impact/
Specialisterne: https://specialisterne.com.au/
Xceptional: https://xceptional.io/

PART III

The Micro Level: Workplaces and Their Contexts

10

Who Are the Engaged Employers?
Strategic Entry-Level Resourcing
in Low-Wage Sectors

Patrick McGurk and Richard Meredith

This chapter examines employers' recruitment of staff via active labour market programmes (ALMPs) through the lens of corporate human resource (HR) strategy. It reviews the available evidence on the characteristics of employers engaged with ALMPs in England and highlights their concentration in low-waged sectors, such as retail, hospitality, social care and cleaning. The chapter draws on HR management theory to propose a strategic explanation for why employers in such sectors invest in the recruitment and retention of low-skill employees through engagement with ALMPs. The HR-based proposition is explored through a case study of a supermarket retailer's engagement with the Work Programme, the UK's flagship ALMP initiative from 2011 to 2017.[1]

The chapter has three main sections. In the first section, the available and most up-to-date evidence of the characteristics of ALMP-engaged employers in England is analysed, highlighting the predominance of large employers in sectors characterized by low wages. The sensitivity of the data is discussed. In the second section, Lepak and Snell's (1999) model of HR architecture is elaborated to propose a set of strategic recruitment and retention practices that may be expected to apply to entry-level employment via ALMPs. In the final section we explore our theoretical proposition through a short case study, which presents the experiences of recruiting staff via the Work Programme at 'Midstore', a supermarket retail chain. The case illustrates how engagement is driven by strategic imperatives and sustained by some local managers, yet also constrained by other local managers and various corporate and extraneous factors.

Who are the engaged employers?

The study of employer engagement is relatively new (Ingold and McGurk, this volume), so empirical research to date in this area is rather disparate, and there are few comprehensive explanations for why certain employers might engage. One important and long-standing generalization made in the relevant policy literature (see for example Snape, 1998; Hasluck, 2011), as well as in the related academic literature (van Gestel and Nyberg, 2009; Simms, 2017; van Berkel et al, 2017), is that engaged employers tend to be motivated by a combination of corporate social responsibility and business efficiency concerns. Other, more specific studies have posited that larger organizations with established HR departments and those linked to employer associations are more likely to engage (Martin and Swank, 2004; Ingold and Stuart, 2015). Deckop et al (2006) studied the effects of particular approaches to engagement rather than its motivations, and evaluated the effects of individual employers' HR policies and practices on the retention of former welfare clients, concluding that wage and benefits policy and development opportunities could have positive effects, while supervisory training proved ineffective. However, overall, there has been a dearth of research, especially on the more detailed experiences of employers, including what motivates and sustains their engagement with ALMPs (Ingold and Stuart, 2015).

In more recent years, localized studies have yielded detailed insights, particularly into the interrelationships between employers, ALMP agencies and the changing regulatory environment (Moore et al, 2017; Sissons and Green, 2017). A smaller subset (see Borghouts and Freese, Hanson and Moore and Hanson, Moore and Gustafson in this volume) offers single-employer case studies that provide insights into how internal strategic choices within individual firms are adapted and changed by engagement with ALMPs. Yet so far, the available research has not enabled a comprehensive contextual or theoretically grounded explanation for employer engagement.

Much of the problem with defining or modelling the engaged employer lies in the lack of good data about the demand side of ALMPs. In Germany, the regionalized organization of the public employment services (PES), which matches local employers and jobseekers, enables fairly comprehensive datasets to be produced on both the supply side and the demand side (Hujer and Zeiss, 2003). In the UK, however, there are *no* publicly available records on employers engaged in employment schemes, in stark contrast to the detailed demographic data on jobseekers on the supply side (Armstrong et al, 2011). Although the UK's PES obtains information via ALMP intermediary agencies, the employer data themselves remain commercial-in-confidence within the Provider Referrals and Payments system of the government's Department for Work and Pensions (DWP). The purpose of that system is to facilitate the smooth exchange of digital information about individual jobseekers and payments with providers, and checks on claimed job outcomes; it does not exist to enable analysis of employer engagement.

ALMP-engaged employers in the UK have generally insisted on remaining anonymous for reputational reasons, lest they be publicly accused of exploiting jobseekers who have been compelled by the new welfare regime since 2011 to take up the employment offered or face benefit sanctions. Only one significant break in such employer anonymity appears to have occurred; this was in September 2014, when the trade body for contractors to DWP and a group of more than 150 Work Programme employers wrote to the *Guardian* newspaper to defend the public value of their engagement (McHugh and various employers, 2014). However, to identify a discrete population of engaged employers has not been possible, even for the government's own commissioned research (see, for example, Armstrong et al, 2011).

A cursory insight into the sectoral characteristics of engaged employers also became available in 2014 in an internal newsletter from the Employment Related Services Association. McGurk (2014) analysed this document to show an almost exact match between the economy's lowest-paying sectors (retail, hospitality and cleaning), including the 'temp' recruitment agencies servicing these sectors, and the biggest recruiters of clients from the UK's then flagship Work Programme. While there were some engaged employers in higher-paying sectors such as law and financial services, the numbers of ALMP recruits in those sectors were minimal, suggesting that engagement by such employers was driven by corporate reputation campaigns and not by core human resourcing decisions. McGurk (2014) therefore argues that employers in low-pay sectors are the most likely to engage on a large scale, as they employ high proportions of entry-level workers as part of their core workforces.

Arguably the fullest characterization of engaged employers is to be found in Osterman (2008), who reviewed various ALMP-type programmes in the USA and made three main generalizations about the engaged employers. Osterman (2008) posits that ALMP-engaged employers tend to be:

1. in low-waged sectors;
2. large, as measured by number of employees; and
3. in industries that value workforce stability for continuity of customer service, such as retail and health and social care.

In other words, Osterman suggests that sector, size and strategy are important influences on individual employer engagement. This analysis also partially supports that of Martin and Swank (2004) with regard to the significance of organizational size (and the accompanying presence of a large HR department), at least in the UK.

The insights from the USA and UK, albeit patchy and incomplete, provide strong indications that, for a more detailed understanding of individual employer engagement, it is fruitful to explore the strategic HR resourcing practices of employers in low-wage sectors. In the next section, we develop and propose a strategic HRM model of engagement at the level of the individual employer.

A model of strategic entry-level resourcing

Lepak and Snell (1999, 2002) advance a firm-level theory that conceptualizes four distinct 'bundles' of HR practices, which make up an organization's 'HR architecture'. Two of the four bundles are relevant for modelling the strategic management of recruits from ALMPs in organizations.

In categorizing the HR bundles, Lepak and Snell distinguish between the 'value' of a firm's human resources on one hand and their 'uniqueness' or 'rarity' on the other. The tasks performed by employees may have either a high or a low value with respect to their centrality to the core operation of the business. Likewise, their skills may be of either high or low rarity on the labour market. This combination of high/low value and high/low rarity produces a four-part architecture of HR practice, as depicted in the matrix in Figure 10.1.

Employees who have neither rare skills nor high strategic value to the organization (in the bottom-left quadrant) are termed 'contract workers'. These workers are 'employed on a contract for services basis, either through outsourcing or, if remaining on a contract of employment, on the strict basis of payment for work done' (Martin and Hetrick, 2006, p 183). Unskilled operatives and 'temps' are likely to fall into this category of employees. The HR bundle usually associated with contract workers is 'externalized', as they may be provided by agencies and are therefore not offered development opportunities beyond basic organizational requirements. The relationship with the employer is likely to be 'transactional', consisting of standardized and routinized work tasks that are closely monitored by managers.

Employees who do not have rare skills, but who are of high strategic value to the organization (in the bottom-right quadrant), are termed 'traditional employees'. These workers are highly important for performing core operations and thus adding value for the organization, although their skills are readily available in the open labour market. They might, for example, be operatives, sales staff or junior managers and supervisors. The HR bundle associated with these employees is 'internalized': they are likely to be on permanent contracts and provided with development opportunities. But there is likely to be a transactional relationship with the organization, not a 'relational' one that aims to secure their identification with and commitment to the organization (Martin and Hetrick, 2006).

Figure 10.1: Human resource architecture

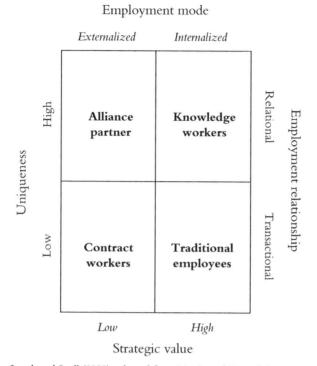

Source: After Lepak and Snell (1999), adapted from Martin and Hetrick (2006, p 184)

Unemployed people participating in ALMPs – namely those with the least bargaining power as they seek to enter or re-enter the labour market – are most likely to be available for employment as contract workers or traditional employees. Employees with highly rare skills – that is, 'alliance partners' and 'knowledge workers' – may well experience unemployment from time to time, but are not representative of jobseekers on ALMPs. At the same time, employers with a strategic preference for human resources of low rarity (that is, traditional employees and contract workers) are most likely to offer entry-level job opportunities to participants of ALMPs. As to whether employers prefer to recruit either contract workers or traditional employees, this depends upon whether employers view them as of low or high strategic value, and thus determines whether they choose to externalize or internalize this source of labour.

Transaction cost economics suggests that a firm will contract out its labour when the 'transaction costs' of maintaining and supervising the contract are lower than the 'bureaucratic costs' of internal staffing (recruitment costs, training, compensation and benefits, and so on) (Lepak and Snell, 1999). Because publicly funded and administered sources of labour should reduce the transaction costs to employers of managing contract workers, this increases the likelihood of engagement by employers who have a strategic preference for contract workers, or who simply seek to fill temporary staffing shortages in low-skill, generic roles. Indeed, such employer behaviour has been highlighted by critics of neoliberal 'workfare' reforms in the UK that compel benefit claimants to take up low-waged or unpaid insecure work, effectively creating an 'industrial reserve army' (Grover, 2003; see also Greer, 2016).

However, the view of employer engagement as an opportunistic externalization strategy, in which employers take advantage of workfare, overlooks the potential strategic benefits of internalization. As Lepak and Snell (1999) note, 'employees can add value if they can help firms offer lower costs or provide increased benefits to customers' (p 35). Thus, it is argued, internalization may be expected when the benefits of reduced employee turnover and the associated consistency in customer service outweigh the accrued bureaucratic costs of increased internal staffing. Lepak and Snell (2002) place a particular importance on customer service, which accounts for six of their twelve measures of strategic human resource value. In their empirical test of the architectural model, they find that '[r]ather than turning over their entire workforce to contractors ... [some] firms are taking steps to ensure they identify and retain those workers who are most critical to their competitiveness' (p 536).

Employers' strategies for the identification and retention of low-skill, yet strategically valuable employees have been well documented in the UK context, particularly in the retail sector where the quality of customer service is central to competitive strategy. For example, Gratton (2003) reports how the UK's largest retailer, Tesco, researched and segmented its workforce into five distinct employee groups. One of the five was the 'work to live' group, identified as mainly long-serving women over 35 years old, uninterested in promotion and willing to do repetitive tasks in return for secure employment close to their home (also cited in Martin and Hetrick, 2006). As with the other four employee segments, Tesco went on to develop tailored strategies to motivate and retain its 'work to live' segment as a means of achieving consistency in customer service (Martin and Hetrick, 2006).

Similar employee segmentation and retention strategies have been observed among employers to whom workforce diversity is an important dimension of their customer service. So, Foster (2004) describes how the retailer Marks & Spencer introduced strategies to recruit ethnic minority staff 'in an effort to lose its white, middle-class English image', and how the do-it-yourself store B&Q targeted older recruits because they 'found that older staff were more likely to have owned a house and carried out home improvements than younger employees and therefore in a position to offer [do-it-yourself] advice to customers' (p 442). Strategies of this kind are familiar as part of a 'business case for diversity', which advocates the recruitment and retention of customer-facing staff who possess the requisite 'soft skills' and share the visible characteristics of the community being served (Foster, 2004; Bleijenbergh et al, 2010; Syed and Ozbilgin, 2019). The real extent to which such strategies are implemented in organizations remains, however, a moot point.

With regard to ALMP initiatives, it is important to investigate the possibility that low-wage, low-skill employee segmentation strategies represent a significant motivation for employer engagement (see also Martin and Swank (2004), with regard to the UK). To this end, sustained employer engagement may be reinterpreted as a process of strategic investment of internalization and development. Such a process would involve ALMP participants being recruited either directly as traditional employees, or as contract workers who are then identified and retained as traditional employees. This would require employers to form ongoing partnerships with active intermediaries. In contrast, weak employer engagement would be represented by occasional dealings with passive intermediaries for the purposes of recruiting temporary contract labour, even if in large volumes.

In summary, the degree of sustained employer engagement may be understood as a continuum along which a firm treats ALMP participants either as contract workers or traditional employees. This continuum is depicted in Figure 10.2.

The central proposition here is that sustained employer engagement is most likely among employers that rely on a large supply of low-wage, low-skill labour for their core operations *and* place a strategic premium on customer service (therefore requiring 'soft skills'), leading them to develop strategies to retain and internalize recruits from ALMPs. The next section of this chapter presents a case study as an exploration of this proposition.

Case study: strategic entry-level resourcing at 'Midstore'

The food retail sector provides a prime site for a case study of a low-wage, customer-service-oriented employer. As McGurk's (2014) research showed, at least at the time, retail was responsible for more job placements of ALMP participants than any other sector in the UK, with food retail representing the largest sub-sector. The national food retail chain 'Midstore' provided the opportunity to study an exemplar case of firm-level, ALMP-related recruitment and retention policies and practices, as well as their outcomes in terms of the experiences of managers and employees at local branch level. Midstore had a history of engagement with ALMP initiatives and, under the Work Programme, had seconded two full-time staff from a private intermediary to work in its national office to coordinate its pre-employment

Figure 10.2: A model of sustained employer engagement

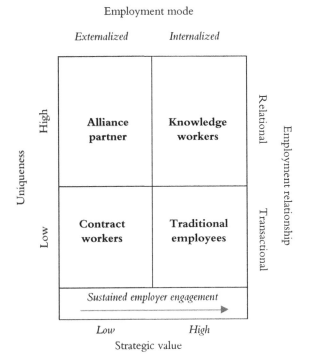

Employment mode

Externalized   *Internalized*

| | Alliance partner | Knowledge workers | |
| | Contract workers | Traditional employees | |

High / Low — Uniqueness

Relational / Transactional — Employment relationship

Sustained employer engagement

Low   *High*

Strategic value

training, recruitment and follow-up support activities (see also retail case study in Baker, Ingold, Crichton and Carr, this volume).

Data collection took place between February and April 2014, involving access to organizational documentation and information system reports, as well as transcriptions from semi-structured interviews with 12 National, Regional, Area and Store Managers (including two staff at national level seconded from the intermediary) and a 'snowball' sample of 21 shopfloor staff, including both Customer Service Assistants and Supervisors. Of the 13 Customer Service Assistants interviewed, ten had been recruited from the Work Programme and three through internal transfers from other Midstore stores. Of the eight Supervisors interviewed, four had been recruited via the Work Programme, with two recruited directly into Supervisor roles and the other two promoted after a few months from Customer Service Assistant roles. In total, 32 interviews were conducted across the four stores.

Partnership with the intermediary

The introduction of the Work Programme at Midstore coincided with a rapid expansion in the business, accompanied by a strategic concern to improve community engagement. From November 2011, Midstore worked in partnership with two private intermediaries. In January 2014, however, the partnership with one of the intermediaries was terminated owing to quality concerns, leaving the other as its sole lead partner. This lead-intermediary then worked together with Midstore's community engagement team at national level to refine a model of recruitment and selection for the long-term unemployed to be applied across Midstore's stores; the intermediary sub-contracted out the model to other regions in which it was not the 'prime contractor'.

Before engagement in the Work Programme, Midstore's Store Managers had been solely responsible for their own recruitment of shopfloor staff. Recruitment methods tended to be informal, using word-of-mouth, personal referrals by staff and job adverts in the shop window. Also, the managers tended to recruit for technical aptitude, such as in handling stock and operating tills, rather than for competence in customer service. Overall, senior managers considered their traditional recruitment practices to be unproductive, ineffective and inefficient. In the words of one Area Manager: "store managers might have just fitted in people for interviews during the normal working day in their small offices next to the filing cabinet … sometimes [they were] interviewing people who couldn't string a sentence together" (Interview with Area Manager X). Another effect of informal recruitment by referral among friends and family was to select disproportionately from among the Store Manager's own ethnic group, a complaint made by all the senior managers interviewed, who expressed concerns about the lack of workforce diversity in many of their stores.

The work of the intermediary secondees was mainly concentrated on 'academies', three-week pre-employment training courses tailored specifically for Midstore. The academies were delivered by intermediary staff, using one of their own offices near to where new Midstore branches were due to open. Each academy had an average of 15–30 participants on referral from the local Jobcentre Plus office. Candidate retention during the academies was typically 60–70 per cent. At the end of each academy, two local Midstore Store Managers – specially appointed as 'recruiting managers' – held a day of selection interviews at the intermediary's local office. The interviews used scenario-based questions designed to demonstrate the candidate's aptitude for customer service, rather than technical aptitude; for example, candidates might be asked how they might handle a particularly demanding customer or delays in the bakery section of the store. Midstore made job offers to an average of 25–30 per cent of the interviewees at the selection days. In 2013, the company filled approximately 10 per cent of its several thousand shopfloor vacancies through these academies although, for new store openings, and in particular areas of the country such as London, the percentage was much higher.

Regional and Area Managers, effectively the local sponsors of the academies, were generally supportive of the new approach to recruitment offered by engagement with the Work Programme. The academies, in a phrase echoed by three managers, had delivered "the right calibre of people" (Interview with Regional Manager X). One Area Manager opined that the academies had "raised the bar" in terms of Store Managers' expectations of the quality of recruits that they should be hiring, and that the intermediary candidates, having been unemployed for more than six months, were often "thankful to be in work", meaning that Store Managers were better able to generate a "sense of pride" in the new stores. This was said to contrast with the "job for life" culture and the disengaged attitude prevalent among many of the more established stores that were staffed by long-serving employees (Interview with Area Manager X). The generally positive perception was summarized by one of the special recruiting Store Managers, working with the intermediary "has ... definitely been a positive process, no question. It's made our lives easier and it has ... brought some good-calibre people into the store that otherwise we wouldn't have ever had the chance to meet" (Interview with Store Manager X1).

Enthusiasm was not completely unequivocal among managers, however. Some considered the traditional, informal methods of local recruitment still to have a place. As one Area Manager explained:

'It is also important for customers to see through posters and word-of-mouth that ongoing recruitment is happening in the local community, say for students and young people and others looking for part-time jobs. We don't want our customers to say "Where have all your staff come from? We didn't know that you were recruiting."' (Interview with Area Manager Y)

Several managers also questioned the suitability and work-readiness of many of the candidates put forward for interview by the intermediary. In the words of one (otherwise sympathetic) Store Manager:

'I've had people put in front of me that I'm told can speak English and clearly can't. I've had people put in front of me that I've actually had to leave the room afterwards, open the windows and smother the room in air-freshener and not been able to go back in for a good ten minutes because their personal hygiene has been that awful ... I've had people put in front of me that I've already seen before and already rejected. So they're the negatives. And then I've had [other] people ... put in front of me who [have] come and been nothing but positive for the store.' (Interview with Store Manager X1)

Overall, the data from the intermediary suggested a successful partnership with Midstore. The proportion of academy candidates being offered jobs was about average for the Work Programme. However, the number of job starters retained for up to six months in 2013 was over 80 per cent, 5 per cent higher than the national average and 10 per cent above Midstore's own annual staff retention (Midstore HR information system). Nevertheless, there was some frustration expressed on both sides of the partnership about a lack of understanding and engagement. On the intermediary side, the secondees complained that Store Managers lost interest in the partnership once their new store was fully staffed and reverted to their traditionally informal recruitment practices, rather than engage with the intermediary for their ongoing churn vacancies. Also, they were of the opinion that engagement was hindered by some Midstore managers who had overly rigid attitudes towards candidates who required more flexible working arrangements, such as parents of young children, people with specific medical needs or college attendees. On the Midstore side, some Store Managers expressed the regret that they were not more closely involved in the design and delivery of the academies, so that interview candidates might be better prepared and knowledgeable about Midstore.

Local HR practices

There was some conflict between Midstore's usual terms and conditions of employment for shopfloor staff and government regulations around the employment of recruits via the Work Programme. Midstore Store Managers generally preferred to offer eight-hour per week contracts to shopfloor staff, under which employees worked four-hour shifts on two different days, thus avoiding the need to pay them for lunch breaks. Government regulations, however, stipulated that recruits from the Work Programme had to be employed for at least sixteen hours per week in order to be removed from unemployment benefit. This constrained Store Managers' flexibility to employ a large number of people on eight-hour per week contracts to staff their weekly shift rotas. In practice, however, although Store Managers tended to complain about this restriction, the shopfloor staff interviewed in this study, almost without exception, were asked to work well over sixteen hours per week. This happened often with less than a week's notice and regardless of whether the staff had been recruited through the Work Programme. It was especially true of the eight Supervisors interviewed, who typically worked 25–40 hours per week. In effect, therefore, Midstore's normal, casualized approach to employment was unchanged by recruitment from the Work Programme.

The casualized approach to contractual hours for shopfloor staff extended to pay and other terms and conditions. All shopfloor staff, whether from the Work Programme or otherwise, were paid the 2014 London statutory minimum wage of £6.50 per hour, with Supervisors receiving approximately £1.00 extra per hour in return for extra responsibilities such as overseeing price reductions and stock deliveries, opening and closing the store and completing paperwork. Training for all new shopfloor staff consisted of a week's basic course prior to starting work. This varied in quality, however, mainly depending on whether it was conducted off-the-job in one of Midstore's training facilities, as was generally preferred by new recruits, or on-the-job in a larger store, where training tended to be more haphazard. Once in store, ongoing development for shopfloor staff was the responsibility of the Store Manager, who mainly relied upon informal, on-the-job methods and on the company's online learning modules, completed by shopfloor staff on an ad hoc basis on the computer in the manager's office during slack periods. Mainly, Supervisors would be asked to attend occasional training days at one of Midstore's regional training centres; these day courses tended to cover technical compliance, on issues such as alcohol licensing. Unlike some of their larger competitors, Midstore did not offer retail apprenticeships. Formal development opportunities were therefore scarce, with opportunities for hourly-paid shopfloor staff limited to promotion to Supervisor (two or three positions per store) and to the rarer, salaried positions of Assistant Store Manager (one or two positions per store) or Store Manager (one position per store).

Despite the casualized, poorly paid and generally 'low-road' nature of the shopfloor jobs at Midstore, morale among the shopfloor staff was reasonably high. Those interviewed were generally positive about their opportunities for interaction with customers, especially the regular and elderly ones. Also, as most had experienced long-term unemployment, the staff generally welcomed being in paid work and the opportunity to mix with colleagues in the workplace. The main negatives were reported as the variability and unpredictability of working hours and the stresses of the job caused by frequent short-staffing and – in some stores – lack of security. The security problem was compounded when having to attend to urgent and physically demanding tasks on the shop floor, such as unpacking stock. Similarly, the supervisors interviewed generally enjoyed the extra responsibility that came with their role, but complained about the lack of specific training and support and the sporadic provision of security staff.

The case of Midstore therefore provides some support for the general proposition: that low-wage, customer-service-oriented employers internalize and retain their recruits from ALMPs as part of their core workforce. Employment at Midstore was so casualized, however, that for the organization there was little distinction between 'contract workers' and 'traditional employees'. This raises the question of the sustainability of Midstore's engagement.

Sustainability of engagement: a tale of four stores

Further analysis at branch level – in two local stores each in two different areas of London, 'X' and 'Y' – sheds light on two main factors influencing the sustainability of employer engagement: i) local manager attitudes and competence; and ii) the quality of the relationship with the local intermediary.

In Store X1, during 2013, five recruits joined from the local intermediary academy, and all were retained at least into the second quarter of 2014. Several proved to be motivated and community-minded individuals. For example, one recruit established a connection with a group of international students who lived in the accommodation above the store and arranged to teach them cooking skills in his free time. There were also examples of the participation of some of the new recruits in local community events such as charity action days. By the end of the first quarter of 2014, customer satisfaction was measured as higher than other store averages for the area, region and country.

Engagement with the ALMP in Store X1 was sustained, in that new recruits were exclusively recruited from the Work Programme and retained as the core workforce. Above all, these recruits were perceived by managers, partly by virtue of their ethnic diversity, to be valuable for customer service. The key to this sustained engagement was the motivation of the Store Manager. His role as one of the area recruiting managers enabled him to see that the Work Progamme provided his best chance of a stable supply of suitable local labour for his store and other stores in his area. The proactive approach of the intermediary to partnering with the local recruiting managers was also an important contributory factor. Store Manager X1 had perceived the previous intermediary as poor, regarding them as presenting inappropriate candidates, just to 'fill gaps' for the opening of the new store. While also not unequivocally complimentary about the new intermediary, he nonetheless recognized that they provided a superior service, allowing the company use of their fit-for-purpose offices for interviewing, offering better-calibre candidates for interview, 'sending us home in taxis [and] giving us lunch'.

In contrast, Store X2 opened in March 2013 under a newly promoted Store Manager, who had spent several years with the company in a number of stores, initially as a Customer Service Assistant while at university. The new store was staffed with a roughly equal mixture of 19 recruits from the intermediary, local enquiries and staff referrals. Two of the intermediary recruits were promoted to Supervisor within 12 months, one of whom was transferred to a neighbouring store.

The store had a difficult first year. It received low customer satisfaction scores in the company's quarterly 'mystery shopper' surveys and experienced the highest staff turnover in the area. At least 50 per cent of the academy recruits did not complete the 13-week probationary period. Although he had access to the same pool of Work Programme recruits as the previous Store Manager, Store Manager X2 continued to recruit from a mixture of sources. On one hand, he recognized the potential value for customer service of Work Programme recruits:

'everyone who's here and … been through the programme, they live nearby. So they … know the community, they know people … [A] customer walks in and goes up to our colleagues and speaks to them, [they] have a conversation … So that really helps.' (Interview with Store Manager X2)

On the other hand, the manager did not sustain his engagement owing to the retention difficulties encountered. While recognizing that the Work Programme had provided some "really good local colleagues", he complained that "we only manage to keep hold of half of the people we get … Either they leave or they just won't go past the probation, they find it really hard". Unlike Store Manager X1, he did not perceive there to be any difference in the quality of service provided by the previous and current intermediaries, but in any case he had little contact with the current intermediary representative.

While the weak engagement at Store X2 may be largely explained by local managerial attitude, the Store Manager's relative lack of interest may have been compounded by a lack of support from senior management in other aspects of the job. For example, he complained about the ongoing problem of lack of security at the store, which he saw as a particular issue given the close proximity of some large housing estates and a drugs treatment clinic. This perception was reinforced by interviews with three shopfloor interviewees, who reported recent violent incidents in the shop and that they sometimes felt unsafe working in the store. As one Supervisor described the security staffing arrangements:

'[The security guard] gets two days off [per week] and people around here know when he's off … [laughs]. Yesterday they came in and took all the cheese. And I went out specifically to get one person who'd stolen yoghurts and when I came back to check the CCTV camera I realized that as I was coming back another person's been stuffing their bags with everything.' (Interview with Supervisor X2)

On balance, however, the interviews with the shopfloor staff suggested that the weak engagement of Store X2 could not be entirely blamed on lack of senior management support. Customer Service Assistants and Supervisors alike complained of poor store management, manifested in bad organization of shifts and working hours, a lack of individual and team communication, and a lack of recognition of staff effort. The contrast with Store X1, which recruited staff via the same intermediary, yet which approached its resourcing and retention differently, demonstrates that demotivated local management, due perhaps in part to a lack of training and support, was the key contributory factor to weak engagement at Store X2.

Store Y1 opened in December 2013 under a newly promoted Store Manager, who (like the manager at Store X2) had spent several years with the company across a number of stores, initially as a Customer Service Assistant while at university. The store's Assistant Manager, three Supervisors and two of the fifteen Customer Service Assistants were recruited via internal transfers from other stores, while the other thirteen shopfloor staff were recruited via the Work Programme. Ten of the thirteen ALMP recruits were retained between January and April 2014, which represented a relatively low staff turnover for the area. The store was struggling to compete with neighbouring supermarket outlets, but both the store and area management considered it 'early days' and were not overly concerned.

Like Store Manager X1, Store Manager Y1 was one of the recruiting managers in his area and had an overall positive attitude towards the Work Programme and its recruits. Although he described the shortlist of interviewees at the academy as a "mixed batch", he considered it "a good experience for me to come across these people" and those he recruited to be "very, very interesting characters". He was also positive about his experience of working with the intermediary: "it was a very, very good experience. They did provide us a kind of an office to get interviews, they did provide us with all the stationery" (Interview with Store Manager Y1). The Store Manager related that he had received two follow-up phone calls in the past three months from the intermediary to check on the progress of the new recruits.

Also notable at Store Y1 was evidence of good practice in people management. The Store Manager described how he held regular team communication 'huddles', informal communications with staff at least once or twice per day and periodic staff recognition sales competitions for £10 or £15 vouchers. His claim was supported in interviews with the shopfloor staff and, despite some complaints about lack of notice about the shift rota and about low pay, the shopfloor staff were appreciative, especially of the efforts taken by the Manager and Supervisors to communicate frequently and in a friendly manner. As one Customer Service Assistant described it:

'[T]he managers [are] not always serious, they like to like juggle round and have fun with you. They don't just, like, put you in a place and say "Look, do this, we're not going to teach you nothing", they actually teach you, they ask you if you need more help … [I]f I have any problems I just go straight to them … I don't have to raise my hand and ask them a question, I just go and speak normally to them.' (Interview with Customer Service Assistant Y2)

Another shopfloor worker emphasized the climate of mutual support that the manager had promoted in the store: "every single one of us, like the manager always tells us, to support each other, like no matter … even if you have a task, help the other colleague if he needs help" (Interview with Customer Service Assistant Y2b).

Like Store X1, therefore, the strong engagement of Store Y1 may be largely explained by involved and motivated store management, combined with the proactive partnership approach of the Work Programme intermediary.

In contrast, Store Y2 opened in March 2013, originally under an experienced Store Manager on temporary assignment from another store. Two further Store Managers followed in quick succession but were transferred to other Store Manager positions within the company owing to a "lack of fit" with this particular store. The fourth Store Manager joined the store in January 2014, having been newly promoted after spending several years with the company across a number of stores, initially as a Customer Service Assistant while at college. Store Y2 was staffed with a roughly equal mixture of 17 recruits from the ALMP intermediary, local enquiries and personal referrals. Although one recruit from the intermediary was retained and promoted to Supervisor within a few months, there had been a high turnover of staff recruited from the Work Programme. After a few months, the store reverted to its traditional method of recruitment by placing job ads in the shop window, after which, according to one Customer Service Assistant, "we were inundated with CVs".

The new Store Manager had a generally positive attitude towards the intermediary, but struggled with the store's legacy of instability in its management and staffing. His short time as manager had been dominated by the need to address sickness and issues of poor performance among the staff, regardless of where they had been recruited from. After a few months, however, he felt that he had managed to stabilize his staffing and provide sufficient training and support, and had reached a point where he could focus on developing the employees' skills and positive workplace relationships: "I respect them and they will respect [me] back" (Interview with Store Manager Y2). Nonetheless, negative attitudes towards staff recruited from the Work Programme persisted in the store, as one Supervisor illustrated: "Earlier, when the store was opened we had some bad people [laughs]. Yeah, they came from Jobcentre, they were just so lazy people … [The] people [who] come from Jobcentre, they are totally different, that's the problem" (Interview with Supervisor Y2).

The interviews suggested that the shopfloor staff were appreciative of the new manager's efforts and that he had helped develop a mutually supportive environment since his arrival. Like in Store X2, however, managers and shopfloor staff both complained of a lack of senior management support, communication and organization. There were similar complaints about violent customer incidents and the lack of consistent security provision in the store: "When we have an incident they have a security guard for two weeks and then they remove [them]" (Interview with Supervisor Y2).

The case of Store Y2 reinforces the conclusion reached in the case of Store X1, that the quality of local management and its associated senior management support play a significant role in the strength and sustainability of employer engagement. However, the case of Store Y2 also demonstrates the limits of well-meaning and positive management if it arrives too little and too late, once the initial resourcing of a new business unit has been completed and less conducive workplace norms have already been established (see also Hanson and Moore, this volume).

Analysis of influencing factors

Overall, the Midstore case illustrates how employer engagement may be less about internalizing ALMP recruits as traditional core employees and more about seamlessly incorporating an increased group of strategically valuable contract workers. The store-level cases also illustrate how the practice of employer engagement is driven by strategic imperatives, sustained by local enablers, and constrained by local as well as corporate and extraneous factors. This analysis is summarized in Figure 10.3.

Figure 10.3: Influencing factors on employer engagement at Midstore

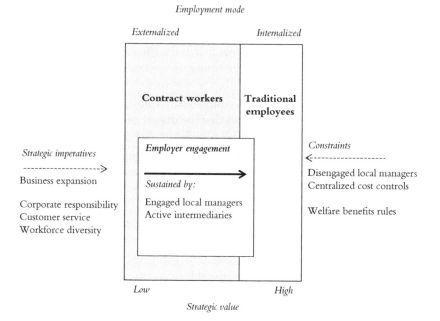

The Midstore case therefore produces some evidence in support of the proposition that engaged employers are likely to invest in the recruitment, retention and development of ALMP recruits as traditional employees because of the consistencies to be achieved in customer service. Staff recruitment and retention for customer service was clearly an important motivation for engagement at corporate, regional and area level, as well as in two of the four store-level cases. However, staff development was not a priority at any level, with almost no evidence of investment in ongoing development or the creation of career ladders for staff. The only 'good jobs' at Midstore were the Assistant Manager and Store Manager roles; all other roles were insecure, hourly paid and often subject to variable hours. In working environments such as the one at Midstore, there was no meaningful distinction between contract workers and traditional employees, as conceptualized by Lepak and Snell. This calls into question the validity of their conceptual category of the internalized, strategically valuable core employee in the contemporary service sector environment.

While the Midstore case does not therefore fully support the concept of sustained employer engagement through internalization, it nevertheless illustrates the complexities of how employer engagement plays out in practice, in three specific ways. First, the case showed that, although corporate responsibility and strategic concerns with customer service and workforce diversity were important drivers of engagement, the principal driver was the strategy of business expansion, fuelling recruitment to staff the company's new stores. This lends further support to previous arguments by Osterman (2008) and McGurk (2014) that employer engagement activity is usually associated with the staffing of new business facilities (often as a condition of local government planning agreements).

Second, through its store-level comparisons, the case demonstrated the influential role played by local operational managers, in combination with active intermediaries, for sustaining engagement through positive and engaged people management. Previous research on managers in the retail sector (Grugulis et al, 2011) suggests that the discretion afforded to the local managers at Midstore is unusual; this may be related to Midstore's medium size, rather than the huge scale operated by many national and international retail chains. Nonetheless, the Midstore case reinforces the arguments of Boxall and Purcell (2011) about the crucial role of managers in implementing HRM. Similarly, it reinforces the arguments made by Osterman (2008) and various ALMP evaluators (for example Hasluck, 2011) about the effectiveness of active rather than passive intermediaries.

Third, the case provides insights into the actual constraints on engagement at firm level. Disengaged or demotivated local managers were shown to be at least as influential in constraining employer engagement as engaged local managers were in sustaining it. Local management disengagement and/or lack of competence is therefore a key constraint, but arguably this is also related to the tight corporate control over costs, exerted often without accompanying support from senior managers. In the case of Midstore, although Store Managers may have had some influence over resource provision at local unit level, it is also arguable that corporate financial controls were responsible for the lack of local control over employee development and reward and over the provision of security staff.

Finally, a significant external, contextual influence on engagement is the changing welfare benefits system, and local managers' navigation of this in partnership with their ALMP intermediary. In the Midstore case, local managers were clearly aware of the upper limit of sixteen hours per week for Work Programme participants and followed strategies to mitigate pressures to issue less casualized, 16-hour per week employment contracts in favour of more flexible 4-hour shifts.

It is instructive to examine the extra managerial flexibilities offered by changes to the UK benefits system since 2017 with the introduction of the system Universal Credit (UC).[2] Partly based on consultations with employers (Rotik and Perry, 2011; Jigsaw Research, 2014), UC reforms ensured on one hand a marked increase in conditions placed on jobseekers and registered carers, accompanied by stronger incentives to accept paid employment. On the other, the reforms ensured a marked decrease in the constraints placed on employers to offer zero- or variable-hours employment contract terms, accompanied by more generous and tailored access to government-subsidized pre-employment training (Royston, 2012; Dwyer and Wright, 2014).

Unpublished research by Meredith (2021) observes how engaged employers, with long-standing relationships with intermediaries, adapted their conditions of employment for new staff to fit to conditionality rules for in-work UC support, based on adverts from the government (DWP, 2014). For example, in sectors such as home care, industrial cleaning and retail, Meredith (2021) found that employers designed employment contracts to fit Universal Credit as an in-work benefit with the aims of addressing instabilities in staffing, reducing training costs and containing costs during periods of peak operational activity (that is, early mornings and late evenings). The role of the PES in supporting ALMP recruits and employers in their retention and progression policies was diminished through the UC reforms, with a stronger and narrower focus on job outcomes and the straightforward averting of unemployment (Meredith, 2021). In short, we may expect the external factor of the changing benefits regime to grow in significance in shaping employer engagement in the UK, further blurring the distinction between contract workers and traditional employees.

Conclusion

This chapter has drawn on strategic HRM theory, in particular that of employee segmentation (Lepak and Snell, 1999, 2002), to propose that the engagement of low-wage, customer-service-oriented employers with ALMP initiatives is sustained as part of core human resourcing strategy. This involves, it has been argued, the ongoing recruitment of long-term unemployed people, as well as their retention and development within the core workforce, as a means of achieving the strategic goal of consistent customer service (compare Osterman, 2008).

Some support for this proposition was provided through a case study of an exemplar low-wage, customer service-oriented employer. The study suggested that, while such employers are motivated to engage by strategic concerns to recruit suitable customer service-oriented staff, and sometimes recruit exclusively from ALMPs for these purposes, engagement is unlikely to be sustained unless intermediaries are active and local managers are motivated and empowered. Moreover, the study suggests that employer engagement, however strong this may be in the short to medium term, will not be sustained over the longer term so long as organizations use low-road employment models. If the core workforce in low-wage sectors are effectively employed as contract workers, rather than 'traditional employees' with permanent contracts and development opportunities, then employers are likely to treat ALMP intermediaries mainly as publicly funded recruitment agencies used to solve short-term staffing needs (Gore, 2005; Greer, 2016; Greer et al, 2017). While some low-wage employers may choose to adopt 'higher-road' employment practices (Appelbaum and Batt, 1994), further research is needed to establish whether employer engagement could be sustained by more professional HR practices and by greater opportunities for employee development and promotion along recognized 'career ladders' (Osterman, 2008).

Our study has been limited to the hypothesis that employer engagement is motivated by the strategic goal of achieving consistent customer service through stable recruitment and retention. Comparative case studies should test this assumption further, by widening the enquiry to low-wage employers in predominantly non-customer-facing operating environments, such as facilities management (cleaning and security), warehousing and distribution. Nonetheless our study has an important implication for policymakers in highlighting the importance of *sustained* employer engagement. It is generally understood that successful employer engagement depends in the first instance on partnerships between competent, active intermediaries and committed, socially responsible employers. But sustained engagement requires sustainable jobs. Unless employers are incentivized to introduce more professional HR practices and offer recognized career ladders to entry-level workers, employer engagement will represent little more than a publicly funded perpetuation of low-road employment practices.

Notes

[1]   The Work Programme was a major payment-for-results ALMP throughout Great Britain from 2011 to 2017, launched under the Conservative-led coalition government of 2010–15.

[2]   Universal Credit is a UK-wide system of means-tested benefit for adults on low incomes, introduced by the Conservative government of 2015. It replaced six means-tested 'legacy' benefits.

References

Appelbaum, E. and Batt, R.L. (1994). *The new American workplace: Transforming work systems in the United States*, Ithaca, NY: ILR Press.

Armstrong, D., Cummings, C.-A., Jones, K. and McConville, E. (2011). *Welfare to work commissioning – Wave Two provider survey*, Research Report No. RR757, Department for Work and Pensions: www.gov.uk/governm ent/publications/welfare-to-work-commissioning-wave-two-provider-sur vey-rr757

Bleijenbergh, I., Peters, P. and Poutsma, E. (2010). 'Diversity management beyond the business case', *Equality, Diversity and Inclusion: An International Journal* 29(5): 413–421.

Boxall, P. and Purcell P. (2011). *Strategy and human resource management*, Basingstoke, Palgrave Macmillan.

Deckop, J.R., Konrad, A.M., Perlmutter, F.D. and Freely, J.L. (2006). 'The effect of human resource management practices on the job retention of former welfare clients', *Human Resource Management*, 45(4): 539–559.

Department for Work and Pensions (DWP) (2014). How Universal Credit can help your business, Guidance, Department for Work and Pensions: www.gov.uk/government/publications/how–universal–credit-can-help-your-business

Dwyer, P. and Wright, S. (2014). 'Universal Credit, ubiquitous conditionality and its implications for social citizenship', *Journal of Poverty and Social Justice* 22(1): 27–35.

Foster, C. (2004). 'Gendered retailing: A study of customer perceptions of front-line staff in the DIY sector', *International Journal of Retail & Distribution Management* 32(9): 442–7.

Gore, T. (2005). 'Extending employability or solving employers' recruitment problems? Demand-led approaches as an instrument of labour market policy', *Urban Studies* 42(2): 341–53.

Gratton, L. (2003). *The democratic enterprise: Liberating your business with individual freedom and shared purpose*, Englewood Cliffs, NJ: Prentice Hall.

Greer, I. (2016). 'Welfare reform, precarity and the re-commodification of labour', *Work, Employment & Society* 30(1): 162–73.

Greer, I., Breidahl, K.N., Knuth, M. and Larsen, F. (2017). *The marketization of employment services*, Vol. 1, Oxford: Oxford University Press.

Grover, C. (2003). '"New Labour", welfare reform and the reserve army of labour', *Capital & Class* 27(1): 17–23.

Grugulis, I., Bozkurt, Ö. and Clegg, J. (2011). '"No place to hide"? The realities of leadership in UK supermarkets.' In I. Grugulis and Ö. Bozkurt (eds) *Retail work*, Basingstoke: Palgrave, pp 193–212.

Hasluck, C. (2011). *Employers and the recruitment of unemployed people: An evidence review*, briefing paper, UK Commission for Employment and Skills: www.gov.uk/government/publications/employers-and-the-recruitment-of-young-people-an-evidence-review

Hujer, R. and Zeiss, C. (2003). 'Macroeconomic impacts of ALMP on the matching process in West Germany', *SSRN Electronic Journal*: https://doi.org/10.2139/ssrn.464683

Ingold, J. and Stuart, M. (2015). 'The demand-side of active labour market policies: A regional study of employer engagement in the Work Programme', *Journal of Social Policy* 44(03): 443–62.

Jigsaw Research (2014). *Universal Credit employers' insight*, Research and Analysis, Department for Work and Pensions: www.gov.uk/government/publications/universal-credit-employers-insight

Lepak, D.P. and Snell, S.A. (1999). 'The human resource architecture: toward a theory of human capital allocation and development', *Academy of Management Review* 24(1): 31–48.

Lepak, D.P. and Snell, S.A. (2002). 'Examining the human resource architecture: The relationships among human capital, employment, and human resource configurations', *Journal of Management* 28(4): 517–43.

Martin, C.J. and Swank, D. (2004). 'Does the organization of capital matter? Employers and active labor market policy at the national and firm levels', *American Political Science Review* 98(04): 593–611.

Martin, G. and Hetrick, S. (2006). *Corporate Reputations, Branding and People Management: A strategic approach to HR*, 1st edn, London: Butterworth-Heinemann.

McGurk, P. (2014). Employer Engagement: A human resource management perspective, Working Paper No. WERU7, Business School Working Paper Series, University of Greenwich: www2.gre.ac.uk/__data/assets/pdf_file/0004/1060933/McGurk-WERU-working-paper-May-2014.pdf

McHugh, K. and various employers (2014). 'Back-to-work help', The Guardian, Letters, 9 September.

Meredith, R. (2021). 'Employer engagement with government employment and skills initiatives', unpublished PhD thesis, University of Greenwich.

Moore, K., McDonald, P. and Bartlett, J. (2017). 'The social legitimacy of disability inclusive human resource practices: The case of a large retail organisation – the social legitimacy of disability employment', *Human Resource Management Journal* 27(4): 514–29.

Osterman, P. (2008). 'Improving job quality: Policies aimed at the demand side of the low wage labor market.' In T.J. Bartik and S.N. Houseman (eds) *A future of good jobs? America's challenge in the global economy*, Kalamazoo, MI: W.E. Upjohn Institute for Employment Research, pp 203–44.

Rotik, M. and Perry, L. (2011). Perceptions of welfare reform and Universal Credit, Research Report No. RR778, Department for Work and Pensions: www.gov.uk/government/publications/perceptions-of-welfare-reform-and-universal-credit-rr778

Royston, S. (2012). 'Understanding Universal Credit', *Journal of Poverty and Social Justice* 20(1): 69–86.

Simms, M. (2017). 'Understanding employer engagement in youth labour market policy in the UK: Understanding employer engagement', *Human Resource Management Journal* 27(4): 548–64.

Sissons, P. and Green, A.E. (2017). 'More than a match? Assessing the HRM challenge of engaging employers to support retention and progression: Challenge of employer engagement', *Human Resource Management Journal* 27(4): 565–80.

Snape, D. (1998). *Recruiting long-term unemployed people*, No. 76; Social Security Research, Department of Social Security.

Syed, J. and Ozbilgin, M. (eds) (2019). *Managing diversity and inclusion: An international perspective*, 2nd edn, Newbury Park, CA: SAGE Publishing.

van Berkel, R., Ingold, J., McGurk, P., Boselie, P. and Bredgaard, T. (2017). 'Editorial introduction: An introduction to employer engagement in the field of HRM. Blending social policy and HRM research in promoting vulnerable groups' labour market participation: Employer engagement in the field of HRM', *Human Resource Management Journal* 27(4): 503–13.

van Gestel, N. and Nyberg, D. (2009). 'Translating national policy changes into local HRM practices', *Personnel Review* 38(5): 544–59.

11

HRM and Social Security: It Takes Two to Create a Transitional Labour Market

Irmgard Borghouts and Charissa Freese

Introduction

Social security and social policy science studies the function, organization, legal basis, costs and effects of social security and labour. The public social security system protects individuals and households against the financial consequences of illness, disability, unemployment and old age. Since the end of the 1980s, socially activating labour market policies in Europe have been aimed at allowing people who do not participate in the labour market to enter the regular labour market as much as possible, so that they no longer have to use social security benefits (typically, a volume policy that aims to minimize the number of people on social benefits). The core idea behind this is that the best form of social security is to be able to obtain and keep work as a source of income. In the mid-1990s, labour market research shifted towards a transitional perspective on labour markets (Schmid, 1995). Social security thinking is no longer about the current labour market status of individuals (employed or unemployed), but also about accounting for the transition people make to, in and from the labour market. This more dynamic view of the European labour market is referred to as the transitional labour market (Schmid and Gazier, 2002). Employment security (the possibility of finding employment and remaining employed, but not necessarily in the same job with the same employer) (Borghouts-van de Pas, 2010) is the new focal concept replacing the concept of job security (expectations of holding a specific job for a long time) (Wilthagen and Tros, 2004; European Foundation for the Improvement of Living and Working Conditions, 2008). The transition from one job to another in the event of redundancy, instead of the transition to unemployment, is a crucial one that enhances employment security (Voss et al, 2009). Employers, not social policymakers, offer jobs and employment. Taking this perspective as a starting point, it is important to focus on the coherence and mutual influence of social security and employer behaviour by means of their human resource management (HRM) policies in facilitating a transitional labour market. In this chapter, we bring together the scientific domains of HRM and social security to gain more insight into how HRM policy can be optimally aligned with social security policy, and how this policy in turn can facilitate HRM policy focused on desired and necessary labour market transitions aimed at creating employment security.

Departing from strategic HRM theory, we expand its boundaries by introducing inclusive HRM, meaning HRM activities that facilitate labour market transitions. Then we discuss the tendency in social security towards moving from *ex post* social risk insurance to *ex ante* proactive risk prevention. After discussing HRM and social security separately, we bring them together in the transition–inclusive HRM–labour market model. This conceptual model describes processes for securing labour market transitions for vulnerable (potential) workers and the connected HRM and social policies. Inspired by transitional labour market theory, as developed by Schmid, we present four transitions and discuss how these transitions relate to the internal, external and 'outside' labour market and how inclusive HRM should be aligned with the public system of social security. Finally, we elaborate on one of the four transitions under this model, that from job to job in the event of redundancy.

Expanding SHRM: inclusive HRM

Strategic HRM (SHRM) policy focuses on the productivity, development and wellbeing of people who currently work in the organization (Boxall and Purcell, 2011). The SHRM literature mentions three groups of outcomes that HRM policy can steer: economic performance, employee wellbeing and social legitimacy (societal outcomes) (Beer et al, 1984). The 'traditional' concept of HRM policies is under pressure as more people on the labour market have no formal bonds with organizations, because they are jobseekers, have loose ties with organizations, are part of the flexible workforce or have different bonds with organizations because they are not directly employed (outsourced). However, organizations' mainstream HRM activities are predominantly oriented at core employees, with a focus on HRM's contributions to organizational performance and their employees' wellbeing. Given the greater diversity of types of labour contracts, confronting organizations with an increase of transitions into and out of their workforce, an HRM focus on societal outcomes is of growing importance. Also, companies face a growing pressure from stakeholders 'to do the right thing' (corporate social responsibility – CSR), emphasizing the importance of social legitimacy as an outcome of HRM in organizations. Research by Helmig, Spraul and Ingenhoff (2016) shows that pressure from primary stakeholders has a strong impact on CSR implementation. Inclusive HRM extends the SHRM perspective from focusing on core employees, to focusing on people who are not yet (or are only temporarily) working in the organization, and contributes to social legitimacy outcomes, such as participation and inclusion. This is of growing importance, as an increasing part of the working population does not benefit from important HR activities such as training and development. Flexible workers receive much less training or work under worse conditions (Fouarge et al, 2012). Other groups, such as people working in SMEs or unemployed, have little or no exposure to HRM activities. For a well functioning labour market and good employment practices, all workers, including vulnerable groups, need to benefit from good HRM policies, even if these are aimed at finding employment outside the current organization. Previously, good HRM policies implied that organizations intended to be good employers and wanted to attract and retain talent for the organization (De Grip et al, 2020). Now, a broader concept of HRM is developing: inclusive HRM. Inclusive HRM focuses on people who do not yet work for the organization (or only temporarily and/or peripherally) (Borghouts and Freese, 2017). The current labour market calls for a different interpretation of good employment practices: not aimed at staying with an employer forever but being able to stay in the labour market. The development of knowledge, skills and sustainable employability in these (potential) workers within the organization is therefore an objective in itself for inclusive employers, to contribute to better functioning in the labour market. This transcends organizational boundaries, and calls for close collaboration with social policymakers, unions and other employers, representing the changing role of the HR function.

Social security

Traditionally, welfare and social security systems aim to respond to labour market imperfections and replace lost income in the event of unemployment or disability. The scope of different definitions of social security varies (Veldkamp, 1978; Viaene et al, 1983; Berghman, 1986; Noordam, 1996). Relief of poverty and meeting needs can be seen as two aims of social security; providing social assistance to those with no other means of supporting themselves. In many countries, social security has the function of income replacement for people and their families at times when they may suffer an interruption of earnings. The narrow definition of social security focuses solely on income replacement. According to Vrooman (2009) social security 'equates to the collective instruments which under certain circumstances offer income protection in the form of benefits and provisions' (p 112). In this delineation, social security provides financial support and compensation for those who have difficulty in meeting fixed costs. It describes transfers in money or in kind (Vrooman, 2009). Other scholars use a broader definition of social security which is not limited to what the government provides through benefits in cash or in kind in the event of a number of closely defined events (for example old age, unemployment, death of breadwinner, maintenance of children, maternity, long- or short-term sickness, disability, employment injuries), but targets all forms of human damage, thus aiming to provide security of income, employment, health and social participation. Social insurance and national provision are one means of doing this, but fiscal, occupational, private and voluntary arrangements can be used equally well. This idea is not new and can also be found in Titmuss's classic work in which three types of social policy are distinguished: 1) institutional–redistributive, 2) achievement of industrial performance and 3) the residual model (Titmuss, 1958). Compensation for losses is the final resort; if possible, interventions aimed at prevention and restoration should take precedence (Vrooman, 2009).

The concept of prevention has been discussed by several scholars (Viaene et al, 1990; Hjort, 1995; Greve, 2006; Sinfield, 2007). As early as 1986, Berghman advocated that preventative forms of measures should be included in the definition of social security (Berghman, 1986; Berghman et al, 2013). McKinnon (2010) summarized and reviewed the prevention debates and concluded that there is no consensus over the concept of prevention. In recent years, attention on prevention in the concept of security has increased and been promoted (Klosse, 2014; van Gestel et al, 2014; Berghman et al, 2018) and more attention is now paid to new social risks such as precarious employment, long-term unemployment and retraining needs (Hemerijck, 2017).

Over the past decade, in scholarly debates and in policymaking the idea of social investment has received more attention. In these streams of literature the prevention function is also addressed, although not defined as such and without indicating a specific order. Hemerijck (2017) defines social investment as 'an encompassing strategy of developing, employing and protecting human capital over the life course for the good of citizens, families, societies, and economies' (p 19) and distinguishes three interdependent functions: (1) raising the quality of the stock of human capital and capabilities over the life course; (2) easing the flow of contemporary labour-market and life-course transitions; and (3) maintaining strong minimum-income universal safety nets as income protection and economic stabilization buffers in ageing societies. The idea of social investment is not new and was developed during the late 20th and early 21st centuries as a new approach to welfare recalibration, to foster economic security and social inclusion: from *ex post* social risk insurance to *ex ante* risk prevention (Hemerijck, 2017). Past work by Schmid and Gazier states that the social investment flow 'imperative', that is, the priority when (re)integrating vulnerable people into the labour market and providing assistance during vulnerable transition, is 'to make transitions pay' (Gazier, 2007; Schmid, 2017, p 116).

Schmid argues that unemployment benefits, or any other benefits maintaining and enhancing the employability of jobless people, must be considered as 'active security' (Schmid, 2017, 2015). Combating long-term unemployment is a major public value in the European Union and its member states. In recent decades, active labour market policies (ALMPs), promoting the employability and labour market participation of unemployed people, have been on the agendas of governments in European countries (Bonoli, 2013). However, these ALMPs apply to people who are already unemployed and do not focus on workers who might lose their job in the near future. In response to the economic crisis in 2008–10 and the COVID-19 pandemic, governments introduced measures to cushion the impact on the labour market and support workers who lost their jobs (Heys, 2013). The European Commission encouraged member states to ensure that the measures were in line with the 'flexicurity' concept: a shift from job security towards employment security by introducing more flexible dismissal regulations at the same time as, for example, ALMP, modern social security systems and lifelong learning opportunities (Madsen, 1999; Wilthagen and Tros, 2004; Bredgaard et al, 2005; Muffels et al, 2014; Bredgaard and Madsen, 2018). This implies a major role for employers in the prevention of unemployment. However, ALMPs focus on the supply side, and generally neglect employer participation (Sinfield, 2007; van Berkel et al, 2017; Orton et al, 2019). From a social security perspective, employer engagement is essential for ALMPs to be effective (Borghouts and Freese, 2017). After all, employers offer jobs, and can use government incentives, for example wage subsidies, to increase the labour market participation of vulnerable groups.

The shift from passive policies aimed at protecting income towards active policies (ALMPs) has been examined extensively in the social policy literature (Hemerijck, 2012; Bonoli, 2013). Bonoli (2010) distinguishes four types of ALMPs: (1) incentive reinforcement (referring to measures that aim to strengthen incentives for benefit recipients to seek work, for example tax credits, time limits on benefit continuance), (2) employment assistance (referring to measures aimed at removing obstacles to labour-market participation, for example placement services, job subsidies, counselling, job search programmes), (3) occupation ('primarily to promote labour market re-entry, but to keep jobless people busy, to prevent the depletion of human capital associated with an unemployment spell' (Bonoli, 2010, p 441)), for example job creation schemes in the public sector, or in training programmes and (4) investment in human capital (upskilling or providing vocational training to jobless people). Passive income protection measures, according to Bonoli (2010), are generally not considered part of ALMP. He argues that 'passive income protection and ALMP measures are financed out of the same budget, as unemployment increases during a recession, increased automatic spending on passive benefits crowds out spending on any type of ALMP' (Bonoli, 2010, p 438). ALMPs hinge on 'making work pay' and are targeted towards the supply side, while the demand side is greatly neglected (van Berkel et al, 2017; Orton et al, 2019).

Transition-inclusive HRM-labour market model

The core idea of Schmid's transitional labour market model is to give a clear normative and analytical direction to the strategy of balancing flexibility and security and to aim at empowering individuals by not only making them ready for the market, but also by making the market ready for the worker (Schmid, 2015). Schmid advocates an analytical approach to studying the dynamics of labour markets rather than focusing on numbers employed or derived figures (for example, employment or unemployment rates). This means looking at transitions from one labour status to another, including combinations of work and education or work and unpaid care. In this section we elaborate on Schmid's model and focus on the mutual influence between HR and employer-oriented social policy. The underlying principles of the transition-inclusive HRM-labour market model are:

- to create employment security, benefiting employees, organizations and society;
- by initiating, stimulating and facilitating transitions on the labour market within and across organizational boundaries;
- this calls for an interplay between government and employers which means organizations should act from an inclusive perspective and social policy actors should take an adaptive, facilitating and stimulating role, responsive to organizational or contextual needs;
- diversifying into the three parts of the labour market: internal, external and 'outside' the formal market; and
- empowering people and organizations: building a fluid workforce and culture in organizations and in the public social domain in which (potential) workers are agile and resilient so that they have the skills or knowledge needed, are motivated and have the opportunity to make a transition into the labour market when desired or necessary. This will unlock (hidden) skills and talents and reallocate resources between declining and growing employers, sectors and the public social domain with the aim of ensuring employment security.

We distinguish four transitions and relate these transitions both to types of employment (or quasi-employment) relationship (including permanent contracts, flexible contracts – i.e. fixed term contracts, temporary agency contracts, on-call contracts – self-employment and call-off contracts) and to positions on the labour market (internal, external, outside the labour market) (Borghouts and Freese, 2017; Freese and Borghouts, 2021). The four transitions, important for the development of inclusive HRM policies and employment security, are:

1. *Future transitions*: to improve security of employment and sustainable employability of workers and organizations in a near future in which functions or jobs change and/or disappear as a result of automation, digitalization, new technologies.
2. *Forced dismissal*: to improve 'from job to job' processes to cope with the consequences of economic crises (cyclical or caused by external events such as a pandemic) in which reorganizations and forced dismissals are unavoidable.
3. *Transition from contract to contract*: to improve the security of employment and social protection of flex workers and self-employed workers.
4. *Transition from inactivity to employment*: sustainable employability/inclusive employment in the labour market; overcoming obstacles to employment; reintegration of sick employees, people with disabilities or long-term unemployed.

In the remainder of this chapter, we examine in particular transitions from job to job (Transition 2 in Figure 11.1) and future transitions (Transition 1 in Figure 11.1), and we link the transition-inclusive HRM-labour market model to various policies aiming to prevent or reduce unemployment, providing a starting point for inclusive HRM policies for groups of vulnerable workers, linked to facilitating social policy. It is important to concentrate on these transitions because in these situations employees are still employed but are vulnerable to unemployment. HR and social policy can therefore adapt proactive policies and practices with the aim of preventing future unemployment.

Unemployment prevention and employment security: the new security

Organizations change in response to crises, globalization and increasing competition. It is clear that, in future, smooth transitions from job to job will be necessary in a globalizing and profoundly changing economy. In order to tackle (long-term) unemployment, responses are required from national governments, employers' associations, trade unions, employers

Figure 11.1: Transition-inclusive HRM-labour market model

1: Transitions in jobs, employment as a result of automation and robotization (Lifelong Learning, agile workforce)
PRIMARY UNEMPLOYMENT PREVENTION

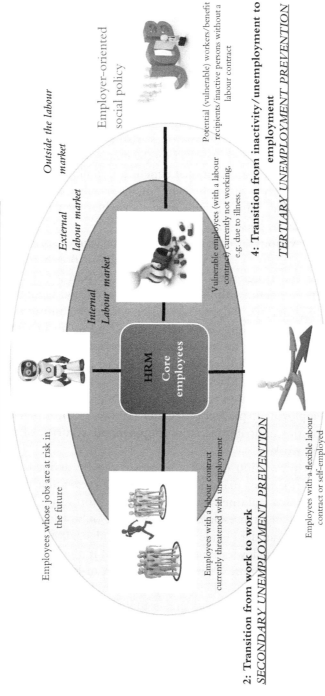

Outside the labour market

Employer-oriented social policy

Potential (vulnerable) workers/benefit recipients/inactive persons without a labour contract

External labour market

Internal Labour market

Vulnerable employees (with a labour contract) currently not working, e.g. due to illness.

HRM Core employees

4: Transition from inactivity/unemployment to employment
TERTIARY UNEMPLOYMENT PREVENTION

Employees whose jobs are at risk in the future

Employees with a labour contract currently threatened with unemployment

Employees with a flexible labour contract or self-employed

2: Transition from work to work
<u>*SECONDARY UNEMPLOYMENT PREVENTION*</u>

3. Transition from contract to contract
PRIMARY and SECONDARY UNEMPLOYMENT PREVENTION

and individual employees. Investments in unemployment prevention and stimulating employment security rather than job security are key.

It is beneficial for people, organizations and society when workers facing or following involuntary dismissals make the transition from the current job to a job with another employer rather than becoming unemployed. The new job provides income and a degree of security, but also reduces the emotional stress of employees who lose their jobs (McKee-Ryan et al, 2009). For organizations, the benefit of investing in smooth job-to-job transitions is financial as labour costs decrease when redundant employees leave the payroll, that is, when the transition starts before the notice period ends. Another benefit is a positive effect on the employer's reputation. Reducing skills depreciation is an additional benefit for employers and workers. The benefit for society is that redundant employees rely less on unemployment benefits or avoid claiming them altogether when the period between two jobs is as short as possible.

There are various forms of unemployment prevention: primary, secondary and tertiary (Evers et al, 2004; Borghouts, 2016; Borghouts et al, 2019). Verschoor and Borghouts (2018) described SHRM activities that Dutch employers engage in with regard to their (potentially) redundant workers, which together try to prevent workers from becoming unemployed. They distinguished four consecutive phases and forms of unemployment prevention, referring to and inspired by previous work of other scholars (Vrooman et al, 1993; Evers et al, 2004; Sinfield, 2007; Borghouts, 2012). In this chapter, we build on this model and expand it by investigating what social policy contributes to preventing unemployment. In each phase of the unemployment prevention model (Figure 11.2), different, inclusive HR activities contribute to the employment security of (potentially) redundant workers.

Primary prevention or risk prevention can be defined as preventing the social risk from manifesting. It is about preventing unemployment before there is a real threat of dismissal in the short term. In this situation, organizations might invest in the 'employability' or 'sustainable employability' of employees (van der Heijde and van der Heijden, 2006; Van Vuuren et al, 2011), so that employees are agile and resilient in the labour market in the event of possible future changes (see Phase A in Figure 11.2). Phase A – investing in employee wellbeing and performance – is at the core of SHRM. In the SHRM literature, considerable attention is paid to employability and sustainable employability (Forrier and Sels, 2003; van Vuuren et al, 2011). At an early stage, the employer can invest in the sustainable employability of employees without the risk of forced dismissal in the short term. We call these 'proactive inclusive HRM activities', such as investment in well-being and training.

Figure 11.2: Unemployment prevention model

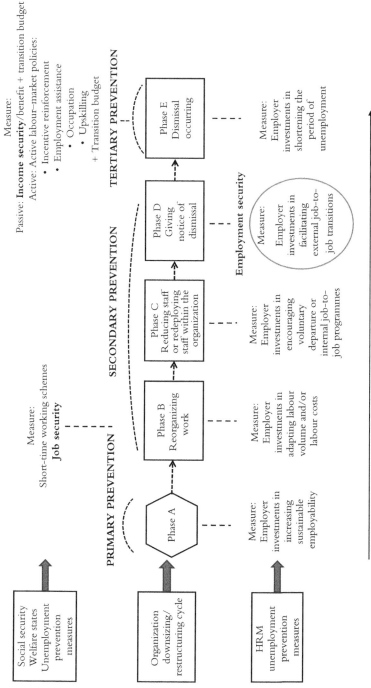

In the second phase of unemployment prevention, secondary prevention is referred to as 'preventing transition to long-term benefit schemes' (Evers et al, 2004; Borghouts, 2012; Verschoor and Borghouts, 2018; Borghouts et al, 2019) and is implemented in the event of impending reorganization or bankruptcy. During the impending dismissal phase (Phase B), an employer can take measures within the organization to prevent or minimize layoffs. Examples include changes to employment volume or employment costs such as reducing overtime, cutting regular working hours or freezing or moderating employment conditions such as pay and benefits. ALMPs also come into play in this phase. During the financial crisis short-time working schemes came into effect in several European countries (Hijzen and Martin, 2013) and during the COVID-19 pandemic many countries introduced support measures aimed at preserving jobs in companies that were temporarily confronted with a reduction in work. These were public schemes aimed at preserving jobs at firms experiencing a drop in demand. In this phase, the welfare state provided income support to workers whose hours were reduced during shortened work weeks. An employer can also encourage employees to leave the organization voluntarily, or promote internal job-to-job transitions (Phase C). During Phase C employees will have learned that early departures will be necessary, but no dismissals have yet been announced. If forced dismissals remain unavoidable despite these measures, then formal notice of dismissal is given. This is followed by another period before employment contracts are actually terminated, because employers must usually give notice (Phase D). Measures to prepare employees for different kinds of job can be implemented during this phase, during which they will learn that their career with the current employer will end soon; such measures aim to prevent unemployment. Finally, once redundant employees have been dismissed, tertiary prevention employers and public authorities can invest in helping to shorten the employees' period of unemployment (Phase E). If it is not possible to help redundant employees move to another job immediately, then it is essential to keep the period 'between two jobs' as short as possible. This also applies to flex workers, and self-employed contractors, who move from contract to contract. Once the (employment) contract has been terminated, the employee (or flex worker or former contractor) may become formally unemployed and if there are no prospects of another job, measures can be implemented to prevent long-term unemployment and the use of benefit schemes. This also can be considered tertiary prevention (Vrooman et al, 1993). In most countries, including The Netherlands, the government is responsible for this phase.

When we link this unemployment prevention typology to the transition-inclusive HRM-labour market model, we see that primary unemployment prevention focuses on transition one. This phase seeks to build up the long-term, sustainable employability and manoeuvrability of staff. Digitalization, automation, technology, flexibilization and cyclical developments can cause a mismatch between future work demands and what people are able and willing to do. The secondary unemployment prevention phase is mainly linked to transition two. In this phase, there is a short-term threat of redundancy. Employees' jobs are now at risk. For employees on a flexible contract, or the self-employed, security is also important (transition three), but policymaking has not paid attention to this. Various recent Dutch policy reports note that the difference between flex and permanent employment relationships has become too great (Commissie Regulering van Werk, 2020; WRR, 2020). The Netherlands is known for its large number of flex workers (Kremer et al, 2017). At the European level, despite decreasing numbers, the number of employees in non-standard employment remains an issue resulting in individual and social vulnerability to labour market adjustments (European Commission, 2021). Tertiary unemployment prevention focuses on preventing long-term unemployment for people who do not, or cannot, actively participate in the labour market. It corresponds with transition four of the transition-inclusive HRM-labour market model.

Investments in inclusive HRM do not start from the idea of keeping one's current job at all costs (job security), but seek to ensure that investments in skills and education, and unlocking talent, allow people to move within the labour market in order to find new work and gain income and employment security (Freese and Borghouts, 2021). In other words, the investment is in transferability and flexibility, but importantly not to the disadvantage of the individuals involved. Although the scope and principles of employer policies may differ from those of the government, they can both contribute to the pursuit of public value on social issues, such as unemployment prevention (van Berkel and Leisink, 2013). Social labour market policies that are aligned with the broader perspective of SHRM can lead to social innovation in supporting (dismissed) employees in moving to another job outside the company and preventing (or reducing) social security claims.

Conclusion and discussion

The global financial crisis between mid-2007 and early 2009 and the COVID-19 crisis that has hit since 2020 have created a sense of urgency and awareness that people cannot always keep their jobs. At the same time, some sectors are desperate for personnel, such as healthcare, ICT and logistics. In addition, in many countries there are millions of outsiders on the labour market, who fail to find employment. There is a mismatch on the labour market, both in quantitative and qualitative terms. The functioning of the labour market is not perfect and there is an urgent need to reflect

Figure 11.3: Unemployment prevention at different levels, different stakeholders, and HR/social policy activities

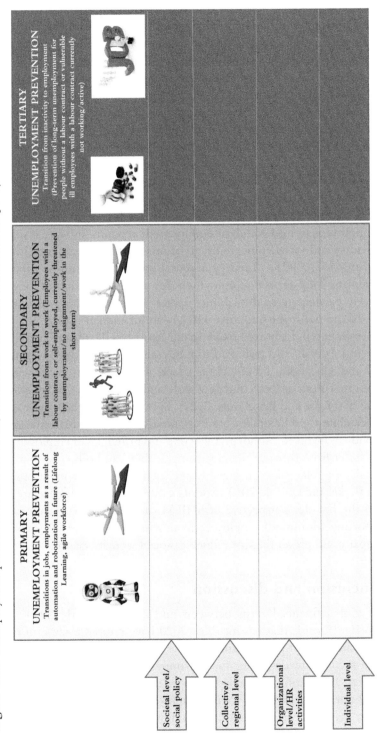

on employment security systems to prevent (long-term) unemployment. By combining social policy and inclusive HRM activities, it is possible to make this move towards an economy based on (unlocked) talents and skills.

The Dutch Economic Council (SER) has drawn up an advisory report, 'Security for people, a flexible economy and recovery of society', which provides a vision for the future labour market in which broad prosperity for all Dutch citizens can be achieved (SER, 2021). This report is in line with the five building blocks published in the European Skills Agenda for sustainable competitiveness, social fairness and resilience, namely: 1) collective action (mobilizing business, social partners and stakeholders, to commit to working together, in particular within the EU's industrial ecosystems), 2) financial means to foster investments in skills, 3) clear strategy to ensure that skills lead to jobs, 4) helping people build their skills throughout life where lifelong learning is the norm, and 5) setting ambitious objectives for up- and reskilling to be achieved by 2025 (European Commission, 2021). The SER advises investing heavily in employment and income security, and emphasizes the importance of an ambitious programme to strengthen the agility and resilience of the economy and to offer people greater security. This has consequences for the way in which the labour market is organized and income policy is shaped, and SER advises the development of adequate infrastructure to provide job-to-job and lifelong learning for people who will have to change jobs in coming years, so that there is always a prospect of new employment. The foundation of such infrastructure requires a new way of thinking: employment security rather than job security must take centre stage. By making not only organizations, but also individuals, more flexible, a 'new security' may be created. At present, almost all the financial incentives offered to employees are geared towards job retention rather than employment security. In a new infrastructure, these incentives must be adjusted to make job-to-job and lifelong learning attractive. This more flexible economy cannot be reached without a proactive, inclusive HR policy. The SER has expressed a major ambition: developing job-to-job and lifelong learning infrastructure, to be ready in eight to ten years (from 2021). This infrastructure, which can be characterized as the 'system world', could be a central way to encourage and facilitate inclusive HRM that connects with the 'living world' of organizations and people. Future research should investigate which HR activities can be offered in different phases at different levels and what the effects will be.

Unemployment prevention has a much greater chance of success if it is set up preventively and proactively at an early stage within organizations, before redundancy becomes an immediate prospect. A crucial condition for this new job-to-job infrastructure is to set up a broad public–private partnership. However promising job-to-job training and lifelong learning may seem, people experience psychological barriers to participating in them. Removing these obstacles starts at the individual level. This requires a system in which individuals can plan their career path horizontally or vertically and in which barriers and risks are eliminated or reduced in the central, collective and individual labour market and social security system. In order to create trust, organizations, trade unions, employers' organizations and society should adapt to this new reality by collaborating on, stimulating and facilitating transitions towards employment security and income security in which people, rather than jobs, are protected (Figure 11.3). Figure 11.3 can be seen as a conceptual tool for policymakers to see at which level policies and practices have been developed in the different unemployment prevention phases, and how they relate to each other at the different levels. It can also show the levels at which policies and practices are still missing.

Many reports stress the importance of lifelong learning initiatives (World Economic Forum, 2020), and investing in the skills of the entire labour force seems logical. This begs the question, why this does not happen yet? An explanation could be that the results of investments in prevention are not immediately visible and the benefits do not automatically accrue to the party that invests. Why would employers invest in their flexible workforce, who only work for their organization temporarily? Why would employers invest in the unemployed?

Public employment services (PES) are organizations that connect jobseekers with employers. PES benefit when employers invest in unemployment prevention and sustainable employability ahead of need, during the employment contract. Experience to date suggests that individuals do not think in sufficient depth about the future outside the organization in which they work, and may only take action when their job becomes redundant or their skills obsolete. These short-term blind spots and the failure to stimulate inclusive HR activities represent a wicked policy problem. Many researchers and policymakers assume that public–private cooperation enables smoother transitions and thus contributes to a better functioning labour market in which people can move easily to and within the market regardless of the economic situation. The crucial (research) question to answer is how to convince different stakeholders to invest in the transitional labour market and patiently wait for the benefits. The societal benefits might exceed the costs, but this has never been measured. Benefits from investments do not automatically return to the stakeholder who bears the costs. There is a micro and macro dynamic when it comes to measuring costs and benefits.

References

Beer, M., Spector, B., Lawrence, P.R. and Mills, D.Q. (1984). *Managing human assets: The groundbreaking Harvard Business School Program*, New York: Free Press.

Berghman, J. (1986). *De onzichtbare sociale zekerheid (The invisible social security)*, Deventer: Kluwer.

Berghman J., Debels, A. and van Hoyweghen, I. (2013). 'Prevention: The cases of social security and health.' In Greve B. (ed) *The Routledge handbook of the welfare state*, Abingdon: Routledge.

Berghman, J., Debels, A. and van Hoyweghen, I. (2018). 'Prevention: The cases of social security and healthcare.' In Greve B. (ed) *The Routledge handbook of the welfare state*, 2nd edn, Abingdon: Routledge.

Bonoli, G. (2010). 'The political economy of active labour-market policy', *Politics & Society* 38(4): 435–57.

Bonoli, G. (2013). *The origins of active social policy: Labour market and childcare policies in a comparative perspective*, Oxford: Oxford University Press.

Borghouts-van de Pas, I.W.C.M. (2010). 'Labour market participation of the disabled: Policies and practices in Europe', *European Journal of Social Security* 12(2): 121–43.

Borghouts-van de Pas, I.W.C.M. (2012). *Securing job-to-job transitions in the labour market*, Nijmegen: Wolf Legal Publishers.

Borghouts-van de Pas, I. (2016). 'Werkloosheidspreventie in Nederland', *Tijdschrift voor Arbeidsvraagstukken* 32(3): 284–302.

Borghouts-van de Pas, I.W.C.M. and Freese, C. (2017). 'Inclusive HRM and employment security for disabled people: An interdisciplinary approach', *E-Journal of International and Comparative Labour Studies* 6(1): 9–33.

Borghouts-van de Pas, I., Bosmans, M., Verschoor, J. and Wilthagen, T. (2019). *Overstappen op de arbeidsmarkt. Een onderzoek naar Van Werk Naar Werk-beleid en – trajecten*, Weert: Celsus, juridische uitgeverij.

Boxall, P. and Purcell, P. (2011). *Strategy and human resource management*, Basingstoke: Palgrave Macmillan.

Bredgaard, T. and Madsen, P.K. (2018). 'Farewell flexicurity? Danish flexicurity and the crisis', *Transfer* 24(4): 375–86.

Bredgaard, T., Larsen, F. and Madsen, P.K. (2005). 'The flexible Danish labour market: A review', CARMA Research Paper, Aalborg: CARMA centre for labour market research.

Commissie Regulering van Werk (Commissie Borstlap) (2020). *In wat voor land willen wij werken? Naar een nieuw ontwerp voor de regulering van werk*, Rijksoverheid.

European Commission (2021). *Joint employment report 2021*, Brussels: European Commission: https://ec.europa.eu/social/BlobServlet?docId=23156&langId=en&furtherNews=yes

European Foundation for the Improvement of Living and Working Conditions (2008). 'Employment security and employability: A contribution to the flexicurity debate', Dublin.

Evers, G.H.M., Wilthagen, A.C.J.M. and Borghouts-van de Pas, I.W.C.M. (2004). *Best Practices in WW-prevemtie (Best practices in unemployment prevention)*, Organisatie voor Strategisch Arbeidsmarktonderzoek.

Forrier, A. and Sels, L. (2003). 'The concept employability: A complex mosaic', *International Journal of Human Resources Development and Management* 3(2): 102–24.

Fouarge, D., de Grip, A. and Smits, W. (2012). 'Flexible Contracts and human capital investments', *De Economist* 160: 177–95.

Freese, C. and Borghouts-van de Pas, I. (2021). 'Inleiding: Inclusief HRM?' In B. Moens, P. Roskam and V. van den Bosch (eds) *Koers naar talent in overvloed: Inclusief HRM als kompas*, Burgge: Die Keure, pp 24–7.

Gazier, B. (2007). 'Making transitions pay. The transitional labour markets' approach to flexicurity.' In H. Jørgensen and P.K. Madsen (eds) *Flexicurity and beyond: Finding a new agenda for the European Social Model*, Copenhagen: DJøf, pp 99–130.

Greve, B. (2006). 'Prevention and reintegration: An overview', *European Journal of Social Security* 9(1): 3–10.

Grip, de, A., Fouarge, D., Montizaan, R. and Schreurs, B. (2020). 'Train to retain: Training opportunities, positive reciprocity, and expected retirement age', *Journal of Vocational Behavior* 117: 1–15.

Helmig, B., Spraul, K. and Ingenhoff, D. (2016). 'Under positive pressure: How stakeholder pressure affects corporate social responsibility implementation', *Business & Society* 55(2):151–87. doi:10.1177/0007650313477841

Hemerijck, A. (2012). *Changing welfare states*, Oxford: Oxford University Press.

Hemerijck, A. (ed) (2017). *The uses of social investment*, Oxford: Oxford University Press.

Heys, J. (2013). 'Flexicurity in crisis: European labour market policies in a time of austerity', *European Journal of Industrial Relations* 19(1): 71–86.

Hijzen, A. and Martin, S. (2013). 'The role of short-time work schemes during the global financial crisis and early recovery: A cross-country analysis', *IZA Journal of Labour Policy*, Discussion paper No 7291.

Hjort, P. (1995). 'Prevention: The wish of everybody, the priority of nobody', *Archives of Public Health* 53(11–12): 489–508.

Klosse, S. (2014). 'Proactive employment policies: A change for the better?' In W. Van Oorschot, H. Peeters and K. Boos (eds) *Invisible social security revisited*, Leuven: LannooCampus publishers, pp 95–109.

Kremer, M., Went, R. and Knottnerus, A. (2017). *For the sake of security: The future of flexible workers and the modern organization of labour*, The Hague: WRR.

Madsen, P.K. (1999). 'Denmark: Flexibility, security and labour market success', Employment and Training Paper No. 53, Geneva: ILO.

McKee-Ryan, F.M., Song, Z., Wanberg, C.R. and Kinicki, A.J. (2009). 'Psychological and physical well-being during unemployment: A meta-analytic study', *Journal of Applied Psychology* 90: 53–76.

McKinnon, R. (2010). 'Promoting the concept of prevention in social security: Issues and challenges for the International Social Security Association', *International Journal of Social Welfare* 19: 455–62.

Muffels, R., Crouch, C. and Wilthagen, T. (2014). 'Flexibility and security: National social models in transitional labour markets', *Transfer* 20(1): 99–114.

Noordam, F.M. (1996). *Inleiding Sociale-zekerheidsrecht (Introduction to Social Security Law)*, Deventer: Kluwer.

Orton, M., Green, A., Atfield, G. and Barnes, S. (2019). 'Employer participation in active labour market policy: From reactive gatekeepers to proactive strategic partners', *Journal of Social Policy* 48(3): 511–28.

Schmid, G. (1995). 'Is full employment still possible? Transitional labour markets as a new strategy of labour market policy', *Economic and Industrial Democracy* 16(3): 429–56.

Schmid, G. (2015). 'Sharing risks of labour market transitions: Towards a system of employment insurance', *British Journal of Industrial Relations* 53(1): 70–93.

Schmid, G. (2017). 'Towards employment insurance?' In A. Hemerijck (ed) *The Uses of Social Investment*, Oxford: Oxford University Press, pp 108–17.

Schmid, G. and Gazier, B. (2002). *The dynamics of full employment: Social integration through transitional labour markets*, Cheltenham: Edward Elgar.

SER (2021). 'Zekerheid voor mensen, een wendbare economie en herstel van de samenleving, sociaal economisch beleid 2021–2025', Advies 21/08, June.

Sinfield, A. (2007). 'Preventing poverty in the European Union', *European Journal of Social Security* 9(1): 11–28.

Titmuss, R.M. (1958). *Essays on the welfare state*, London: Allen and Unwin.

van Berkel, R. and Leisink P. (2013). 'Both sides now: Theoretical perspectives on the link between social and HR policies in promoting labour market participation.' In P. Leisink, P. Boselie, M. van Bottenburg and D. Hosking (eds) *Managing social issues: A public value perspective*, Cheltenham: Edward Elgar.

van Berkel, R., Ingold, J., McGurk, P., Boselie, P. and Bredgaard, T. (2017). 'Editorial introduction: An introduction to employer engagement in the field of HRM – blending social policy and HRM research in promoting vulnerable groups' labour market participation', Special Issue: Employer engagement, *Human Resource Management Journal* 27(4): 503–13.

van der Heijde, C.M. and Van der Heijden, B.I.J.M. (2006). 'A competence-based and multidimensional operationalization and measurement of employability', *Human Resource Management Journal* 45(3): 449–76.

van Gestel, N., Vossen, E., Oomens, S. and Hollanders, D. (2014). *Toekomst van de sociale zekerheid: Over provisie, preventie en participatie (The Future of Social Security: Provision, Prevention and Participation)*, The Hague: Boom Lemma.

van Vuuren, T., Caniëls, M.C.J. and Semeijn, J.H. (2011). 'Duurzame inzetbaarheid en een leven lang leren (Sustainable employability and lifelong learning)', *Gedrag & Organisatie* 24(4): 357–74.

Veldkamp, G.M.J. (ed) (1978). *Sociale Zekerheid: Inleiding tot de sociale zekerheid en de toepassing ervan in Nederland en België*, Deel 1: *Karakter en geschiedenis (Social Security: An introduction to social security and its implementation in the Netherlands and Belgium*, Part 1: *Its character and history*, Deventer: Kluwer.

Verschoor, J. and Borghouts, I. (2018). 'Inclusief HRM: Het nemen van maatregelen ter preventie van werkloosheid van boventallige werknemers (Inclusive HRM: Taking measures to prevent unemployment of redundant workers)', *Tijdschrift voor HRM* 3: 55–75.

Viaene, J., Laheye, D. and van Steenberge, J. (1983). *Een begrippenkader voor de hervorming van de sociale zekerheid (A conceptual framework for social security reform)*. Sociaalrechtelijke Kronieken.

Viaene, J., Huys, J., Justaert, M., Lahaye, D., Simoens, D. and van Steenberge, J. (1990). 'Een begrippenkader voor de hervorming van de sociale zekerheid.' In J. Viaene et al (eds) *Hervorming van de sociale zekerheid: vanuit een nieuw begrippenkader*, Annex, Brugge: Die Keure.

Voss, E., Wild, A., Kwiatkiewicz, A. and Farvaque, N. (2009). *Organising transitions in response to restructuring. Study on instruments and schemes of job and professional transition and re-conversion at national, sectoral or regional level in the EU*, final report, European Commission.

Vrooman, J.C. (2009). *Rules of relief: Institutions of social security, and their impact*, The Netherlands Institute for Social Research, The Hague: SCP.

Vrooman, J.C., van Wijgaarden, P.J. and van den Heuvel, F.G. (1993). 'Prevention in social security: Theory and policy consequences', research memorandum, Tilburg University, Department of Economics; Vol. FEW 631.

Wetenschappelijke Raad voor het Regeringsbeleid (WRR) (2020). *Het betere werk. De nieuwe maatschappelijk opdracht*, The Hague.

Wilthagen, T. and Tros, F. (2004). 'The concept of "flexicurity": A new approach to regulating employment and labour markets', *Transfer: European Review of Labour and Research* 10(2): 166–86.

World Economic Forum (2020). *The Future of Jobs report 2020*, Geneva.

12

Conditions, Processes and Pressures Promoting Inclusive Organizations

William Hanson and Jeffrey Moore

This chapter examines the environmental conditions, pressures and processes that promote an inclusive, adaptive organization. An adaptive organization is necessary for recruiting and retaining marginalized groups in the labour market. We begin with theoretical concepts in well-established leadership theory, and transition to real-world examples. Based on years of research findings from multiple cases involving large corporations, we lay out important strategies for organizations to successfully integrate large numbers of disabled members into the workforce. Specifically, we draw from three studies involving global industries: 1) three distribution centres for Walgreens, a retail and wholesale pharmaceutical corporation; 2) three distribution centres for Sephora, a cosmetics corporation; and 3) a manufacturing plant in North America, part of a multinational automotive supplier. All three global corporations have undergone recent, radical change improving inclusivity. The first two of the example corporations have each developed three distribution centres – where in a single 500-employee distribution centre, there are between 100 and 200 employees with disabilities. In the third example, the multinational automotive supplier changed the culture in a large manufacturing plant containing over 800 employees generating $US1 billion in sales (Moore and Hanson, 2022). In all three corporations, production, retention, and job satisfaction increased from previous conditions, with absenteeism and turnover rates declining, while productivity increased.

Internal and external pressures can create the need for organizations to adapt to new conditions. Some pressures are helpful, while others stymie organizational purpose. Furthermore, pressures can be created within the organization to promote changes that make a better fit with the environment, leading to outcomes such as innovation, increased productivity, and faster solutions to company challenges. In part, leaders are able to shape a unit's pressures and conditions for building a successful, inclusive organization.

In this chapter we begin by discussing the importance of moving away from traditional styles of leadership, and adopting a more comprehensive model that better supports inclusive organizations. We introduce elements of complexity leadership theory, which we argue provides a stronger framework for adaptability – the creation of an inclusive organization. After a short introduction, we integrate case study examples while discussing the importance of organizational conditions, pressures, and processes – all critical elements in creating a successful, inclusive organization. Finally, we present important policy considerations in supporting an adaptive shift toward the integration of a disabled workforce.

Leadership models and challenges to inclusiveness

North American inclusive organizations have the same business pressures to be competitive and financially viable as do other organizations. Like all organizations, they must also deal with a workforce shortage. Large employee turnover is endemic to many industries in North America as well as the difficulties in recruiting effective employees during historically low unemployment levels. Shrewd business leaders look to recruit from among the disabled population as having significant competitive advantages. Notably, disabled employees boast higher productivity rates, lower absenteeism, and lower safety incidents (Moore et al, 2020a, 2020b).

Developing an inclusive organization requires adopting a different management philosophy than the traditional leadership model with origins in the early 20th century (see Taylor, 1919). A traditional bureaucratic model of leadership is more suited to the industrial age (Uhl-Bien and Marion, 2007, 2009). In the traditional model, the organization's primary focus is low costs, efficiency, and high production numbers. This task-centred model attempts to codify behaviours and methods to achieve a uniform and efficient method of mass production, thereby suppressing adaptivity. Characterized by centralized authority, leaders often practise a directive and controlling style, disenfranchising front-line workers and shutting off communication of front-line issues. Tight control of resources and decision making, as well as focus on efficiency and predictive outcomes, often hamper adaptability (Moore and Hanson, 2022). This is one reason that Hanson and Ford (2011) highlight the criticality of minimizing control while balancing administrative demands – in order to reduce barriers for adaptability.

Complexity leadership theory offers leaders opportunities for a successful, adaptive, inclusive culture. While this theory offers many facets for leadership, we will discuss a few of the most important ones for industry leaders and governmental policymakers: In particular, the creation and nurturing of the needed *conditions, processes, and pressures* for an organization to thrive. Just as important, these concepts are critical for implementation to achieve a successful inclusive company (Moore et al, 2020a).

Complexity leadership theory

Complexity leadership provides an excellent framework for inclusive organizations. It recognizes that front-line employees and mid-level managers are the heart of adaptivity – for solving unique problems and new ways to operate. Complexity leadership centres on a more flexible, innovative organization.

Complexity-oriented leaders invoke healthy pressures and processes to encourage peers and employees to seek timely outcomes fitted to the organization's environment. For example, they make a concerted effort to adjust necessary policy and decision-making latitude to invoke change favourable to adaptive *processes*. At the same time, such leaders also allow policy implementers to work around less important barriers (rules, procedures, and other control measures). Complexity leadership theory is a comprehensive model with fewer policy and rule encumbrances, clear priorities to enable front-line initiative, and specific leader-functional roles. These roles consist of *administrative, enabling*, and *adaptive* functions – activities to foster the necessary conditions for the new inclusive culture to emerge (Uhl-Bien et al, 2007; Uhl-Bien and Marion, 2009). In this adaptive capacity, both formal and informal leaders perform some or all of these functions (Uhl-Bien et al, 2007; Uhl-Bien and Marion, 2009).

Formal and informal leaders, in complexity leadership terms, enable lower-level centres of interconnectivity, interdependence, consensus, creativity, innovation, organizational learning, and joint problem solving (Uhl-Bien et al, 2007; Uhl-Bien and Marion, 2009). Employees participate in shared goal building, vision and value creation, and other activities often reserved for executives (Hanson and Ford, 2011). Complexity dynamics bond leaders and employees in closer relationships, as well as recognizing the roles of informal leaders and front-line adaptivity. In these contexts, Robert Lord (2008) stresses that we view 'leaders as participants' (p 176). This is similar to James Burns's (2003) perspective that transformational leaders share the same wants, needs, and goals as employees. Strong relationships established between managers and employees have been shown to lead to more productive outcomes (Moore et al, 2020a; Moore and Hanson, 2022).

For complexity leadership to work, organizations must accept certain levels of higher risk; mistakes are considered part of a learning organization and a natural product of the innovation process (Senge, 2006). The acceptance of errors when solving problems and developing innovative solutions enables the workforce to create new knowledge and new opportunities.

Normally, in a traditional model of leadership many of these activities might be considered as hampering productivity – using more time, more resources, and being generally inefficient. However, for adaptability and for change or innovation to occur some latitude must be given for risk taking. For example, in Walgreens distribution centres, where disabled employees comprise at least 30 per cent of the workforce, managers encouraged front-line teams to work on production challenges. While this 'problem solving' initially took time away from production, improvements made by team members led to increased production levels in the long term. The same can be said of the manufacturing plant case, where front-line members began to serve on a new culture committee. While initial production was slowed, implementation of suggested improvements soon increased production to higher levels. The side effects in both cases was a greater sense of satisfaction by workers, improving retention, and increasing productivity (Moore et al, 2020a; Moore and Hanson, 2022).

As a side note, while not addressed directly, recruiting and retention are a major factor in effective leadership. Complexity leadership creates the environment for these to be successful. It encourages leaders to work in tight partnership with the front line. It also opens leaders to understanding that external agencies are important to their organizational pursuits, and encourages unconventional ideas to challenge the status quo. In the Walgreens case, this corporation formed strong relationships with employment agencies and other social programs to recruit and train disabled workers. Also, outcomes of success – in terms of adaptation toward higher productivity or competitiveness – provides actualization to team members, thus improving retention. As much research shows, employees tend to enjoy being part of a successful organization (Bakke, 2005; Zhang et al, 2014).

Conditions

Complexity leadership conditions emanate from collectively practising the three leadership functions – administrative, enabling, and adaptive – to support adaptive outcomes. Over time, these leadership functions nurture an environment open to adaptive processes, hence optimizing organizational fit, or competitiveness (Uhl-Bien and Marion, 2009; Arena and Uhl-Bien, 2016). Specific conditions needed are elusive; they are the behaviours and environmental elements that promote, or do not stifle, the needed adaptive processes. As Uhl-Bien and Marion (2009) argue, adaptive leader roles 'promote adaptive dynamics' and help 'incorporate adaptive outcomes' (p 647). They go on to stress that for adaptivity to take place, leaders must protect and foster those conditions. We can be more specific in the sense that injecting the proper tension and interaction are part of these conditions, and that establishing good human relations such as trust, respect, and open communications are important (Uhl-Bien and Marion, 2009).

So, how do we know when the right 'conditions' are in place? We would propose that it is when the adaptive processes are in operation: interconnectivity, interdependence, consensus, creativity, innovation, organizational learning, as well as shared goal building and problem solving. These embedded processes are indications that a strong complexity leadership culture exists. Table 12.1 provides some insight into the general responsibilities of each complexity leadership function in order to foster the conditions for organizational adaptivity (see Uhl-Bien et al, 2007; Uhl-Bien and Marion, 2009). These functions are operationalized by practising behaviours which define adaptive conditions (see Moore et al, 2020a; Moore and Hanson, 2022). Once these practices become routine and extensive, adaptive processes emerge.

Table 12.1: Complexity leadership functions and conditions

	Administrative function	Enabling function	Adaptive function
	Loosens formal structures – supports front-line effort	Promotes adaptive process and occurrence	Stimulates initiative and ideas – the doers
Adaptive conditions leading to adaptive processes	• Supportive planning and coordination • Minimize non-critical rules and policy • Encourage group decision making and innovation • Recognize informal leaders as helpful rather than harmful; leverage their influence and ability • Push down decision making, power and resource control • Challenge norms and status quo; raise productive tension • Provide general direction and sense making • Accept mistakes as 'learning'	• Cultivate conditions for interaction and collaboration • Champion new ideas from the lowest level • Leverage collective knowledge and ability • Support informal leaders • Reduce barriers to front-line problem-solving, learning and creativity (accept some risk and inefficiency) • Encourage supportive environment • Protect front-line adaptive movement • Buffer employees from over-regulation and control	• A change movement in which adaptive outcomes emerge from agentic interaction • Engage collective processes: creativity, organizational learning, innovation, and problem solving (bottom-up) • Generate ideas and solutions • Engage in initiative and collaborative action • Produce shared ideas, information, products, resources, and so on

Source: Adapted from Uhl-Bien et al (2007); Uhl-Bien and Marion (2009)

Adaptive processes

The primary role for all leaders is to foster necessary conditions for adaptivity. Once a supportive environment is established, adaptive processes work to produce important outcomes in an unpredictable, self-ordered manner. Said differently, the organization leverages the cognitive and skill capacity of the workforce to solve challenges and discover faster and better solutions grounded in daily work. This counters a tightly controlled process where executive teams sort issues and orchestrate the bulk of initiatives and products, limiting the rapidity and robustness of solutions. Marginalized groups have distinct characteristics that, in their integration of workers, require new methods of leadership and management. Innovating solutions and changes by those involved with daily challenges creates timely, well-grounded outcomes.

Earlier, we mentioned the various adaptive processes produced by complexity leadership: interaction, interdependence, consensus, creativity, innovation, organizational learning, as well as shared goal building and problem solving. These processes are critical for inclusive environments – they help workers and managers to learn about each other, unite them in common objectives, and raise production. Synthesized here are the key features of adaptive processes:

1. *Interaction as the key to successful change.* Communication and creating shared meaning are key in all three of the following case studies.
2. *Interdependence, or the moderate reliance on others, as vital to collective achievement.* Often classified as low, moderate or high, usually moderate levels of interdependence are sought, to strike the right balance for successful and timely outcomes (Marion and Uhl-Bien, 2003). If interdependence is too great, then completing the simplest task is weighed down by the bureaucratic nature of hierarchy or other factors such as conflicting constraints (Uhl-Bien et al, 2007). If too little, partners in shared ventures may have little interest in completing them as they are focused on their own projects. In each of our cases, senior management had to work longer with the front line for adaptive processes to occur. This was an effort by the three corporations to raise the interdependence of the workers from low to moderate. Said differently, leaders gave up control over various processes in order for the company to be adaptable.
3. *Consensus as often not only required for strong proposals, but also for buy-in and follow through success.* Group agreement in policy, rules, and objectives, ensure a good chance of success. In all three of our case studies, when the front line became involved in processes, more robust solutions emerged and became embedded in company life.
4. *Creativity as it arises from the group's ability to interact and share ideas.* From this interaction, ideas represent no single person, but a collective effort;

yet ideas are not always put into practice (Baer, 2012). This is a major reason complexity stresses the need for leaders to champion front-line ideas and solutions. At the manufacturing plant, their front-line culture committee became a problem solver for managers and employees, proposing solutions grounded in front-line issues.

5. *Innovation as the wellspring of creativity – where ideas and proposals are accepted and championed.* While the core of innovation emerges from both the individual and collective levels, it remains the result of interaction – shared knowledge, ideas, or the ability to implement (Uhl-Bien et al, 2007; Marion, 2008).

6. *Organizational learning as required for new knowledge and adaptation* (Marion, 2008; Bennis, 2013). By nature, learning is one area in which mistakes are made. Often a barrier to change, leaders sometimes retreat from a possibility of making a mistake – to seek 'stability' in pursuit of efficiency and effectiveness.

Corporate examples

Over the past ten years our research team has worked with three corporations in different industries who employ thousands of people. This work has been focused on organizational change through leadership development. We have studied Walgreens' inclusive culture transformation through the intentional hiring of people with disabilities. Working with the company's executive team and specifically with operations and human resources in their distribution centres, we collected data through face-to-face interviews, group interviews, and member checks. Similarly, we were invited to research Sephora and study the impact that hiring people with disabilities would have on their organization. We conducted face-to-face interviews, group interviews, and member checks, analysed employee production numbers, surveyed employees on their perceptions of their supervisors, teams, and employees with disability. One outcome of our work was to elicit, using data, the positive impact of inclusion on disabled employees and non-disabled employees alike. Furthermore, we did a time study of managers' leadership styles, before and a year after the inclusion initiative. Lastly, we worked with the leadership of a large automotive manufacturing facility with over 800 employees to facilitate their leading a change of culture. We gathered data through face-to-face interviews, group interviews, and member checks, and developed leadership training and human resource tools for supervisors. This action research embedded the researchers with the leadership and assisted them to incorporate complexity leadership principles.

Walgreens provides one example of adaptive emergence. At Walgreens, the shift in hiring disabled employees placed the leaders in a situation where they needed to share information and decisions while learning the nuances of working with various disabilities. This organizational learning process was dependent in part on mid-level managers creating an informal working group to help each other – thus increasing manager *interdependence*, while stimulating *innovative* solutions (Moore et al, 2020b). The group also *shared learning*, about both success stories and shortfalls in employee motivation, communication, and outcomes. An important note is that senior leaders did not intervene to direct or stop what emerged. This is important as adaptivity emerges from employee interaction (Marion, 2008; Moore et al, 2020a, 2020b).

Sephora offers another example of adaptive emergence by the creation of pathways for onboarding disabled individuals. The company increased its external interactions with local agencies serving disabled citizens to create a nine-week onboarding program with a training centre. The human resource department worked with local agencies to have input into the training content and bring in their agency coaches to become part of the training team. This guaranteed a continuity for the disabled employee coming to join the team. Sephora and local agencies increased their interdependence in order for this adaptive process to work (Maxey and Moore, 2017; Moore et al, 2021).

A third example emerges from a manufacturing plant of an international corporation. One of the eight major initiatives in their culture change was the creation of a culture committee. Composed of volunteer hourly team members, its role was to *interact* with top management over critical plant issues. This increased communication and *interaction* between hourly-paid employees and top management. Originally, it recommended various process changes. Once its impact became recognized, the committee's influence grew, working on *shared goals* and production issues. Top leaders then empowered the committee to work on *innovative solutions* assisted and supported by the executive team. The outcome of these actions was *consensus* around what the real issues were and how to go about solving them. Committee members were empowered to represent their colleagues' perspectives, while managers led through humility by resisting intervention to take control and provide their own solutions. Their humility, or deference in building *consensus*, enabled a strong team (Moore and Hanson, 2022).

In short, leadership-function practices and processes are needed conditions for adaptivity to emerge. Table 12.2, derived from research studies involving three large corporations, provides some examples of how these processes work.

Pressures

Organizations must sometimes create *pressures* that promote productive, lasting change. Complexity leadership theory describes this as tension (Marion,

Table 12.2: Examples of adaptive processes from three case studies

Adaptive process	Leader role	Employee/team role
Interaction/ interconnectivity	• Managers encourage teams to interact and innovate • Partnerships with local agencies serving disabled people to build an employment solution • Develop break/lunch areas to facilitate dialogue (large space, beverages, food options)	• Team helps shorter members reach tools (building a step) • Visual aids created for each station (images vs. written instructions) • Culture team works with employees to understand perspectives and concerns; share findings in quarterly all-employee meetings
Interdependence	• Top leaders push decisions to mid-level managers • Learn to 'ask the person' instead of making assumptions about their perspectives/wants • Learn about employees in order to find out what motivates them	Mid-level managers seek peer assistance in understanding/ resolving new challenges (create ad hoc council)
Creativity/ innovation	Build teams through improvement initiatives from team ideas	Team creates changes that allow employees to strike button instead of a key on a keyboard
Consensus	Intentionally recognize they cannot be an expert in every disability; listen to employee perspectives	Seek to understand the other person's perspective before giving an opinion
Organizational learning	Mid-level managers seek peer assistance in resolving employee shortfalls	Mid-level managers create ad hoc council to discuss lessons learned and resolve specific issues
Initiative	Managers seek ways to motivate or communicate to employees	Team members volunteer as disability mentors, providing additional training and support
Shared goal-building	Top leaders foster partnerships with local agencies serving disabled citizens to build training centre	Team creates new target goals
Shared problem-solving	Leader discusses issues on the team with managers and front-line culture committee	Front-line culture team presents executive committee with suggestions to improve relations with managers; later used for management training

2008). This tension may emanate from external sources (competition, new laws, new policy, among other things), or it may arise internally. At the manufacturing plant, it was generated internally when the plant manager recognized that current efforts to change were futile. The company hired consultants and that was the catalyst for successful change. Either way, the tension, or pressures, moved the organization toward change.

At Walgreens, corporate policy created change efforts in supply distribution centres through a policy requiring a 30 per cent disability employment rate while maintaining current production levels. This external pressure led the distribution centre to create new hiring and training procedures, and foster leadership styles by managers. At the same time, the corporation realized the pressure inflicted on the distribution centres and allowed local leaders to 'bend' various conflicting rules or policy. In most cases, it was simply reflective of loosening control and allowing the leaders to be more 'adaptive.' A third pressure on the company was to find and recruit disabled employees. This pressure led to the creation of a strong bond between community employment agencies and the supply distribution centre.

These three pressures on the distribution centre were immense, and as a result required the managers to discard many of the traditional leader-practices they had learned and applied during their career. These pressures forced them to reorganize and rely more on each other for knowledge, ideas, and plans. They began to learn about various disabilities and develop front-line consensus on solving motivational and work-station challenges. They also learned to depend on informal leaders and disability champions.

A second example of pressure helping to create an adaptive organization is the case of the manufacturing plant in the south-east United States, where employees and managers were not working together. Research discovered low levels of respect and trust, high turnover, production levels marginal, and little leadership or employee development (Moore and Hanson, 2022). In this case, some pressures came from the corporation, which was displeased with poor results from its culture survey, and the manufacturing plant attempting (and failing) to invoke change. One of the many initiatives bearing positive results was an overhaul of formal organizational values. Eventually, when employees and managers worked on improving levels of respect and development, trust was re-established, turnover dropped, and production increased.

One of the key pressures in distribution centres is productivity rates, since their margins are in the single digits. Sephora has balanced the pressure of productivity with the employment of disabled team members, who have completely changed their teams. During a two-week period, we analysed daily production numbers of teams at Sephora. Findings showed that disabled team members boast a 152 per cent productivity rate, while their non-disabled counterparts had a 116 per cent rate. However, disabled team

Figure 12.1: Operationalizing complexity through pressures in tension

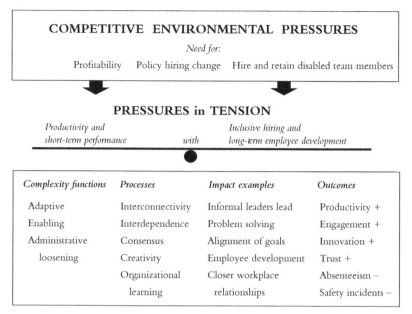

Source: Adapted from Uhl-Bien et al, 2007; Uhl-Bien and Marion, 2009

members showed more difficulties handling change. Leaders would then balance team needs so non-disabled team members would take on new tasks or deal with production changes. Groups considered their teams to be a success because the high productivity of some and the adaptability of others consistently allowed teams to exceed production standards (Moore et al, 2022).

Figure 12.1 presents the impact of pressures in tension upon organizations adopting complexity leadership functions. In this instance, the competitive environmental pressures that are driving the organization are profitability, a need to change hiring policies, and learning how to lead inclusive teams. Managers and supervisors balance short-term productivity pressures with the need to have a long-term focus on employee development. Using the complexity leadership functions, organizations realize an increase in productivity, employee engagement, innovation, and trust with a decrease in absenteeism and safety incidents.

Policy considerations for adaptability

Organizations face strong cultural mindsets when forming and implementing an inclusive workplace. These include three major patterns of thinking that collide in the inclusive organization: societal norms and biases about disabilities, perspectives of the non-disabled employees, and the perspectives of the employees with disabilities themselves. Within these clashing cultural mindsets, an inclusive workplace creates ethical resonance by aligning company core values with employees' values. Core values such as respect and care for others are essential qualities of an inclusive workforce (Moore and Hanson, 2022). We find that the hands providing assistance, coaching, and support are the hands of fellow team members who become the disability champions (Moore et al, 2020a). This ethical resonance becomes the catalyst for conditions and pressures producing the inclusive workplace (Doughty and Moore, 2021).

There are a number of possible solutions in improving the adaptability of companies in order to integrate a large number of disabled employees into the workforce. One major force to overcome is the experience most managers have in a traditional leadership model of control and efficiency, which often neglects employee concerns and relationships. Healthcare has begun to address this shortfall through development of *complexity management competencies* (Hanson and Ford, 2011). Complexity processes involve important people-focused processes that are required for inclusiveness and adaptability.

Taking this analysis into account, some key recommendations for successful adaptive integration of marginalized groups of disabled employees are suggested:

1. *Showcase inclusion success in local context*: Visit a successful inclusive organization to gain an internal understanding of hiring, training, and retaining new employees and managers to support your inclusive initiative. Walgreens distribution centres provide an excellent model for hiring, training, and retaining new employees, as well as how to lead and work in an inclusive environment. This organizational learning will impact the creation of new methods of operation and problem solving.

2. *Develop partnership with local resources*: Gain an understanding of external resources in hiring and training a disabled workforce. Maxey and Moore (2017) discuss the importance of building a bridge to inclusive hiring by partnering with local agencies in Chapter 13. Different cities and countries may well have different agencies, funding, and other resources to hire and train marginalized workers.

3. *Design and deliver inclusive leader training*: Teach and define key complexity concepts for managers – how it is different from traditional methods, what functions and processes are needed to make the initiative work. If interested, explore healthcare's discussion and development of complexity competencies (Hanson and Ford, 2011).

4. *Ensure policy orientation for the executive*: Create a system of policy flexibility, minimizing unnecessary rules. Social capital strategies – the connectivity

between employees – drives both performance and innovation within complex organizations (Arena and Uhl-Bien, 2016). Innovation and problem solving are encouraged by minimizing encumbrances. Organizations are better able to maximize teamwork between workers, and between workers and managers, building an adaptive organizational culture. When building a complex process organization should reflect the earlier processes outlined in Table 12.1.

5. *Support leader adaptivity*: Ensure adaptive processes occur, reinforce leader functions. Research results from work with Walgreens, Sephora, and the manufacturing corporation showed these processes result in an increase in production and invention. When managed well, this culture becomes accepting of change and inclusivity.

Conclusions

Complexity is the study of enabling the organizational conditions for adaptivity. It is about organizational change, and can only take place through agent interaction (Moore and Hanson, 2022). Complexity provides a scaffolding for movement toward significant improvement in inclusivity, and is a change in mindset, structure, and process where leaders enable the conditions needed for change to occur.

As organizations promote inclusive initiatives to become more competitive in their environment, they turn to adopting complexity leadership practices. Frequently, these organizations face external pressures for change in labour practices regarding the disabled workforce and other marginalized labour groups; or the company creates its own internal pressure to make the change. It may hire consultants as a form of tension to assist in organizational change, involving specific recruiting, training, and retention strategies. These changes often seek to balance the tension of productivity and short-term performance with creating an inclusive culture and long-term organizational outcomes. Adopting complexity leadership principles leads to changed behaviours that have a transformational impact on the workplace, producing effective outcomes for both employees and the company.

We posit that organizations integrating large numbers of employees from a marginalized group such as disabled employees may find greater success in changing into an adaptive culture. We suggest this is directly tied to the need for leaders to become more interdependent (involved) in the change effort. That is, leaders are collectively engaged in the change, exploring various strategies and building strong relationships with organizational members. When integrating a large number of marginalized employees, managers do not always have the knowledge to accurately understand each disability or marginalized employee's viewpoint. Therefore, managers are forced to be more grounded in employee perspectives. This includes developing organizational learning in a way that increases the development of all employees, builds consensus, increases creativity in problem solving, and binds company members in the daunting challenge of building an effective team. This inclusive leadership practice balances the pressures of productivity and employee development, the key to successful inclusive hiring. Research shows that successful inclusive hiring initiatives create a new culture that boasts higher productivity rates as well as employee trust, engagement, and satisfaction.

Does this apply to me? Whether a large business or a small one, agriculture, government, education, or business, the short answer is 'Yes.' While specific details might be different, processes remain the same. The 'how' might vary, but leaders are challenged to ensure adaptive processes emerge. For example, 'how to nurture interaction' in a distribution centre may differ from 'how to nurture interaction' in a manufacturing plant, but the end result needed for an adaptive organization is still interaction. Also, as we have seen, pressures take different forms, but they must result in some sort of change effort. While the details might also shift with the level of analysis, general processes do not.

Moving organizations away from a hierarchical, bureaucratic model of leadership to a more employee-focused model opens the way for group-focused change that resonates with members. It embeds cultural considerations and collective purpose in the adaptive effort, making it more robust and powerful. This model can be generalized to other marginalized groups and other initiatives imposing a need for change. Front-line participation is essential to creating an environment open to change, partnerships, and accepting 'differences.' It works to resolve barriers by rooting solutions in organizational culture.

In conclusion, cultural change is more difficult when only a few are brought into a strong culture. The welfare of two or three employees may impinge on the ability of a large organization to take the transition seriously. In the large-scale operation of Walgreens' supply distribution groups, the size of the transition was large enough for managers to realize that many things had to change, and they had the backing of corporate leadership in the effort. Rather than a distraction, research identified the disabled workers in Walgreens as a catalyst, enabling successful change into an inclusive culture (Moore et al, 2020b).

With increasingly complex and unpredictable business environments, organizations are forced to turn to adapting their organizational culture to counterbalance these external pressures. Strong organizational leaders choose strategic initiatives that embrace the tension between operational pressures and 'employee-focused leadership', which pushes the organization toward healthy culture change. Our findings point to organizations being transformed through intentionally hiring and integrating marginalized groups, such as employees with disabilities. However, we posit that any strategic initiative by complexity leaders that embraces operational pressures with long-term employee development provides a proven way to bring, adaptivity, innovation, employee engagement, and competitivity to the organization. These inclusive organizations loosen formal structures, promote adaptive processes, and stimulate ideas and initiative. Embracing the challenge of hiring marginalized groups and leading through complexity leadership, increases productivity, employee engagement, innovation, and trust, while decreasing absenteeism and safety incidents.

References

Arena, M. and Uhl-Bien, M. (2016). 'Complexity leadership theory: Shifting from human capital to social capital', *People + Strategy* 39(2): 22–7.

Baer, M. (2012). 'Putting creativity to work: The implementation of creative ideas in organizations', *Academy of Management Journal* 55(5): 1102–19.

Bakke, D. (2005). *Joy at work: A revolutionary approach to fun on the job*, Seattle, WA: PVG.

Bennis, W. (2013). 'Leadership in a digital world: Embracing transparency and adaptive capacity', *MIS Quarterly* 37(2): 635–6.

Burns, J.M. (2003). *Transforming leadership*, New York: Atlantic Monthly Press.

Doughty, S.E. and Moore, J.R. (2021). 'Understanding inclusive organizations through ecological systems theory', *International Journal of Research in Business Studies and Management* 8(1): 7–14.

Hanson, W.R. and Ford, R. (2011). 'Embedded in complexity: Leader competencies in healthcare', *British Journal of Healthcare Management* 17(7): 284–90.

Lord, R. (2008). 'Beyond transactional and transformational leadership.' In M. Uhl-Bien and R. Marion (eds) *Complexity leadership*, Part 1: *Conceptual foundations*, Charlotte, NC: Information Age Publishing, pp 155–84.

Marion, R. (2008). 'Complexity theory for organizations and organizational leadership.' In M. Uhl-Bien and R. Marion (eds) *Complexity leadership, Part 1: Conceptual foundations*, Charlotte, NC: Information Age Publishing, pp 1–15.

Marion, R. and Uhl-Bien, M. (2003). 'Complexity theory and al-Qaeda: Examining complex leadership', *Emergence: A Journal of Complexity Issues in Organizations and Management* 5: 56–78.

Maxey E.C. and Moore, J.R. (2017). 'Impetus for culture transformation: Disabled employee pre-hire training.' In S. Frasard and F.C. Prasuhn (eds) *Handbook of research on training evaluation in the modern workforce*, Hershey, PA: IGI Global, pp 116–26.

Moore, J.R. and Hanson, W.R. (2022). 'Improving leader effectiveness: Impact on employee engagement and retention', *Journal of Management Development*: https://doi.org/10.1108/JMD-02-2021-0041

Moore, J.R., Hanson, W.R. and Maxey, E.C. (2020a). 'Disability inclusion: Catalyst to adaptive organizations', *Organizational Development Journal* 38(1): 89–105.

Moore, J.R., Maxey, E., Waite, A. and Wendover, J. (2020b). 'Inclusive organizations: Developmental reciprocity through authentic leader–employee relationships', *Journal of Management Development* 39(9/10): 1029–39.

Moore, J.R., Hankins, S. and Doughty, S. (2021). 'Successful employees with disabilities through the lens of Bronfenbrenner's ecological systems theory: A case study at Sephora', *Journal of Business Diversity* 20(5): 10–19.

Moore, J.R., Hanson, W.R. and Maxey, E.C. (2022). 'Beyond inclusion: Team impact of hiring people with disabilities at Sephora and Walgreens', *Organizational Development Journal*, Fall: 66–76.

Senge, P. (2006). *The fifth discipline: The art and practice of the learning organization*, New York: Random House Books.

Taylor, F.W. (1919). *The principles of scientific management*, New York: Harper and Brothers.

Uhl-Bien, M. and Marion, R. (2009). 'Complexity leadership in bureaucratic forms of organizing: A meso model', *Leadership Quarterly* 20(4): 631–50.

Uhl-Bien, M., Marion, R. and McKelvey, B. (2007). 'Complexity leadership theory: Shifting leadership from the industrial age to the knowledge era', *Leadership Quarterly* 18(4): 298–318.

Zhang, T., Avery, G.C., Bergsteiner, H. and More, E. (2014). 'The relationship between leadership paradigms and employee engagement', *Journal of Global Responsibility* 5(1): 4–21.

13

Practice Case Study: Sephora's Journey to an Inclusive Workplace and the 'Let Us Belong' Philosophy

Jeffrey Moore, William Hanson and Tom Gustafson

An inclusive workplace with a diversity of disabilities

Sephora North America created an adaptive and engaged employee culture in response to shortages of entry-level employees. This case study reveals the best practices Sephora used when developing an inclusive initiative aimed at hiring individuals with physical or cognitive disabilities. Our objective in this chapter is to illustrate an inclusive roadmap for companies seeking to operationalize similar inclusive initiatives which will transform their culture and improve their productivity.

Sephora, owned by LVMH Moët Hennessy Louis Vuitton, the world's leading luxury goods group, was aggressively expanding in North America, which necessitated building a strong, loyal, and productive employee culture. A brand-new distribution centre in Las Vegas was created in 2019 to support the west coast while implementing an inclusive workforce that would decrease employee turnover. Our findings reveal that, through the development of an inclusive workforce on a large scale, Sephora achieved employee engagement while also improving productivity and employee retention. Our findings present the four-stage journey, namely to (1) establish the vision, (2) build the bridge, (3) launch and (4) optimize.

The real-world problems facing Sephora were the shortage of human capital and the need to have an engaged, adaptive, and innovative employee culture. This was in the context of a crisis in employee loyalty across America with a majority of employees not trusting their employer (Aityan and Gupta, 2012; Wharton, 2012). In the manufacturing industry, and especially for the distribution centre, retaining and hiring employees was one of the key human resource crises which elevated the essential role of the manager (Ellinger et al, 2002; van Hoek et al, 2020; The Conference Board, 2021). Furthermore, COVID-19 has led to employment shortfalls in migrant workers who fill seasonal operator positions, putting pressure on farming, service, and manufacturing sectors (Barrero et al, 2020; Corbishley, 2020; Maurer, 2021). Another impact of COVID-19 has been the increase in online shopping that increased distribution centres' volumes. Hourly-paid employees working in these entry-level positions were rarely loyal to their employer and left for just a little better remuneration. Logistics research shows that emotional intelligence in managers is essential to facilitate the connection with employees and build a better workplace environment (Hohenstein et al, 2014; Keller et al, 2020).

Owing to high turnover in entry-level positions in large-scale facilities, managers often focus primarily on production metrics as they lead teams of between 20 and 50 employees. These operational realities create negative workplace environments in which employees feel disengaged and not valued. Researchers have found that organizations that seek to be complex adaptive systems are more likely to survive (Uhl-Bien, 2021). Creating an engaged and adaptive culture is a competitive advantage that counterbalances powerful operational pressures (Novak et al, 2021). If left unchecked these operational pressures condition managers to use authoritarian leadership styles, uniquely focusing on metrics (Uhl-Bien et al, 2007).

Inclusion intelligence: Sephora inclusive roadmap

Sephora North America radically changed the culture in its distribution centres. The four stages of this journey – vision, bridge, launch, and optimize – were the result of cooperation between leaders and supervisors and their teams, within strategic and operational imperatives.

Vision casting

The inclusive initiative was born when the Sephora Senior Vice-President of Supply Chain saw Randy Lewis present on Walgreens' large-scale hiring of people with disabilities at a professional conference (Lewis, 2014; Walgreens, 2016). Walgreens, the largest drug store chain in the United States, created multiple inclusive distribution centres where a large proportion of their workforce are individuals with disabilities, cognitive and/or physical limitations (see Chapter 12). He proceeded to ask his Vice-President of Human Resources to visit the Walgreens distribution centre in Connecticut where an inclusive workplace was a vibrant reality with 30 to 40 per cent of its 500 employees having a disability. Sephora Human Resource team members witnessed an inclusive workplace transforming the culture of that

Figure 13.1: Sephora's inclusive roadmap

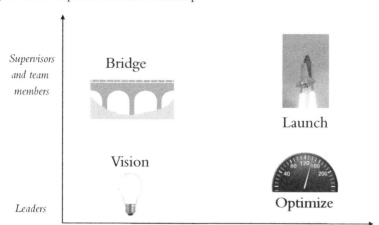

facility (Figure 13.1). The VP of Human Resources sent Sephora's Disability Coordinator, who had previously been a behaviour interventionist, to train with the Walgreens Inclusive Director. Behavior interventionists specialize in developing individual treatment plans to help autistic clients develop the skills they need to function in society (ACES, 2021).

The second step for Sephora's executive team was to sponsor the inclusion initiative and create an environment of trust. It is essential for the executive team to convince managers and supervisors that they are completely behind the priority of a new organizational culture. Executives create an environment of trust where managers and supervisors can learn how to lead in new inclusive teams without fear of reprisals because of their errors or mistakes. Executive champions lead the way in addressing the big questions and fears that managers and employees have so they can overcome their fears and biases and learn how to interact in a new inclusive team.

The primary barrier in this stage is fear. Fear of the unknown surrounding the plethora of disabilities, fear of doing the wrong thing or saying the wrong thing. A common reaction is: "I am not a disability specialist! Let the professional disability specialists take this on." The powerful emotion of fear is often successful in stopping an employee from starting the journey to adapt and change.

Sephora understood that the inclusion initiative was much bigger than just another corporate social action but was a transformation of its very organizational culture. They connected to their core values and earlier slogan to 'inspire fearlessness' (Sephora, 2021). Sephora executives highlighted how a largely unrepresented and often cast-aside segment of the workforce could be integrated and fearlessly reached out to 'the least of these'. They believed that, at the core, their employees wanted to do a good job, and that managers' goal was to help employees be successful. They connected with the powerful emotion of joy, rooted in a desire to improve others and oneself – doing a good job, and creating a better place to which the 'least of these' could belong. Sephora provided a way to self-actualize, where employee and company joined in the practice of creating a better world.

Building the bridge to inclusion

With the vision well established and championed by the executive team, the work of transforming the culture of the organization took shape by building a bridge to hire candidates with disabilities. This was achieved by hiring an inclusion consulting company to build a pipeline of candidates and to create training materials to support the adaptation of managers and employees.

The human capital pipeline of candidates was created by networking with local government and community agencies that serve the people with disabilities. Identifying which agency was open to adapting their processes in order to partner was essential. As Sephora's executive team champion argued:

> This is a win–win–win situation. The employee wins by belonging to a workplace, the company wins by receiving a loyal and productive employee, the state wins by having an individual no longer need their stipend.

Creating a strong partnership is the greatest challenge of the inclusive organization at this stage. Community and agency partnerships are essential to providing a regular pipeline of candidates to join the workforce. Owing to the uniqueness of federal, state, and local agencies in the USA, there is not a standard method and partner agency.

Creating an onboarding training for candidates with disabilities was accomplished by dedicating a training room and developing a nine-week onboarding curriculum. The first weeks were used for training soft skills. Next, the training focused on core job functions with a gradual transition on the operations floor. The consulting team broke down the job activities into smaller units and provided adapted learning aids to help disabled candidates learn their jobs. They trained agency job coaches on the core job functions so that they could train their job candidates. The onboarding training therefore was carried out by agency job coaches who brought a number of their clients into the onboarding process (Maxey et al, 2017). Candidates entered as agency clients, became interns as they integrated with the operations floor, reached 100 per cent productivity standards, then finally became full Sephora employees. As new employees they received the same pay for doing the same work as their co-workers.

Additionally, the consulting agency created training support for managers and employees in the facility. Managers were provided with an orientation to leading an inclusive team, which highlighted the benefits of disabled team members to their teams. This orientation focused on showing how disabled employee metrics consistently exceed 100 per cent of standard, and how disabled employees have almost no absenteeism, and work in a much safer manner. Training also focused on how to make your employees successful through understanding employee motivations and learning how to assess attitude, behaviours, and productivity. They were shown how to use the 'ask the person' (ATP) model (Moore et al, 2020a) and discuss observations and potential solutions. They were putting into practice the reflective supervision they received (see next paragraph) by creating a positive dialogue centred on making the employee successful, which can be applied to disabled or non-disabled team members alike.

Another aspect of creating an environment of trust is helping managers, supervisors, and employees understand what the new inclusive culture is all about. Often called reflective supervision, a leader would start an open dialogue and inquire about what fears and frustrations exist in the manager/supervisor. Opening the dialogue in a non-punitive way allows fears to be acknowledged, discussed, and overcome. The goal is to help employees deal with workplace emotions – fear created by change, the disability unknown – and open up to adaptation, learning, and change. Larger open dialogues with a few people were led by inclusion leaders who in small breakout groups discussed the fears and frustrations of the managers/supervisors. These sessions focused on dealing with fear.

Finally, Sephora created an inclusion coordinator position, part of the human resource department, to step into the management of the inclusive project started by the consulting team. The inclusion coordinator has four major duties: (1) managing the relationship with the agencies, (2) liaison with the managers and supervisors, (3) advocating for the program in the community and (4) supporting other companies wanting to start an inclusion initiative.

Launch: creating a new culture

Sephora developed the inclusion initiative in both a start-up facility and an existing facility. In the start-up scenario, adoption of the inclusive culture was immediate and natural as, from the start, managers, supervisors, and employees were aware of the workplace inclusion in the hiring process. However, when the inclusion initiative was introduced at an existing facility, the change was much slower, as managers and supervisors had to adjust to the new reality.

During this phase the inclusion coordinator worked almost exclusively with the managers and supervisors to apply the training previously developed.

Continuing to meet with small groups of managers/supervisors the coordinator discussed the problems and challenges of inclusion, and how to overcome them, bringing participants to a place where they chose to learn from each other, step out in courage, and adapt. The inclusion coordinator was modelling what it means to focus on the employee and help them be successful. Coordinators equip managers and supervisors to understand and assist the employee first of all, rather than jump to a corrective action as a first step.

Essential to the launch stage of the inclusion journey is that managers and supervisors need to adopt a new style of management, focusing on the employee as well as on performance (Moore et al, 2020b). Previously, managers only valued performance. Now managers were expected to maintain the tension of production with a focus on employee success. They were expected to make their team members successful and were forbidden to dismiss any employee without extensive efforts to develop them. Supervisors were pushed to coach their team members and focus on creating balanced teams in which disabled and non-disabled could share each other's strengths. This new way of thinking did not try to make everyone fit into one mould but rather to use the specificities of each team member to support the team objectives. New leadership skills – mentoring and coordination – were required. The outcome was a new leadership style where supervisors took ownership of employee relations, non-disabled employees provided coaching and support, and the inclusion coordinator strengthened the supervisor–employee relationship by providing support.

The main challenge of distribution centres is the business pressures of productivity and efficiency. Disabled team members needed to be as productive as their non-disabled counterparts, doing the same work for the same pay, a key tenet in the social contract of these employees. Sephora compared the productivity of its disabled and non-disabled employees, finding that the disabled employees typically outperform their counterparts. Tables 13.1 and 13.2 compare productivity and absences at the two facilities. Looking at a month at the beginning of the pandemic fewer than 2 per cent of disabled team members had an unexpected absence while 24 per cent of their peers were unexpectedly absent. Safety incidents were also measured to reveal that employees with disabilities have markedly fewer such incidents.

These findings clearly show how over 120 employees with disabilities are on average more productive and show less absenteeism and fewer safety incidents than over 650 non-disabled counterparts. High absenteeism is expensive as the organization may have to pay overtime to the non-absent employees.

Optimize

After the launch of this initiative, a new CEO arrived in Sephora and fully supported the inclusion initiative, making it one of the company's

Table 13.1: Productivity and absenteeism comparisons in Mississippi

Date	% EWD	Absenteeism		Safety		Productivity	
		Non-EWD	EWD	Non-EWD	EWD	Total non-EWD	Total EWD
01/04/2020	25%	22%	2%	0	0	113%	116%
01/05/2020						126%	120%
01/06/2020	19%	25%	7%	1	0	111%	111%
01/07/2020						105%	114%
01/08/2020	16%	22%	5%	0	2	106%	112%
01/09/2020						110%	115%
01/10/2020	23%	24%	4%	1	0	98%	112%
01/11/2020						95%	106%
01/12/2020	24%	24.70%	6%	0	0	103%	108%
2020	**21%**	**23.54%**	**4.80%**	**2**	**2**	**114%**	**114%**
01/01/2021	19%	28%	7%	2	1	109%	119%
01/02/2021	18%	25%	6%	3	0	109%	115%
01/03/2021	15%	24%	7%	6	2	109%	115%
01/04/2021	15%	28%	6%	2	0	99%	107%
01/05/2021	15%	29%	5%	4	1	105%	113%
01/06/2021	15%	30%	5%	3	0	113%	117%
01/07/2021	16%	31%	6%	2	0	110%	118%
01/08/2021	19%	33%	7%	3	0	108%	113%
01/09/2021	20%	33%	7%	4	3	103%	112%
01/10/2021	21%	29%	5%	2	0	106%	110%
01/11/2021	19%	30%	4%	6	1	89%	100%
01/12/2021	19%	33%	6%	7	0	97%	105%
2021	**18%**	**29%**	**5.9%**	**44**	**8**	**105%**	**112%**
01/01/2022	20%	31%	5%	5	0	105%	108%
01/02/2022	20%	33%	4%	4	0	113%	110%
01/03/2022	22%	29%	6%	3	1	99%	107%
01/04/2022	20%	32%	5%	4	0	94%	105%
01/05/2022	11%	22%	3%	1	0	118%	119%
01/06/2022	12%	20%	6%	0	0	103%	127%
01/07/2022	15%	21%	4%	0	0	111%	121%
01/08/2022	15%	26%	4%	5	0	115%	112%
01/09/2022	12%	26%	6%	1	0	110%	116%
2022	**16%**	**26.7%**	**4.8%**	**23**	**1**	**108%**	**114%**

Note: EWD = employee with disability

Table 13.2: Productivity and absenteeism comparisons in Las Vegas

Date	% EWD	Absenteeism		Safety		Productivity	
		Non-EWD	EWD	Non-EWD	EWD	Total non-EWD	Total EWD
4/1/2020	8%	3.07%	0.71%	2	0	113%	116%
5/1/2020						126%	120%
6/1/2020	10%	2.96%	1.40%	2	1	142%	116%
7/1/2020						139%	119%
8/1/2020	11%	2.00%	0.00%	2	1	134%	121%
9/1/2020						130%	120%
10/1/2020	12%	2.00%	0.68%	2	0	107%	114%
11/1/2020						105%	100%
12/1/2020	11%	2.00%	0.67%	1	0	117%	105%
2020	**10%**	**2.41%**	**0.69%**	**9**	**2**	**126%**	**115%**
1/1/2021	12%	3.00%	0.00%	4	0	135%	117%
2/1/2021	11%	1.00%	0.00%	2	0	138%	121%
3/1/2021	13%	6.00%	3.00%	3	0	132%	124%
4/1/2021	12%	2.00%	3.00%	5	0	110%	116%
5/1/2021	12%	3.00%	0.00%	0	0	134%	112%
6/1/2021	12%	2.00%	0.00%	0	0	132%	114%
7/1/2021	14%	3.00%	1.00%	0	0	129%	114%
8/1/2021	20%	3.00%	1.00%	1	0	112%	108%
9/1/2021	17%	3.00%	1.00%	0	2	112%	108%
10/1/2021	12%	5.00%	1%	3	0	108%	101%
11/1/2021	8%	8.00%	1%	6	0	91%	83%
12/1/2021	8%	2.00%	1%	6	0	102%	100%
2021	**13%**	**3.42%**	**1.00%**	**30**	**2**	**120%**	**110%**
1/1/2022	21%	18.00%	1.00%	1	0	122%	113%
2/1/2022	19%	9.00%	2.50%	2	0	120%	108%
3/1/2022	19%	9.00%	1.00%	2	0	103%	107%
4/1/2022	21%	10.00%	1.00%	0	0	97%	98%
5/1/2022	21%	6.00%	1.00%	0	0	122%	117%
6/1/2022	23%	6.00%	1.00%	0	0	117%	113%
7/1/2022	20%	3.00%	1.00%	2	0	105%	114%
8/1/2022	21%	3.00%	2.00%	0	0	127%	111%
9/1/2022	25%	3.00%	1.00%	0	0	113%	107%
2022	**21%**	**7.44%**	**1.28%**	**7**	**0**	**116%**	**111%**

Note: EWD = employee with disability

key strategic initiatives. This was very effective in moving employees companywide in supporting the inclusion initiative.

During the optimize stage of the inclusive journey Sephora relied on the inclusion coordinator to liaise with managers and supervisors. Continuing to meet small groups of managers/supervisors they discussed the problems and challenges of inclusion. These sessions continued to focus on dealing with fear and how to overcome it.

Inclusive teams continued to thrive and co-workers became mentors to a disabled team member. This volunteer mentoring emerged from within the teams as employees embraced the joy of making a difference in the lives of their disabled co-workers who had overcome such hardship – they identified with helping them be successful. These inspirational stories continued to appear all over the organization. Sephora's video crew shot inspirational vignettes, connected to the theme 'Belonging', which were then used in training and community outreach efforts. Some examples are posted on the Sephora inclusion webpage.

In one facility, managers had let the productivity standard for the disabled team members slide down to 80 per cent while their non-disabled peers kept to the 100 per cent standard. These managers had not been willing to have coaching conversations but reduced the standard instead. Once the inclusion champion found out about this discrepancy, immediate action was taken to have the 103 disabled employees retrained to reach standard. Local managers were amazed to discover that all these employees were able to make the standard. In this part of the journey Sephora discovered that accountability is a critical area that must apply to all employees without differentiation. This inclusive dynamic between managers and team members is a reality in all of their inclusive distribution centres.

We collected data from Sephora's four North American distribution centres. This data was both qualitative and quantitative. First, we looked at all of the hourly-paid employees' daily performance rates over two weeks. Second, we interviewed all of the hourly-paid employees about their perceptions concerning their managers, their non-disabled co-workers, their disabled co-workers, their work, and their engagement, collecting over 700 responses. Third, we interviewed all of the hourly-paid employees' supervisors and managers, collecting over 80 responses. Finally, we were able to correlate a large percentage of the hourly-paid employees' responses with their productivity rates.

Results of the four-stage inclusion roadmap

Our survey of all Sephora distribution centre employees revealed that employees felt strongly that there should be no differences in performance standard between disabled and non-disabled, as Figure 13.2 shows. Figure 13.2 describes the impact of employee thoughts about disabled

Figure 13.2: People with disabilities should be held to the same performance standards as non-disabled employees

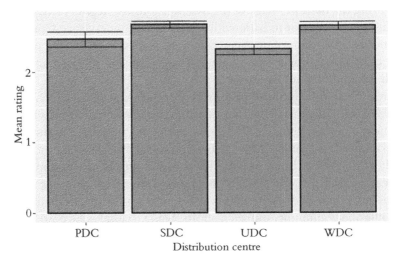

employees as very significant with ANOVA results: $F_{(3,702)} = 6.567$, $p < .001$, based on 706 respondents from 4 distribution centres. Sephora labelled their four distribution centres SDC, UDC, WDC, and PDC. Furthermore, we made pairwise comparisons of the four distribution centres and found that the two employing people with disabilities significantly differ from UDC (which has no employees with disabilities) in their agreement that all employees should be held to the same standards, regardless of disability: SDC ($p = .00037$) and WDC ($p = .00117$).

Interestingly, as Sephora creates inclusive organizations, many managers, supervisors, and employees are drawn to them because of their inclusive practices. Sephora clearly articulates its inclusivity within its hiring messaging and process. Inclusion has become a competitive advantage in drawing human capital who value inclusion and who identify with creating an inclusive workplace, a better world.

Productivity metrics

Productivity metrics contrast the differences between employees with a disability (EWD) and employees without a disability (non-EWD). We found strong EWD metrics in absenteeism, safety, and productivity in the Mississippi and Las Vegas facilities. Overall, two factors push down the EWD percentage: the number of non-EWD employees in the facility increased over the period surveyed, and EWD employees have a nine-week onboarding phase while non-EWDs only receive two-week onboarding.

Figure 13.3: Employees with a disability have made the team more effective

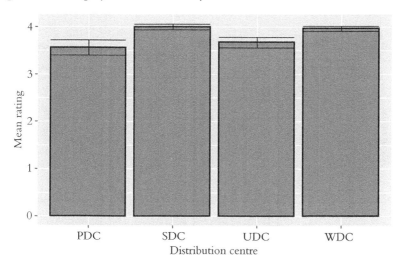

Impact of employees with disabilities on the team

We turn our focus to the impact on the culture of the organization and the impact of inclusion. Figure 13.3 illustrates employees talking about the performance on the job of their team members with a disability, finding that the team members with disabilities have made a significant contribution toward making the team more effective. ANOVA results: $F (3,455) = 5.737$, $p < .001$) with 459 respondents from the 4 distribution centres.

Looking at the pairwise comparisons of the four distribution centres we found that the two centres employing people with disabilities differ significantly from both UDC and PDC (neither of which have employees with disabilities) in their agreement that employees with disabilities have made the team more effective: SDC:UDC ($p = .0184$) and WDC:UDC ($p = .0385$), SDC:PDC ($p = .0076$) and WDC:PDC ($p = .0184$).

Figure 13.4 shows the same 459 employees agreeing that their disabled team members performed their assignments as well as people without a disability. This question also gained a significant response with ANOVA results: $F (3,455) = 3.278$, $p = .02$) based on 459 respondents from 4 distribution centres.

Finally Figure 13.5 reports that the 459 employees agree that their disabled team members made them a better person in other aspects of their life. This question was marginally significant with ANOVA results: $F (3,455) = 2.225$, $p = .08$, across 459 respondents from 4 distribution centres.

Figure 13.4: Employees with a disability perform their assignments as well as people without disabilities

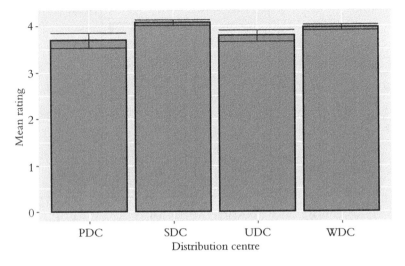

Figure 13.5: Team members with disabilities made me a better person in other aspects of my life

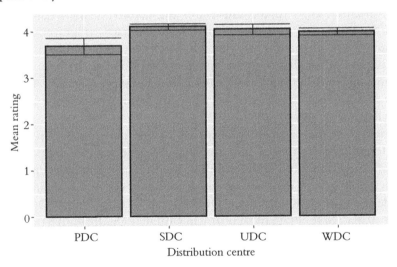

Lessons and implications for inclusive employer engagement

Sephora has intentionally pursued creating inclusive workplaces to help increase retention of employees while improving the workplace culture for all employees. Its solution was to create a four-step process to successfully identify, recruit, and onboard disabled employees. This strategic hiring practice requires a nine-week onboarding program as well as necessitating strong partnerships with local organizations to keep the candidate pipeline full. The human resource inclusion coordinator in each facility provides the support needed to maintain local partnerships and internal inclusion training.

Organizations which desire to create an inclusive workplace need to have strong ties to their core values to inspire this organizational culture change. Furthermore, an executive champion needs to lead the inclusion initiative while overseeing the planning and execution of this vision. Successful executive champions embed culture change into the strategy of the organization. Building the bridge to inclusion often requires external assistance in establishing the first inclusive facility. Once the bridge between local organizations serving the population of people with disabilities is made, a training centre can be built, enabling an effective onboarding training experience. Finally, as disabled employees are onboarded, supervisors and team members begin the process of adapting to each other, resulting in greater openness, cooperation, innovation, and productivity.

Sephora has found that becoming an inclusive workplace has aligned with their company motto 'We belong to something beautiful.' This alignment has produced ethical resonance with many of their employees. Belonging necessitates respect and care for others, which are essential qualities of an inclusive workforce. We find that the bands of fellow team members who assist, coach, and support become the voluntary disability champions.

References

ACES (2021). 'Elevating the standards in the treatment of autism': www.acesaba.com/autism-treatment/what-is-a-behavioral-interventionist/

Aityan, S.K. and Gupta, T.K.P. (2012). 'Challenges of employee loyalty in corporate America', *Business and Economics Journal*, 12.

Barrero, J.M., Bloom, N. and Davis, S. (2020). 'COVID-19 and labour reallocation: Evidence from the US', *voxEU.org*, 14 July.

Conference Board, The (2021). 'As COVID-19 recedes, labor shortages return as a key challenge for US companies and opportunity for American workers', press release, 28 May.

Corbishley, N. (2020). 'Farm-labor crisis under COVID-19 sends countries scrambling', *Wolf Street*, 13 April.

Ellinger, A.E., Ellinger, A.D. and Keller, S.B. (2002). 'Logistics manager learning environments and firm performance', *Journal of Business Logistics* 23: 19–37.

Hohenstein, N.-O., Feisel, E. and Hartmann, E. (2014). 'Human resource management issues in supply chain management research: A systematic literature review from 1998 to 2014', *International Journal of Physical Distribution & Logistics Management* 44(6): 434–63.

Keller, S.B., Ralston, P.M. and LeMay, S.A. (2020). 'Quality output, workplace environment, and employee retention: The positive influence of emotionally intelligent supply chain managers', *Journal of Business Logistics* 41(4): 337–55.

Lewis, R. (2014). *No Greatness without Goodness: How a Father's Love Changed a Company and Sparked a Movement*, Carol Stream, IL: Tyndale.

Maurer, R. (2021). 'Labor shortages: The disconnect and possible solutions', *Society Human Resource Managers: Talent Acquisition*, 4 August.

Maxey E., Moore, J. and Hanson, W. (2017). 'Impetus for culture transformation: Disabled employee pre-hire training.' In E. Maxey, J. Moore and W. Hanson (eds) *Handbook of research on training evaluation in the modern workforce*, Hershey, PA: IGI Global.

Moore, J.R., Hanson, W.R. and Maxey E.C. (2020a). 'Disability inclusion: Catalyst to adaptive organizations', *Organization Development Journal* 38(1): 89–105.

Moore, J.R., Waite, A.M., Maxey, E.C. and Wendover J. (2020b). 'Inclusive organizations: Developmental reciprocity through authentic leader–employee relationships', *Journal of Management Development* 38(1).

Novak, D.C., Wu, Z. and Dooley, K.J. (2021). 'Whose resilience matters? Addressing issues of scale in supply chain resilience', *Journal of Business Logistics* 42: 323–35.

Sephora (2021). 'Sephora stands: We belong to something beautiful': www.sephorastands.com/

Uhl-Bien, M. (2021). 'Complexity leadership and followership: Changed leadership in a changed world', *Journal of Change Management* 21(2): 144–62.

Uhl-Bien, M., Marion, R. and McKelvey, B. (2007). 'Complexity leadership theory: Shifting leadership from the industrial age to the knowledge era', *The Leadership Quarterly* 18: 298–318.

US Department of Labor (2021). 'Persons with a disability: Labor force characteristics – 2020', press release, Bureau of Labor: www.bls.gov/news.release/disabl.toc.htm

van Hoek, R., Gibson, B. and Johnson, M. (2020). 'Talent management for a post-COVID-19 supply chain: The critical role for managers', *Journal of Business Logistics* 41: 334–36.

Vogel, N. (2012). 'Disability best practices: Who's doing what?' *Profiles in Diversity Journal* 72.

Walgreens (2016). 'The Walgreens experience': https://youtu.be/avNykR3FsUc

Wharton, K. (2012). 'Declining employee loyalty: A casualty of the new workplace', *Online Business Journal*: https://knowledge.wharton.upenn.edu/article/declining-employee-loyalty-a-casualty-of-the-new-workplace/

14

Conclusion: Making Active Labour Market Policies Work

Patrick McGurk and Jo Ingold

The overriding theme of this book on employer engagement has been 'making active labour market policies work'. This is to say that, while our collection offers a broad and varied intellectual exploration of employer engagement – including its meaning, interpretation and practice in comparative context – our ultimate aim has been to arrive at a clearer understanding of how employers may contribute to ALMPs in a way that successfully secures sustained employment for people who are often widely left outside the workplace. We have approached this by exploring the issues at three levels: macro (institutional and national policy), meso (regional and implementation through partners) and micro (workplace organization).

It is clear from the material in this book that there is no magic formula for engaging employers to make ALMPs work. The diversity of policy orientation and institutional machinery across countries and within regions is simply too great and complex, as is the variety of partners, programmes and the employers themselves. Yet despite the complexity and diversity of employer engagement policy, implementation and practice, we can conclude that some general, and critical, lessons that may be drawn in order to shed light on the pragmatic question facing all countries about how employers may be engaged more effectively in active labour market policies. Firstly, we synthesize the lessons from the different country contexts in the collection's chapters. Secondly, we offer some ingredients for successful employer engagement at macro, meso and micro levels. Finally, we set out an agenda for future research and scholarship in this area.

General lessons from the country cases

Three of the chapters in the collection are devoted to international comparison, specifically between the UK, Denmark and The Netherlands (Bredgaard, Ingold and van Berkel), then between the UK and Australia (Baker, Ingold, Crichton and Carr) and finally between the UK and Germany (Wiggan and Knuth). The remaining chapters are all based on single-country studies, though the only country beyond this set of countries is the USA (Hanson and Moore; Moore, Hanson and Gustafson). This is helpful in that the conclusions drawn in the comparative chapters provide a useful set of starting points on which the conclusions from the single-country chapters may then build, to create a richer set of contextualized insights. The country selections themselves are also distributed between the more liberal market economies (UK, Australia, USA) and the more coordinated market economies (Germany, Denmark, The Netherlands), therefore allowing conclusions to be drawn from a varieties of capitalism perspective (Hall and Soskice, 2001). Our international comparative perspective is far from exhaustive. However, based on the variety of national institutions captured, in the spirit of the overall question how employer engagement can 'make ALMPs work', we suggest that effective and sustainable employer engagement seems to be based upon: (1) bounded voluntarism; (2) connections to wider political-economic changes involving worker security and job quality; and (3) local collaborative relationships.

Bounded voluntarism

The three-country comparative chapter by Bredgaard, Ingold and van Berkel spans both the liberal and coordinated types of market economy. However, the authors conclude that the policy instruments designed to ensure employer engagement in ALMPs in all three countries studied – the UK, Denmark and The Netherlands – are *predominantly voluntary* rather than obligatory in nature. It is helpful to view such voluntarism on a continuum, along which voluntarism is bounded to different degrees. At the more bounded end are the Danish and Dutch cases, which exhibit clear national programmes and frameworks to negotiate a balance between disadvantaged unemployed and employers, such as the Flexible Jobs schemes and the Job Agreement. Towards the less bounded end, as Bredgaard et al show, is the UK, in which no activation policy exists that provides an institutionalized basis for this type of negotiation; instead, initiatives are regulated but tend to emerge from 'the bottom up' and so are less systematic and more piecemeal than the Danish and Dutch cases. Indeed, McGurk and Olaleye further illustrate the fragmented and weak nature of employer engagement, in England at least, even when subjected to relatively strong 'sticks' such as a compulsory apprenticeship levy. Extrapolating further down the less bounded end, it may be argued that the US context represents the most extreme form of voluntarism. The US cases in our collection concentrate only on single-organization examples, so necessarily are not concerned with wider institutional structures. However, it is arguably significant that all of the single-case examples in the US chapters depict highly voluntaristic engagement by socially responsible employers, who appear to be making strategic investments in ALMPs almost entirely on their own terms.

It is important, nonetheless, not to overstate the bounded nature of engagement in countries such as Denmark, and to appreciate the *complexity of the boundedness*. Dall, Larsen and Madsen, for example, illustrate how, in Denmark, effective employer engagement can be achieved through political, economic and organizational prioritization but with very low regulation of, and obligations for, the employers. They argue that employer engagement cannot easily be produced through standardized policies and implementation models. Local autonomy and flexibility in the solutions applied become important preconditions for brokered engagement processes, and unusual demands are made on the efforts of employer engagement staff in labour market intermediaries (for example employment services providers, or 'ALMP agencies'). The authors' analysis of the Danish case therefore implies that it is possible to create employer engagement even in a context of voluntary engagement. However, they also illustrate how the limits of voluntary engagement are easily exposed as employer priorities and complex social aims collide. Dall, Larsen and Madsen go on to show how employers who are mainly motivated by short-term goals – productive (or free) labour – might be less motivated to sustain relational and reciprocal engagement over a prolonged period. If, for example, the aim of the ALMP is to promote the labour market participation of unemployed individuals who have social, mental and/or physical challenges, then employers may need to be bound to different ultimate goals, beyond the establishing of standard work placements and/or temporary, subsidized employment for specific individuals.

Connections to wider political-economic changes involving worker security and job quality

There is an understandable, problem-solving-oriented temptation to seek a neat set of answers to the question 'how to engage employers to make ALMPs work'. The overriding insight from this collection, however, is how inextricably linked are questions of employer engagement and ALMPs to wider political economy issues, in a way that eludes any reductive answers. The strongest contemporaneous political-economic theme to emerge from the various discussions in the preceding chapters is how arguments about employers' roles in ALMPs and their sustainability are increasingly bound up with wider debates about worker security and job quality.

The political-economic theme, and its centrality to understanding employer engagement, is most strongly evident in the Danish case, as analysed by Etherington and Jones. Dovetailing with Dall, Larsen and Madsen's chapter, Etherington and Jones explain how Danish employer engagement can only be clearly understood *in relation to the structural roles played by other actors*, namely the trade unions and local government. The authors set out four key elements of the Danish system that are crucial in shaping employment and skills. The first element is high union density and membership, which make trade unions important actors in the welfare system, in which they manage unemployment insurance benefits (the Ghent system), thereby connecting trade unions strongly to unemployment policies. Second, and linked to this, is trade unions' active involvement in social dialogue and bargaining around employment policy (Valizade et al, 2022). Third is a developed system of collective agreements in which unions negotiate changes and improvements to welfare and skills policies. The fourth and final element is the central role and importance of local government (including the local welfare state) and devolved authorities in labour market policy. In other words, the Danish case exhibits a highly devolved system where institutions and actors operate within the same geographical boundaries, thus enabling smooth coordination and collaboration between employers and jobseekers, the opposite of the fragmented and often misaligned structures in the UK, for example. In short, the Danish case can be said to exemplify how employer engagement can only be understood through the complex geographies of labour market development.

In a further demonstration of the political-economic basis for employer engagement, Wiggan and Knuth, in their comparison of the UK and Germany, highlight the importance of *changes and varieties of labour markets*, because of influences as diverse as changes in business cycles and unexpected political crises related to integration of refugees. As the authors put it, employer needs are 'neither fixed, nor divorced from (shifting patterns of) labour market stratification, segmentation and demand'. In other words, our understanding of employer engagement is necessarily temporal and context-dependent not only in terms of countries but also of political and business cycles. The UK–Germany comparison presented suggests that the types and quality of jobs and work placements provided, and their sustainability through ALMPs, are related not just to individual employer (or hiring manager) choices but also to the structures of the employing businesses – their size and sector and their connection to the required vocational training qualifications. Wiggan and Knuth show, for example, how in Germany owner-managed small and micro enterprises were more willing to take on candidates from under-served groups than in the UK, where there was an emphasis on engagement with larger employers. To some extent this echoes Martin's (2004) classic work on the importance of employer associations, employer size (and the presence of an HR department); however, Wiggan and Knuth also offer the tentative explanation that the German labour market is more structured along formal and documented vocational qualifications and professionally structured career paths than the UK market. This represents again perhaps a nod to the varieties of capitalism typologies still having salience.

Borghouts and Freese's chapter on The Netherlands highlights the importance of understanding employer engagement in the context of *policy responses to wider changes in the labour market*. The authors draw attention to recent measures enacted by the Dutch Economic Council (SER) in response to growing concerns about the large number of flex workers and the resultant advisory report 'Security for people, a flexible economy and recovery of society'. The report provides a vision for the future labour market in which broad prosperity for all Dutch citizens can be achieved (SER, 2021) in line with the five building blocks published in the European Skills Agenda for sustainable competitiveness, social fairness and resilience, namely: (1) collective action (mobilizing business, social partners and stakeholders, to commit to working together in particular within the EU's industrial ecosystems), (2) financial means to foster investments in skills, (3) clear strategy to ensure that skills lead to jobs, (4) helping people build their skills throughout life where lifelong learning is the norm, and (5) setting ambitious objectives for upskilling and reskilling to be achieved by 2026 (European Commission, 2021). The SER advises significant investment in employment and income security and emphasizes the importance of an ambitious programme to strengthen the agility and resilience of the economy and to offer people more security throughout their working lives. This is a compelling blueprint to follow and clearly has important implications for employer engagement with ALMPs, which should increasingly be framed in terms of wider structures of employment security, rather than job placement and retention.

Even in the liberal market economy of the UK, employer engagement with ALMPs is increasingly being discussed *in relation to job quality* arising from an increasing emphasis on issues of employment sustainability and in-work progression. Green and Sissons show how, until relatively recently, the predominant focus of UK employment policy was bound up with a concern for employment quantity (with less consideration of the quality of work) and ALMPs had developed around a more active approach to out-of-work benefit claimants, increasing use of mandation and an over-arching work-first emphasis. Although the UK ALMP framework remains to a large extent disconnected from wider policy debates about 'good work', there is growing scope to ask how elements of the current context might allow

ALMPs to capitalize on some upwards pressures on job quality. There are also a number of other regional and local factors, which are opening up new directions around job quality, including in entry-level roles (although within this discussion there also needs to be consideration of career pathways). Successful implementation of such workforce strategies requires good knowledge of the local area and the characteristics of the local labour force, together with strong local partnership working, demonstrating that local stakeholders other than public employment services can take the initiative in developing new projects and programmes without direct public employment services' involvement (although this necessarily relies on staff having knowledge of such initiatives and, where applicable, the ability to offer the relevant support). Recent developments in the UK and elsewhere may indicate an important opportunity to capitalize on and ensure that employers play a crucial role, to create and/or promote good-quality jobs, alongside addressing unemployment.

Local collaborative relationships

Intersecting the wider questions of national regulation and the related political-economic structures and processes is the very strong, common theme of local collaborative partnerships, which enable effective and sustained employer engagement. This theme is central to both the comparative UK–Australia chapter by Baker, Ingold, Crichton and Carr, and the single-country chapters focusing on The Netherlands, Australia, the UK and the USA (respectively Dall, Larsen and Madsen; Hamilton; McGurk and Meredith; Hanson and Moore; Moore, Hanson and Gustafson).

Baker et al show how, in both the UK and Australia, selected ALMPs brought together multiple stakeholders for the purposes of better job matching and sustainability of jobs by working directly with employers to service their needs and also through better preparation of candidates. The case studies from both countries demonstrate how barriers to employer engagement arising from government commissioning models may be overcome by putting in place *innovative local structures*. More specifically, the country case studies highlight the need for government departments to work together, in order to meet employers' labour demands as well as to consider collaboration at the stage of policy and programme design, rather than expect providers to 'retrofit' their delivery within highly competitive commissioning models. In the Danish context, when opening up the 'black box' of employer engagement but with underpinning institutionalized rules and incentives, Dall, Larsen and Madsen show the central importance of relationship-building between local stakeholders for successful and sustainable job outcomes. The authors show how employer engagement is developed *relationally over time in negotiated collaborations* between employer engagement staff, employers and unemployed individuals, and contextually in the specific circumstances of the unemployed, the workplace and the active labour market policies.

The centrality of relationship-building to successful employer engagement resonates throughout the other localized case studies in the collection. In particular, Hamilton's account of improved employer engagement with an Australian non-profit disability enterprise demonstrates the importance of *facilitated interventions* for stakeholders. The author relates how a multi-agency group including employers was brought together by specialist facilitators to make collective sense of the opportunities and challenges presented by changes to the National Disability Insurance Scheme and other national policies in Australia, such as the lifting of the cap on the number of supported disabled employees.

The intersection of macro, meso and micro levels of ALMPs

Our exploration of the question of effective employer engagement for sustained employment of jobseekers through ALMPs has been structured according to macro, meso and micro levels. Such distinctions are of course artificially sharp in considering how employer engagement plays out in practice. However, the general lessons about sustained employment outcomes that permeate this collection lead us to offer the following idealized framework in Table 14.1 for successful employer engagement characteristics.

Table 14.1: Characteristics of successful employer engagement

Engagement level	Main actors	Key characteristics
Macro	• National governments • Employer associations • Trade unions	• Blend of policy 'sticks', 'carrots' and 'sermons' • Institutionalized social partnerships • Regional/local devolution • Societal concern with the quality of working life
Meso	• National regulators • Intermediaries • Sectoral bodies • Regional and local government	• Simplicity in programme operations • Holistic recruitment and retention intermediary services • Co-production partnership approach and local autonomy • Occupational career ladders
Micro	• Individual firms • Human resource management experts • Local partnerships	• Inclusive leadership and human resource management • Shared responsibility for local, social outcomes

Macro-level employer engagement

As Bredgaard, Ingold and van Berkel argue, it is the role of national governments to shape – to varying degrees – the regulation, facilitation and negotiation of arrangements for employer engagement. This happens through blends of policy 'sticks' (such as rules and taxes), 'carrots' (such as financial subsidies and other incentives) and 'sermons' (such as information and influencing) directed at employers. Of course, different political parties that form national governments will have varying ideological preferences and changing priorities; these will affect the *blend of sticks, carrots and sermons* that is used in complex, context-specific ways. Similarly, there are no easy, optimal blends for any particular national institutional context, or to fit certain varieties of capitalism. As already noted, there is a general preference for voluntary carrots and sermons, rather than sticks, even in the more coordinated market economies of The Netherlands and Denmark, let alone the more liberal ones like the UK. There is no 'big book' of policy preferences. We merely recognize that national governments seem to require a blend of all three types of strategy in order to implement ALMPs and adapt them to changing circumstances.

With regard to different types of national institutional arrangements, our collection nonetheless suggests that *institutionalized social partnerships*, which formally bind national governments, employer associations and trades unions in decisions that shape ALMP design, enable meso-level approaches that have the potential to lead to more sustained employment outcomes for a greater number of jobseekers. This is most notable in Denmark, where trades unions have played an integral role in both design and implementation of policy (see Etherington and Jones). Conversely, at the other extreme, the UK experience illustrates how voluntaristic arrangements tend to be accompanied by either short-termist and/or transactional attitudes towards ALMPs, or well-meaning but short-lived engagement by employers (see McGurk and Olaleye). This does not mean that sustained employer engagement cannot occur amidst such settings but requires significantly more activities by actors on the ground.

A third general observation with regards to the macro level is that successful employer engagement appears to be enabled by *regional and local devolution*. While devolution is in any case integral to governance in most of the countries featured in this book – notably Germany, The Netherlands and Denmark – it is striking that the most powerful examples of ALMPs tend to be associated with innovations born out of regional and local stakeholder partnerships, regardless of the country in question (see Dall, Larsen and Madsen; Borghouts and Freese). In the UK's highly centralized system, for example, as highlighted by Green and Sissons, arguably the most sustainable approach to engaging employers in ALMPs is to be found under a devolved arrangement in Wales.

A final characteristic at the macro level, albeit more aspirational than real, may be identified as *a societal concern with the quality of working life*. This manifests itself for example in The Netherlands, in the attempt to mobilize employers as social partners to commit to a new system of labour standards designed to achieve greater employment and income security over the working lifetime, in part-acceptance of the employer-driven contemporary trend towards non-standard and more flexible jobs (see Borghouts and Freese). Other manifestations of this more general societal concern are illustrated in the potential shift, as observed by Green and Sissons, away from 'work-first' ALMPs towards 'career-first' ALMPs, thereby incentivizing higher job quality and in-work progression over low-quality job outcomes. Relatedly, we see, for example in Germany, how employers may be engaged as partners in national campaigns to (re)integrate marginalized groups such as refugees or older workers into the mainstream workforce (see Wiggan and Knuth).

We recognize that this last proposed characteristic of successful employer engagement at the macro level may seem overly idealistic and gloss over very real contradictions in stakeholder interests. However, the discussion serves to re-emphasize an important general point: that successful employer engagement has to be recognized and negotiated as part of a set of wider social and political relations – it is not sustainable if treated as a separate, transactional process between government and individual firms.

Meso-level employer engagement

For all the consideration of macro-level characteristics of employer engagement, our collection accentuates the overriding importance of the practical concerns of ALMP implementation at the meso level. Key to successful implementation are the interrelationships between the labour market intermediaries and the commissioners and regulators responsible for ALMPs, sectoral employer bodies, as well as the machinery of regional and local government. Observations from across our collection lead us to surmise that, for productive and efficient relationships between these actors to develop, four factors are important.

Firstly, as ALMP evaluation studies and ground-level accounts persistently point out, employer engagement initiatives have been constantly stymied by instability and complexity in government schemes, which intermediaries have to interpret and then offer to employers. The ALMP arena has fallen victim to 'policy hyperactivism' (compare Dunleavy, 1995). Instead, for ALMPs, there is a strong case to be made for *simplicity, transparency and continuity in programme operations*. Quite how such positive features of ALMP implementation could be attained amidst such contemporary political volatility is hard to imagine: however, the long-term collective aspiration is worth stating if effective and sustainable employer engagement is to be approximated. The example by Baker et al of provider- and commissioner-led collaboration in the UK is testament to the long lead time needed for such initiatives to gain ground, speaking to somewhat incremental change (or recalibration) in policy (Hemerijck, 2012) and practices.

Secondly, meso-level studies indicate that effective and sustainable employer engagement is best achieved when intermediaries are able to offer – and deliver – *holistic recruitment and retention services to employers*. The Dall, Larsen and Madsen study from Denmark particularly illustrates how, if intermediaries develop competency beyond the standard pre-employment and job placement services, then it is possible to achieve a more effective and tailored approach to meeting the employers' ongoing workforce needs. As Osterman (2008) has argued, intermediaries ideally need to develop specialist human resource (HR) knowledge, usually in a particular sector, in order to understand how best to support employers with their recruitment and retention needs.

Thirdly, and related to the previous point, it is suggested that successful employer engagement ideally relies on a strong partnership relationship between the intermediaries and their employers, rather than a transactional exchange in return for HR services. In particular, the case studies from the UK and Australia (see Baker, Ingold, Crichton and Carr; Hamilton) demonstrate how effective ALMP implementation is enabled via a 'co-production' or co-opetitive partnership approach, in which both the aims and the ongoing execution of the programme(s) are jointly owned and negotiated between the intermediary, employers and local government representatives. Such arrangements require autonomy to be afforded to the local partnership, so that the stakeholders may be empowered to work creatively together, which is not common in the ALMP regulatory environment.

A final characteristic resides more at the sectoral level and concerns the creation and recognition of *occupational career ladders* within countries. The opportunity for newly recruited employees to achieve incremental qualifications in a particular vocational area helps facilitate workforce progression and retention, and therefore a more sustained basis for employer engagement. Also, as Wiggan and Knuth indicate, a relatively developed system of vocational qualifications across different sectors in Germany appears to help small- and medium-sized employers to engage with and make informed recruitment decisions about unemployed applicants, thereby widening the potential pool of engaged employers. Incremental qualification structures and therefore career ladders tend however to be less available in the low-wage sectors, such as cleaning and security, in which entry-level recruitment from ALMPs is likely to be more prevalent (see McGurk and Meredith). Nevertheless, the German example shows that in other low-wage sectors, such as retail and social care, it is quite possible to plan for sustainable careers, which can also help strengthen employer engagement.

Micro-level employer engagement

It is hardest to generalize about the characteristics of successful employer engagement at the micro level: the individual employer. However, our observations in this collection lead us to conclude that the quality of the relationships between individual leaders/managers, key personnel within local intermediaries and partner agencies, and the individual jobseekers themselves, is pivotal to the success of any ALMP. The personalities and relationships involved cannot of course be legislated for within policy design or implementation processes. Yet there are arguably two general features of these relationships which policymakers and practitioners can support to pursue more effective and sustainable employer engagement.

Firstly, as particularly our US case studies demonstrate, firms should be encouraged to practice *inclusive leadership and HR management*. This is to say, that the most engaged employer organizations adopt a strategic stance that recognizes the need not just to fully integrate marginalized groups into their workforces (see Hanson and Moore; Hanson, Moore and Gustafson), but also to train and support operational managers in recruiting and retaining employees from ALMPs though close collaboration with representatives of local intermediaries (see McGurk and Meredith). This unconventional approach to leadership and HR management is often challenging, especially for local managers, and can be difficult to operationalize; for this reason, specialist HR expertise may need to be brought in to train and support the employer organization.

Second, and related to inclusive leadership, is a wider concern for social responsibility beyond the organization. In particular, the case study from The Netherlands (Borghouts and Freese) suggests that, ultimately, sustainable employer engagement entails acceptance and promotion among individual employers of *shared responsibility for local, social outcomes*. This is to say that individual employers see themselves as part of a community ecosystem of organizations and networks that support the economic and social wellbeing of the local population, of which engagement with ALMPs is an important part. Such congruence of socially responsible interests between local stakeholders is exemplified in Hamilton's case study of the engagement of the Australian non-profit disability enterprise. The partnership required expert facilitation and intervention but, to a large extent, the stakeholders pushed against open doors. In other, more mainstream instances, stakeholders' social responsibility may be propagated by government and its agencies through 'sermons', but ultimately the employer has to make a strategic choice to subscribe to it; more direct sticks and carrots are unlikely to be appropriate. There is potential here to align ALMPs with notions of 'shared value' (Preston, 2020) that seek to align profitable outcomes with positive social outcomes. This concept goes beyond much-critiqued nods to corporate social responsibility (CSR) although the presence of CSR policies has been a prospective 'logic' for employer engagement in ALMPs (Simms, 2017).

Finally, turning to the question of employers' strategic choices to share responsibility for local social outcomes, it is important to recognize the harsh reality: that in fact most employers show little sign of behaving in this way. This reality does not necessitate quotas or hard regulation, although these have been introduced in countries including The Netherlands. However, it is critical that employer engagement strategies should not accept the status quo, especially if this perpetuates the growing number of 'bad jobs' involving poorly paid, insecure and/or 'dead-end' jobs with associated poor mental and physical health in the jobholder (Warhurst and Knox, 2020). It is instructive to note here the work of 'HR disruptor' Lucy Adams (2017), in her call to 'put the human back into human resources'. Just as it is past time to disrupt HR, likewise, ALMPs need to be a 'disruptive strategy' to 'expand the pool of better jobs' (O'Regan, 2015, p 17) rather than perpetuate existing workforce inequalities. This is the compelling and urgent opportunity for employer engagement. The next and final section seeks to set out an agenda for research in order to capture these important developments across countries.

Future research agenda

As noted in our introduction, this collection is the first to address the topic of employer engagement with ALMPs in a comprehensive way. It has necessarily required a multidisciplinary approach, combining contributions from academics from the fields of social and public policy, political economy, employment relations, HR management and leadership, as well as from practitioners from the employability sector and management consultancy. The result has been a collection of rich insights into the motivations and behaviours of different types of employer, and how they interrelate with a variety of national, regional and local policies and institutional arrangements. With many caveats, we have offered some general international lessons – bounded voluntarism, connections to wider political-economic changes involving worker security and job quality, and local collaborative relationships – together with a framework of some ideal characteristics of employer engagement at macro, meso and micro levels.

More than this contribution, however, we believe that our seminal collection rightly points to more questions than answers. We contend that there are four main areas identified that should shape future research into employer engagement, while necessarily continuing to adopt a multidisciplinary approach. Any single discipline on its own simply fails to capture the full range of external and internal factors that influence how employers interact with ALMPs to co-produce good, sustainable work for all. The four main areas we recommend for future research are: (1) policy design, (2) policy implementation, (3) employer behaviour and (4) empirical evidence of effectiveness.

Firstly, with regard to policy design, our current understanding of different national models of employer engagement, or groups of them, is still very limited. As Bredgaard, Ingold and van Berkel argue, a fruitful direction for future research would be to build on the demand-regulation, -facilitation and -negotiation framework to compare activation approaches across a wider range of countries, including at different levels of governance and service delivery, to examine the development of the institutional and contextual characteristics that help to explain specific employer engagement configurations. Such configurations, as Etherington and Jones argue, should most meaningfully be observed in terms of evolving systems of power and negotiation between key interests and actors (after Esping-Andersen, 1990), thereby revealing the social and political dynamics of changing labour regulation, rather than taking a more narrow, static perspective on how many employers or how much they engage with ALMPs.

The second area recommended for future research concerns policy implementation. While much employer engagement research to date has tended to focus on intermediaries rather than the employers themselves, there is still much that we do not yet know about the variety of 'micro-processes'. In particular, ALMP intermediaries are practising a range of approaches, including collaboration and co-opetition (see Baker, Ingold, Crichton and Carr), and helping to implement a range of labour market strategies, including job rotation (Etherington and Jones), job carving and job fit (Dall, Larsen and Madsen). Yet there has been no comprehensive research to date into how much, why and how these different approaches and strategies may be adopted under various conditions. Similarly, intermediaries are increasingly expected to have the competence to deliver a wide range of services beyond job placement, and therefore to have relatively wide skill sets within their own workforces, including specialist and sector-specific HR knowledge and skills (McGurk and Meredith). To what extent and under which conditions do, or can, public employment services or ALMP agencies meet such expectations?

The third area relates to our key stakeholder group, namely the employers themselves. As Wiggan and Knuth argue, employer attitudes towards jobseekers and the labour market generally can vary considerably across different types of employer, such as by sector and size, as well as by time. Similarly, McGurk and Meredith show how the internal dynamics can lead to quite different engagement outcomes within the same employer, depending on changing strategic and operational factors. Questions of how and why employer behaviours vary are therefore suggested as likely to be fruitful for future research. This might also help address Borghouts and Freese's more general call for a better understanding of how employers and other stakeholders may be convinced to invest in the transitional labour market and patiently wait for the benefits. How, for example, might employers be convinced to become co-producers rather than purchasers of ALMP services (see McGurk and Olaleye)? Can clear 'business cases' for engagement be made, as Hamilton argues? Part of understanding employers better and convincing them to engage would include research into which strategies might best be used to educate, persuade, negotiate and challenge employers to improve their workplace practices.

Finally, we recommend more empirical research into and evidence on the effectiveness of different employer-engagement-related interventions. At the higher levels, as Bredgaard et al suggest, studies should examine the impact of varieties of employer engagement and the extent to which they contribute to a more inclusive labour market. Different aspects of ALMP implementation also require deeper investigation. As Green and Sissons highlight, more research is needed on how to design individual employment support for progression and on the appropriate timing of interventions: where are the critical junctures, and over what period is the process viewed? How might elements of the current context allow ALMPs to capitalize on some upwards pressures on job quality? And how can this be captured by research? Lastly, at the workplace organizational level, there is a need for more action research studies such as those by Hanson and Moore and Moore, Hanson and Gustafson, which document through data and evidence examples of good workplace practices that demonstrate different roads to better employment.

References

Adams, L. (2017). *HR Disrupted: It's time for something different*, London: Practical Inspiration.

Dunleavy, P. (1995). 'Policy disasters: Explaining the UK's record', *Public Policy and Administration* 10(2): 52–70.

Esping-Andersen, G. (1990). *The three worlds of welfare capitalism*, Princeton, NJ: Princeton University Press.

European Commission (2021). *Joint employment report 2021*, Brussels: European Commission: https://ec.europa.eu/social/BlobServlet?docId=23156&langId=en&furtherNews=yes

Hall, P.A. and Soskice, D. (2001). *Varieties of capitalism: The institutional foundations of comparative advantage*, Oxford: Oxford University Press.

Hemerijck, A. (2012). *Changing welfare states*, Oxford: Oxford University Press.

Martin, C.J. (2004). 'Reinventing welfare regimes: Employers and the implementation of active social policy', *World Politics* 57(01): 39–69.

O'Regan, F. (2015). *Sector workforce intermediaries: Next generation employer-engagement strategies*, Washington, DC: The Aspen Institute.

Osterman, P. (2008). 'Improving job quality: Policies aimed at the demand side of the low wage labor market.' In T.J. Bartik and S.N. Houseman (eds) *A future of good jobs? America's challenge in the global economy*, Kalamazoo, MI: W.E. Upjohn Institute for Employment Research, pp 203–44.

Preston, P. (2020). *Connecting profit with purpose: How to create a world-changing business*, Melbourne: Michael Hanrahan Publishing.

SER (2021). 'Zekerheid voor mensen, een wendbare economie en herstel van de samenleving, sociaal economisch beleid 2021–2025', Advies 21/08, June.

Simms, M. (2017). 'Understanding employer engagement in youth labour market policy in the UK', *Human Resource Management Journal* 27(4): 548–64.

Warhurst, C. and Knox, A. (2020). 'A manifesto for quality of working life', *Human Relations* 75(2): 304–21.

Index

References to endnotes show both the page number and the note number (139n14).

Printed and bound by CPI Group (UK) Ltd, Croydon, CR0 4YY

17/01/2024

08223611-0002